AT HOME IN ASIA

---- ✳ ----

Expatriates in Southeast Asia
and Their Stories

by

Harold Stephens

with a foreword by

Mort Rosenblum

AT HOME IN ASIA: Expatriates in Southeast Asia and Their Stories, by Harold Stephens

Front cover: *Women Carrying Offerings,* Oil on canvas, by Han Snel, Neka Museum, Bali, Indonesia

Photos by permission

Printed in Bangkok, Thailand, by Allied Printers

ISBN: 0-9642521-1-2

Library of Congress No: 95-060152

First Printing: November 1995
Second Printing: August 1996
Third Printing   July 1998
Fourth Printing   February 2001

Published by:

Wolfenden

U.S.A.
P.O. Box 789
Miranda, CA 95553-0789
Tel: (707) 923-2455 Fax: (707) 943-3955

Book design & layout: Robert Stedman Pte Ltd, Singapore

Also by **Harold Stephens**

⟋⟋≈⟍

Who Needs a Road, with Al Podell
Discover the Orient
Destination Singapore
Turn South at the Equator
Malaysia
Asian Portraits
Asian Adventure
Three Decades of Asian Travel & Adventure

3

AT HOME IN ASIA

is dedicated to
Tasnai Sudasna na Ayudhaya
of Thai Airways International

The people in this book are real; their actions and deeds are related as the author remembers them, or as the people themselves told him. The text of their conversations is as close as the author can recall. Little has been left to the imagination.

Some of the stories presented here have been previously published in part in the *Bangkok Post, Asia Magazine, Signature Magazine, Accent* and Thai Airways International's in-flight magazine *Sawasdee.*

The author would like to thank all those who have assisted with the publication, and in particular to Prajak Jamrusmechoti for his kind assistance over the years.

CONTENTS

Foreword by

MORT ROSENBLUM

A Word About The Author

As a foreign correspondent, my job involves the usual upheavals, small wars and workaday mayhem. Every so often, however, the mail includes a pleasant surprise which takes me away from that boring routine; a letter from Harold Stephens, filled with some real excitement.

You can spot Steve's letters from across the room: The address is written in urgent printed characters, with the no-nonsense, slightly askew strokes of a man who has struck gold and is racing to catch the last burro to Eureka. The envelope seems to twitch and quiver from all the energy within.

I remember one which reached me in Singapore, full of the usual chatty news: "chased by crocodiles . . .," "capsized off Tioman Island . . .," "pirates nearly got us near the Celebes. . . ." At the end, when he added, "Wish you were here," and I thought: me, too. If it was merely a matter of voracious reptiles, shipwrecks or killers afloat, I'd bet on Steve, hands down.

What always struck me was the tone of the letters. Always humble, courtly, full of derring-do but absent of bravado. But this is only to be expected. Adventure is Harold Stephens' natural state. To boast of his exploits would be like bragging about breathing

A product of long nights with Conrad on a Western Pennsylvania farm, he grew up with a code of honor and a sense of ingenuous wonder. He is burly and broad-shouldered—in "Mutiny on the Bounty" he doubled for Brando when action got intense—but his buckles don't swash. Handsome, with eyes that, in fact, twinkle, he is no ladykiller. His code, in that regard, is more Sir Walter than Flynn.

Steve can give you *Lord Jim* by heart: "He saw himself saving people from sinking ships . . . cutting away masts in a hurricane, swimming through a surf with a line, or as a lonely castaway, barefoot and half-naked, walking on uncovered reefs in search of shellfish to stave off starvation." He can tell you about everyone of Maugham's rubber planters and district officers.

He is always after something that eludes normal men. If someone tells him a prehistoric, enigmatic Big Kneecap is running loose in the Burmese backcountry, he'll be off before the informant finishes his sentence. If he hears of an ancient Greek olive oil convoy lost in the Mariana Trench, he'll head out with snorkel and swim fins. Unlike quixotic amateurs, Steve most likely will bring back the kneecap and olive pits.

One day Steve announced to friends that he would build a vessel to take him on his odysseys to forgotten archipelagos and against currents that others avoided as a bad idea. It would be made of cement. Of course, we thought. Months later, we were spending our weekends slapping concrete across a transom.

Steve's *Third Sea* must have done a million miles, its low-slung pirate-brown schooner hull crashing the reefs in every lost corner of the Southern Hemisphere. He racked up adventures even he hadn't dreamed of, from the nastiest straits of the Philippines to Cook's favorite waters across the Pacific.

One day, in another of these letters, the news was bad. The *Third Sea* was blown onto the rocks off Hawaii in a hurricane. Even Lord Jim couldn't have saved her; it must have been a hell of a blow. If there was ever the time for a little self-pity, this was it. Not a trace of it. Steve had lost a love of his life, but he had others.

Once I tried to write a book about Steve. But who would believe it? Anyway, he writes his own books, and they're good ones. But my notes spill out of a large crate. Steve lied about his age to join the Marines so he could fight in the Pacific. He exaggerated his language skills so he could be a translator in China. Imprisoned by the Chinese communists, he escaped and swam out to a passing junk. He rode a motorcycle across Australia, a jeep across Russia and — was it a pogostick across the Arctic?

Occasionally, word slipped out about his affairs of the heart. A gentleman, he does not talk much of these matters. Only later, for instance, his family back home discovered why he returned from Tahiti with a cast on his arm. A Tahitian woman, distraught at his leaving, drove him off a cliff.

Once Steve was married to a woman of Philadelphia high society, with a respectable job in naval intelligence. The marriage ended. That was when he went to Tahiti. One ranking government officer tried to talk sense into him. He invited Steve home to a family dinner and sat him down to watch a television series called, "Adventures in Paradise," to explain the ridiculous Hollywood romanticizing of a dull reality. Soon afterward, Steve was in the cast of the series. And in paradise.

Part of the time, he now lives among the redwoods in Northern California, in what ought to be a tame environment. But this is Harold Stephens. When I telephoned him just before delivering these lines to his publishers, he and his wife, Michelle, an island girl herself, reported an earthquake that very morning, and the rains were causing havoc. The Eel River was overflowing its banks and flood waters raged all around, carrying off power lines and outing the roads. Normal people had evacuated.

But even more than he amasses adventures, he collects characters. He is drawn to people who distinguish themselves from the chairs they sit in. And anyone in that category is drawn to him. With a writer's skills and a friend's warmth, Steve describes the remarkable lives of those who populate his world.

9

At Home in Asia is more than a collection of his best Asian sketches. It is a fat, rich sheaf of those Steve letters, to be savored and treasured and kept at hand for long nights when the ordinary world most of us know is just not enough.

Mort Rosenblum,
Associated Press, Paris

INTRODUCTION

OTHER PLACES

By The Author

"We wander in our thousands over the face of the Earth, the illustrious and the obscure, earning beyond the seas our fame, our money, or only a crust of bread...." Lord Jim by Joseph Conrad.

Given the chance, we all like to travel, to go beyond the sea, to visit foreign places. And oftentimes when we do travel, we try to imagine what it would be like to live there. How would it be to live in Singapore, the busiest seaport in the East, or maybe Bangkok, with its palaces and thousands of temples. And what about Kathmandu, high in the Himalayas, or Bali, where artists and poets go to live. Now that's a place we have all dreamed about. And how many other such places are there whose names ring with romance? Can you picture your own Thai house, made of polished teak, with a high sloping roof and carved eaves and lintels, with tiny brass bells that tinkle in the breeze? Or perhaps a Malay house overlooking the Malacca Strait with a pandanas roof to keep it cool. And can you imagine having your own boat and diving beneath the sea for sunken treasure, or hacking through primeval jungle in search of lost cities? Or perhaps owning a plane and flying around Southeast Asia as simply as one takes to the freeways back home in Los Angeles?

There are people who live this way and do these things, people who have gone beyond the sea and taken up residence in foreign lands. These are the people I would like to tell you about.

You will meet John Everingham, an Australian, who wanted to fight in the Vietnam war. The army said he was too young, so he went to the war on his own. In the end

John probably had more combat experiences, on land, sea and air, than most G.I.s stationed there. You will read how he became a noted war correspondent and photographer, fell in love with a Laotian woman, Kao, and to free her from the Pathet Lao, swam with her beneath the Mekong River. Hollywood came to Bangkok to make a movie about his adventures – with Michael Landon playing his part – and *National Geographic* included his life story when they featured him in a special issue on Australia. He married Kao and they have two children and live in a lovely house with a lush tropical garden outside Bangkok.

You will meet Hans Hoefer. He arrived in Asia driving a Volkswagen van, stood on a mountain peak in Nepal and vowed he would never go back to cold winters in Germany. He sold the van, donned a backpack and roamed around Southeast Asia for the next few years, with little money and few cares. On Bali he produced a guide book about that lovely island, and during the next twenty-five years produced more than two hundred other such guides in a series called *Insight Guides*, making him one of the most successful publishers of travel guides in Asia, if not the world. Hans lives in Singapore in a great colonial house with thick Persian rugs on the floors and rare tapestries on the walls. He has offices around the world.

Bill Heinecke, the son of a war correspondent, graduated from high school in Bangkok, and decided he'd rather not waste his time attending Georgetown University in Washington, as his father hoped. "Then get a job, and go to work," his father demanded. Bill did, and by the time he was twenty-one he had become a self-made millionaire. When he reached forty, a few years ago, he was one of Asia's most successful entrepreneurs, with hotels and fast food chains and more than fifty restaurants scattered around Thailand. He drives race cars in motor rallies, flies his own plane and dives with a camera looking for great white sharks off Australia's Great Barrier Reef.

Can you dream of spending a lifetime in an earthly tropical paradise? What would that be like? Would it become boring? Han Snel has spent more than fifty years on the island of Bali, and he is not bored. He's a painter and his oils hang in galleries around the world. His wife is a beautiful island woman, and his home is carved stone with a lotus pool in the garden. He defied the Dutch army and government authorities to do what he has done. Over the years his best friends have included all the great artists who at one time or another have lived on Bali – Arie Smit, Donald Friend, Theo Meier, and others.

For years I had been reading in newspapers the flash reports about an intrepid, daring seaman who carried his boat up over the Andes in South America so he could sail the tiny craft upon the highest body of water on Earth. Then he carried it back down again and sailed it in the Dead Sea, the lowest body of water. He has done everything a sailor can do. He has lectured at the Explorers' Club in New York and has authored fourteen books about his adventures. Today he is housebound in Phuket in southern Thailand, writing more books, and suffering a tragedy few of us could endure. You will read about his successes and his agonies too.

There are others I have chosen to tell you about. Kurt Wachtveitl has met every important person who ever came to Asia. He is the manager of what many savvy world travellers consider the "Best Hotel in the World"—the Oriental Hotel in Bangkok. What does he attribute his success to, and what about his lifestyle? Could you spend a lifetime living in such luxury? And other managers of great hotels, Axel Goerlach and Frans Schutzman. What happened when they found themselves involved in international espionage and political intrigue? If you think managing a great hotel would be boring, you may change your mind when you read about these gentlemen.

As a boy in England, Robin Dannhorn read Conrad and Kipling and Maugham and dreamed of one day finding adventure and romance in the Far East, but as he grew to manhood he was told to put away his boyhood dreams. He didn't, and instead made them come true. How he did is his story.

And then there are the three women of Nepal. I went to Kathmandu hoping to convince Barbara Adams to let me write about her, and then found Lisa Choegyal and Inger Lissonevitch. Don't let the last names mislead you. Lisa is English; Inger, Danish. They have their own incredible tales to tell. Lisa is married to the son of an eastern ruler of Tibet, and Inger's husband was the famous Boris of Kathmandu. Barbara Adams—that American woman—defied all protocol and fell in love with the brother of the King of Nepal, and he with her. Each of these three women's lives is a tale of adventure, and each an adventure story waiting to be told.

There was another fascinating woman I have to tell you about, Della Butcher. For decades she has helped struggling artists, and did everything possible to promote the arts in Asia. I wrote about her struggles, and as this book was going into print, we learned that Della had suddenly and unexpectedly died in her home in Singapore. In memory of her, I have kept the chapter about her in the book, unchanged.

You will also read about Bill Mathers. I wrote about Bill in an earlier book, *Asian Portraits*, which is also about "expats" living in Asia. I have written more about him in *At Home in Asia* for a very special reason. Formerly a U.S. Navy salvage engineer in Vietnam, Bill became a salvage diver with his own company in Southeast Asia. When he located the British battleship *HMS Repulse*, sunk by Japanese dive bombers off the coast of Malaysia during the opening days of World War II, he invited me to join the salvage expedition. I concluded after that experience that Bill had reached the pinnacle of his salvage diving adventures. How mistaken I was. It was only the beginning.

You will read about Karel Van Wolferen. I met him many years ago when I was exploring northern Thailand by Jeep;

that was before there were paved roads in the north. Karel is Dutch, and was teaching English in Japan. We made the trip together, and for a week he kept me enthralled with his stories, and insights, on Japan. Karel returned to Japan, and a few years ago published a book that has shook the world—*The Enigma of Japanese Power*. Since then he has lectured in universities around the world, and has been invited to brief the U.S. Congress about the state of affairs in Japan. I had to go to Japan a half dozen times to talk to him before I could finally get his story. He was always off somewhere telling countries how to deal with Japan. Karel's story is an example of how the pen can be mightier than the sword.

There are, of course, many others I wanted to include. My very good friend John Willoughby lives with his lovely Malay wife, Ijah, in a beautiful house high on a cliff in Port Dickson in Malaysia. John came to the Far East during the war, met Ijah and has never left. He's retired now but not inactive. He and Ijah spend their time sailing Asian waters in their yacht or else they are off somewhere exploring the remote regions of Burma or Indonesia. John is an amateur archaeologist and a warehouse of knowledge about Asia. He keeps his life private.

In *Asian Portraits* I wrote about Jessie, a Hawaiian who became sumo champ in Japan. I didn't think it was possible for anyone else to equal his performances. Then came another American, a Hawaiian leviathan who fights under the name Konishiki. Having bullied his way to crunching victories in the Japanese sumo world, he is forcing that country to face the long-dreaded prospect that a foreigner might become their national champ. At 238 kilos (524 pounds), Konishiki, twenty-seven, is the largest combatant ever recorded in the centuries-old history of sumo. I went to Japan to get to know him better–his real name is Salevaa Antinoe–but once there I realized that there was little I could add to his life's story that hasn't already been told. In a few years it may be different.

For years I have been going to Eddie's Log Cabin in Cebu in the Philippines. Eddie Woolbright, owner of the bar and restaurant, serves up the best steak dinners in the Far East. He has great tales to tell about how he came to the Philippines as an American G.I. during World War II. There was a young girl in a small village that he helped liberate, and they became friends. Her name was Imelda. In later years she became the First Lady of the Philippines, Mrs. Marcos. But Eddie did well on his own; he married Miss Philippines. That was his first wife; he had half a dozen others, and has a grand house on Woolbright Avenue in Woolbright Estate, where all his dozen children live. He agreed to let me write about him, but when I went to see him in Cebu he was vacationing for the summer and fall, with all his kids, in Los Angeles, close to Disneyland.

I wanted to tell you about Mike Yamashita. Mike is a Japanese-American who was groomed to take over the family business in New Jersey. But Mike wanted to be a photographer. His father gave him a year to make his mark, or shape up. I met him when he came to Bangkok. He sold his first picture to a magazine there, for fifteen dollars. He joined my crew and helped me sail my schooner through the South China Seas. I watched him dive in ninety feet of water, without scuba, to free an anchor, and I was there when he hacked through the Malay jungle with the Wildlife Department in search of the elusive white rhino. I saw him again in Singapore, years later. Now he was receiving top dollar for a two-month assignment to photograph the city. And on my desk is a copy of the February 1993 *National Geographic*. The lead article is "Mekong River." Mike has the photo credits. To do this, he and writer Thomas O'Neal became the first Western journalists to reach the headwaters of the Mekong River which they then followed for twenty-six hundred miles to the delta in Vietnam. When I last talked to Mike, he was preparing to photograph in southern Japan. He has a country home in New Jersey but he spends most of his time in Asia. "Where in Asia?" I asked. "Anywhere," he answered.

We often hear, in our modern day, that they don't make people like they once did. Don't believe that. The trouble is not with others but with ourselves. We don't take the time to meet these people. We don't take the time even to talk to the person who sits next to us on the jet that brings us to Asia. I have been rather fortunate. As a travel columnist for the *Bangkok Post* and travel correspondent for Thai Airways International, I have been able to travel around Asia and meet these people. I have come to know them over the years, and they are not so different from the district officer, the rubber planter or the government servant that Somerset Maugham wrote about in his novels and short stories at the beginning of the century.

The ease of travel has certainly made the world much different from Joseph Conrad's time. Nevertheless, they wandered in Conrad's day, and they continue to wander today. But with a difference. Conrad lived in a world in which it took six weeks by steamer to reach Asia from Europe. Today you can cover the same distance in twelve hours or less. Back then, in a lifetime, you might make one or two trips to Asia. Today you can do it a couple times a year. It is no longer a question of time but of money. No more six-week voyages on the P&O Line or the Messangerie Maritime. Singapore is now as close to Peoria, Illinois, as the nearest airport.

In Conrad's time, few people remained in foreign lands to live out their lives. Eventually, their duties fulfilled, they returned home, and as Conrad said, "like going to render an account closed, for man was rooted to the land from which he drew his faith together with his life." And once home, their wandering days were over. No more boundless horizons, no more hot quests for the ever-undiscovered country over the hill, across the stream, beyond the wave.

Until the end of the 19th century, few people travelled for pleasure. It was only after horsepower had been

Stephens standing on the Bund in Shangahi. (Photo by Robert Stedman)

replaced by steam engines that the travel industry was born. We reached the golden age of travel in the 1920s and 1930s, when the rich boarded luxury liners and railroad cars with thirty or more pieces of luggage, and Louis Vuitton became a household word. The increasing accessibility of world travel for pleasure whetted a public taste for the exotic, and for adventure.

Soon the highest mountains were climbed, the darkest jungle explored, the deepest cave discovered. We might imagine, then, that the thrill of travel would diminish, but we know the contrary to be true. The desire to travel is as great as it ever was, and more and more people are doing it. We continue to search for the rainbow's end, and some choose to live in foreign places. Why? What is it that makes one want to remain in distant lands, to become an expatriate? It's not the lack of love for one's own country, or from the desire to flee from an unhappy home. Nor is it for political, economic or social reasons. The motives are deeper, and more complex. The answers to why the people in this book have become "expats," I leave you to discover for yourself as you read about their extraordinary lives. But keep in mind, these people were not born into the lives they lead; they created them.

Harold Stephens,
Bangkok, 1995

Photographer—John Everingham on assignment.

Chapter 1

JOHN EVERINGHAM
From Laos with Love

In 1969, the road between Phnom Penh and Saigon was a hazardous stretch of deep ruts and endless potholes. Every so often traffic had to turn off the road to skirt the many shell holes that marred the pavement. Lines of military vehicles slowed all movement down to a walking pace. Trucks with Cambodian soldiers rumbled up and down on one side of the border while Vietnamese and American troops moved along the other. Travel was further delayed by military barricades that appeared every few kilometers, fuel drums, painted white and filled with cement. Off to the sides of the barricades, behind sandbags piled waist high, stood armed sentinels with automatic rifles at the ready. Guards checked the papers of all those who used the road.

John Everingham knew every kilometer of the road from Phnom Penh to Saigon, and he knew at which roadblock he could expect trouble. He spoke some Cambodian, and this always helped, for the soldiers never expected a white man to speak their language. He joked with the guards when he stopped at a blockade; they bantered back with him, laughed and always waved him on.

John wondered how long he could keep up the charade. Making these runs between the two capitals while both countries were looking at each other down gun barrels was risky business. But he had no alternative, unless he wanted to go back to Australia and go to work, or worse yet, go back to school. Maybe even end up in jail.

One morning he checked out of his hotel room in Phnom Penh and locked up his motor bike in the hotel parking lot. He patted the bike fondly, a Suzuki two-stroke trail bike that he had used to travel from Australia and up the Malay Peninsula to Thailand. Then he shouldered his overnight bag, clutched tightly a long cylinder wrapped in a rice sack, and headed for the bus station that would take him to the Cambodian-Vietnamese border. Once aboard the bus, he felt confident; he had made this run with his precious tube so many times he couldn't remember the exact count.

Some guards at the barricades knew him and simply waved him past; others who were new checked his papers carefully. Cambodia was easy this day; no one stopped him. Now came the Vietnamese checkpoint. He was aware there might be American guards at the other side, and American G.I.s, especially officers, didn't like guys with long hair. A kilometer before the border he carefully tucked his blond, shoulder-length hair under his hat, checked that the tube was still safe in the overhead rack and waited.

There were no Americans with the Vietnamese this day. A soldier with an MP armband checked his papers and let him pass. Once again he had made it; he was safe. The bus continued on across the Mekong Delta to Saigon.

That night after he checked into his hotel he went to the bar on top of the Caravelle Hotel. On a raised stage above the bar a bosomy Australian singer in a tight sequined gown sang "I Left My Heart in San Francisco." John paid little attention. He walked past the bar and by habit went out on the balcony where he could watch the gunfire. On most nights when he was in Saigon he'd go to the top of one of the hotels and watch the fireworks; helicopters strafing, rockets coming in, shells exploding in thundering flashes somewhere in Cholon. Watching the war from a rooftop, with a Bud or whiskey in hand, was a favorite pastime for those living and stationed in Saigon. It was Fourth of July every night.

But on this night John wasn't thinking about the gunfire. He had two people he wanted to meet. The first person was the Master Sergeant who ran an NCO Club in town. Exactly at nine, the hour they were to meet, the man came into the club, saw John standing out on the balcony and walked directly over to him. Without greetings, he barked, "You bring 'em?"

"I have them," John replied.

"Where?" the sergeant asked with urgency in his voice. It was apparent he didn't like John, nor any of the civilians who came into the military club, but there wasn't much he could do about it. John had a press pass and could come and go through military installations as he pleased.

"I'll bring them to your office in the morning," John said and turned away from the sergeant. The sergeant grumbled and left. John then saw the reporter, the other person he was to meet.

"It's all fixed," the reporter said after they shook hands. "No more runs to Phnom Penh for you."

John couldn't hold back his excitement. "You mean with Walter Cronkite?"

The reporter nodded and put an arm around John's shoulder. "With Walter Cronkite," he repeated.

It wasn't much of an assignment, being a sound man for American TV, but he needed a break, and he thought he could turn this one to his advantage. John was a photographer and new to the game. Freelance press photography paid little in the beginning, and he needed money to live, or he'd have to go back to Australia. More than once he thought about getting out of Vietnam, but the old pros encouraged him to hang in there.

At first John did whatever he could to earn a few dollars. He translated for those who needed a Cambodian interpreter; he assisted movie and TV companies; he served as a guide for VIPs. Then came the discovery in Cambodia.

John was in Angkor Wat walking among the Khmer ruins, when he noticed students taping square sheets of thin rice paper over bas-relief temple carvings. Once the paper was in place they rubbed the surface with hunks of charcoal thus creating an impression of the carving on the paper. The results were rather crude but interesting art forms.

John didn't think much about it until he was in Saigon and watched G.I.s buying up souvenirs – fake antiques, native artifacts, handicrafts of every sort. Why not temple rubbings? He went back to Cambodia, hired a couple of students and was in business. Whenever he had a couple dozen rubbings, he headed to Saigon.

As an Australian, he had no trouble crossing the borders in Southeast Asia. He traveled freely throughout Thailand, Cambodia and Laos. Vietnam was even easier. With a press pass he could travel anywhere he pleased. Temple rubbings were new and John was one of the first people to bring them out of Cambodia. In a few months he had enough cash to go to Hong Kong and purchase new camera equipment and supplies.

Now as a "gopher" with CBS he could give up the risky business of running the border between Cambodia and Vietnam. The next morning he delivered his last batch of temple rubbings to the club manager. He was lucky to be done with it. He was certain Prince Sihanouk would soon lose his hold on Cambodia and the border would close. A few months later, in April 1970, it happened. U.S. and Vietnamese forces invaded Cambodia in an effort to rout Viet Cong and North Vietnamese troops that were using bases inside Cambodia to overthrow the South Vietnamese government.

With a CBS assignment, John Everingham was able to put all his energies toward making his mark as a war correspondent. Within six months he was one of the most successful combat photographers in Vietnam. He began winning awards. His first prize was from the *San Francisco Chronicle.*

In time his photographs appeared in major magazines and newspapers around the world. The editors of *National Geographic* gave him assignments, and in one issue devoted to Australia they printed an article specifically about him. His life was also chronicled in *Reader's Digest.* When he wasn't covering the war in Vietnam, he was in Laos or Thailand. He became proficient in both the Laotian and Thai languages and traveled widely in both countries. He came to know the Thai Royal Family and was able to capture them on film. His collection of Royal Family photographs is probably more comprehensive than that of any other foreign photographer in Southeast Asia. For his understanding of Laos, he was called to Washington to testify at Senate hearings about America's MIAs. And Twentieth Century-Fox came out from Hollywood with a crew to do a film on his life. The late Michael Landon played the part of John Everingham and Priscilla Presley his American girlfriend.

But I am getting ahead of my story. Let's go back a few years to when John Everingham left Australia for Southeast Asia. He wasn't looking for fame, nor a name for himself. At the age of sixteen he had dropped out of high school because he couldn't make the rowing team.

John was an idealist from the start. He couldn't get on the team so he quit school and went to work in the cane fields of Queensland to toughen up. "It was the best way I knew to get fit," he said. But once out of school he was no longer interested in joining the rowing team. He now had a taste for another life. In the sugar fields he met tough laborers from New Guinea and the South Pacific islands, and from them he heard about far off lands where customs differ and age-old traditions don't die. He couldn't go back to school now. Instead he went to New Guinea to discover a new world for himself. That was in 1966.

It wasn't all glamor in New Guinea. Work was hard to come by, and to support himself he was forced to take a job washing dishes and waiting on tables in a restaurant in Port Moresby. Nevertheless, New Guinea was his lodestone to adventure. He got to know the highlands and the bush country. He became fascinated by the Kokoda Trail.

During World War II, the Japanese invaded New Guinea, but they never managed to capture Port Moresby, although they got very close at one time. As the tide of the war turned, the Japanese were pushed back in a long and gruelling fight up the Kokoda Trail. Energetic bushwalkers today can follow that same trail from the south to the north coast, and John became one of them. He hiked it not once but twice. The first time he covered it from end to end in one week; the second time he did it in the record time of three and one half days. In New Guinea, John established the pace he followed from then on.

Eventually John returned to Sydney, undecided in what direction to turn. Before long he was caught up in the patriotism that was taking over Australia. The conflict in Vietnam had escalated into a full-fledged war. Australia, New Zealand, South Korea, Thailand and the Philippines were sending military personnel to South Vietnam as part of what the Americans called the 'Free World Military Forces.' Australia's participation in the Vietnam War constituted the most significant commitment of Australian military forces overseas since the 1940s. Eventually the overall number of Australian military personnel to serve in Vietnam would reach 46,852.

But the army didn't want John Everingham. They told him to go home, finish school and come back when he was older.

John was not about to wait out the years. The war would be over by the time he was old enough to join the service. He decided he would go to Vietnam on his own. His plan was to spend a month or two in the country, and then continue on to London. He would work for a year in England and then return home. This was not unusual; many young Australians did the same—except that most did not stop off in Vietnam to check out a war.

"For six months I worked my butt off," John said. "I saved every cent I could." Then he bought a Suzuki two-stroke motorbike, a 35mm camera and some film. He shipped the motorbike to Singapore, hitch–hiked to Darwin and flew from there to Singapore. His adventures were about to begin.

"I knew absolutely nothing about Southeast Asia when I arrived in Singapore," John admitted. "I never heard of Angkor Wat nor did I even know there were any such places as Laos or Cambodia."

He drove up the length of the Malay Peninsula to Bangkok, more than a thousand miles, some of it through dense jungle. It was the Fall of 1967. At that time Bangkok was the most exciting city in Asia. "The town was pulsating, bubbling at the seams," John recalled. "G.I.s on R&R, war correspondents, con-men, photographers, war profiteers, wives coming to meet their army husbands on leave from Nam, foreign entertainers either on their way to Saigon or returning from Saigon, and girls, there were girls galore in Bangkok, girls from all over Thailand. I don't know where they got all the pretty Thai girls but they were there, doing their thing on Patpong and later on Soi Cowboy."

John soon discovered the many worlds of Bangkok. He met serious reporters and writers who were covering the war in the field; and he met others who were content to file their reports while sitting in Tiger Lucy's on Silom Road. John listened to their tales, and he was more eager now than ever to go to Vietnam. In late December he left Bangkok on his motorbike. He drove across war-torn Cambodia to Phnom Penh. He checked his bike at his hotel and caught a bus to Saigon. His arrival in Vietnam coincided with the second wave of the 1968 Tet Offensive. John Everingham was soon to see what war was all about.

The Tet Offensive of early 1968 marked a crucial turning point in the war. On the evening of January 31, as the country celebrated the New Year, the Viet Cong launched a stunning offensive attacking more than one hundred cities and towns, including Saigon. As the TV cameras rolled, a VC commando team took over the courtyard of the US Embassy building in downtown Saigon.

"Half of Cholon was under the communists and shells were exploding everywhere," he said.

John thought he might have difficulty with the authorities. "I had just turned eighteen. I went as a tourist, a young idealist who believed in what we were doing. The West had a mission I thought, and that was to save the world. And then I saw the killing. It didn't take long for me to realize that something was wrong. World War II was black-and-white, but not this. This didn't make sense."

John is still baffled by what happened next. He had no accreditation as a photographer or as a correspondent, yet in the next three months he made forty-nine military flights into war zones. He was just a kid hopping around Vietnam, following one battle after another, and no one ever questioned him. "All I had to do was walk up to a plane, and if there was space, I was on. No questions. I was a kid viewing the war."

But the war in Vietnam added to John's confusion. The senseless killing, the degradation of it all. Only when he went back to Australia to visit his family in 1970 did he know what he wanted to do. "No one back home had any idea what was going on," he said. "And no one would listen to me. But I could make them see with pictures. I could show the world things as they were."

John made up his mind to return to Vietnam, but this time as a bonafide news man. He knew he was short on formal education, but there were those in Saigon who were willing to help him. He had to get back to Southeast Asia as quickly as he could. But then fate took a strange turn.

Now that he was eighteen the law required that he register for the draft. Two years before he had begged to join the army but the army wouldn't take him. Now the army wanted him, but he didn't want the army. He could not fight for a cause he totally opposed. He decided that he would rather go to jail than fight a meaningless war. He had seen the conflict as few of his countrymen had. He had risked his life to learn the truth. He refused to sign up for the draft.

His refusal to register presented a serious problem. He could not leave Australia without a clearance from the draft board, and without signing up he couldn't get a clearance. Then he heard about a long shot.

There was a weekly air flight from Darwin to Dili, the capital of East Timor. It was a route that all the young radicals in Australia knew about. For some unknown reason the authorities in Darwin seldom checked the papers of passengers leaving the country. It was his only hope. He hitchhiked to Darwin and luck was with him. He caught a flight to Dili. He made it, but in doing so he had burned the bridges behind him. He couldn't return home without facing arrest and the possibility of a jail sentence.

Back in Vietnam John fell in with the press. "I was right up with the best teachers. Photography was the easiest. I got my press pass and I worked for the little dispatch news services. Mike Morrow taught me how to write a news story. He spent a great deal of time with me and gave me help. Once I got that down, and could take pictures, I was all over the countryside – Laos, Cambodia, Vietnam. Unlike before, this time I had a purpose. With money coming in I gave up selling souvenirs to G.I.s. No more temple rubbings, but I have to admit, I did start a craze. Today temple rubbings are in every tourist outlet in Asia."

John's future became obvious to him. "I was certain now I wasn't going to return to Australia and be an accountant or sit in an office the rest of my life." His road to adventure led him to Laos.

Why Laos?

"The Laotian people had the greatest impact on me," he said. Vietnam and Cambodia had drama, but Laos held the fascination. "After Prince Sihanouk's fall and Cambodia closed its doors, I moved my base of operations to Laos. I set up an office in Vientiane, the news center of Laos, but I spent much of my time in Luang Prabang." At this northern town, the second largest in Laos, three tributaries—the Nam Khan, the Nam Ou and the Nam Suong—flow into the Mekong River. It's a sleepy town where the streets are lined with old French colonial buildings. John loved the peace and quiet of Luang Prabang. The location also gave him access to the north. He liked to go cave exploring in the nearby Pak Ou Caves, and he enjoyed hopping on his motorbike and exploring places like Phonsawan and the mysterious Plain of Jars.

He came to know the south as well, such towns as Savannakhet, Salavan and Champasak. In Salavan Province he spent time with the hilltribe people living in villages on the Boloven Plain, villages that are arranged in circles. John became part of the yearly hilltribe festival in which water buffaloes are sacrificed in the middle of the village circles.

He loved to roam around the tenth century Khmer ruins at Pak Se. "These were lost, forgotten cities," he said. "The jungle here had reclaimed man's work. You could look up and see in the branches of banyan trees, in deathlike grips, the heads of long forgotten Khmer kings, smiling down at you."

But what John enjoyed the most was visiting the hilltribes of the north. He trekked to distant villages, villages that clung to the sides of steep hills, and others that looked down from misty mountain tops to winding rivers far below. He came to know the people, the Hmong and Mien, and he learned to speak their languages. John Everingham was happiest when he was among the hilltribes, far from the torment of war in Vietnam.

But the peace and joy of northern Laos did not last for long. The war in Indochina was heating up and the innocent mountain people would soon be caught in the middle of someone else's madness. John grew more and more anti-war with each passing day. The villages he knew and loved were now being bombed.

The U.S. established air bases in Thailand, and bombers were soon crisscrossing eastern and northeastern Laos on their way to and from bombing missions in North Vietnam and along the Ho Chi Minh trail. The missions attempted saturation bombing of Pathet Lao strongholds but with little effect. The Pathet Lao simply moved their headquarters into caves near Sam Neua. Still the bombing did not stop. B-52 captains had instructions to unload their bombs when returning from Vietnamese air strikes, and without specific targets, they would open their bomb-bay doors over civilian centers in eastern Laos. From 1964 to 1973, U.S. planes dropped more than two million tons of bombs on Laos, more than the total used by U.S. Forces during World War II. Laos has the distinction of being the most heavily bombed nation in the history of modern warfare.

Many of the hilltribe villages that John had visited were indiscriminately bombed. "As soon as the Pathet Lao moved into a village," he said, "the people had little time to get out before the bombs began falling. Sometimes they never got the word and got blasted, and oftentimes the old people refused to move. It was mass murder."

The control of an area was not always clearly defined, and often John ran into Pathet Lao troops in village streets. He would talk to soldiers and listen to their side. One day he met two Pathet Lao and learned that the Americans had just bombed Long Pot, a Hmong village he knew and had often visited. He could feel his anger building. "These were innocent people," he said. Thinking they might need his help, he immediately set out for Long Pot village.

On the trail he met Hmong who were fleeing from the ravaged north. He stopped them to ask questions. They were angry and upset. "They were peaceful people who wanted no part of the war," John said. "Young men from their villages had been forced into the Pathet Lao forces. The only thing they now asked was for everyone to go away and leave them alone."

Whenever the Pathet Lao took over a village, it was certain to be bombed soon after. Those who survived were forced into refugee camps. John knew he had to reach Long Pot village as quickly as possible. If he could photograph the terror brought about by the bombings he could hopefully convince the world of the wrong being done.

When he reached the village he found it deserted. Fires were still smouldering and the dead had not been buried. He began shooting pictures, roll after roll. Suddenly a half dozen Pathet Lao soldiers appeared. Like others he had met, they were friendly, but cautious.

They didn't know how to confront a white man speaking their language and taking pictures.

The soldiers asked that John accompany them to the next village. He could hardly refuse. Once they arrived at the village, the soldiers handed him over to another Pathet Lao unit. They too were uncertain what to do with this stranger, and in turn led him to still another village farther north. Here the soldiers were less friendly. They looked at him with suspicion. For two days his journey continued, from one check point to another, and each time he was handed over to someone else. With each transfer the story changed. Soon forgotten was the truth: that he was an Australian journalist. Somewhere along the route he had become a downed American pilot.

Guards now tied his hands behind his back and pushed him ahead of them, prodding him with rifle butts. He came upon villages completely bombed out. Villagers were no longer polite; now they vented their anger against him; they jeered and threw stones and spit at him. Those who had fled into the forests for protection, came out from cover to see the white man who had dropped bombs on their homes and schools. They came to see the American pilot the Pathet Lao had shot down from the sky.

"I tried telling them I was Australian, a journalist," John said, "but it did no good. These people had never seen a newspaper and they had no idea what I was talking about. To them there were only three kinds of foreigners. There were the French, but now they had gone home, and there were the Russians and the Americans. I wasn't Russian so I had to be American."

A young boy, no more than ten years old, was given a rifle and to the satisfaction of the villagers was instructed to walk behind the prisoner and make sure he didn't escape. "I was nervous as hell," John said. "He kept jabbing me with the rifle barrel, and the more he jabbed the more the people enjoyed it. He had his finger on the trigger. I knew that had I done anything at all, had I even stumbled, he would have shot me."

On the third day John arrived at a village he hadn't seen before. A mob gathered and jeering soldiers shoved him into a bamboo cage. There were no windows and only a small opening for a door. There was not enough room to stand nor to lie down. He had to sit with his knees up to his chin. Ventilation came from cracks between the bamboo. And through these cracks villagers came from miles around to see the white captive. John was aware of eyes peering in at him. At times guards opened the door slightly so someone could get a better look, and once they put an egg in the opening to see what he would do. He felt like an animal in a cage, and to them he was.

John surmised that he could have broken out during the long nights, but what purpose would it have served? How far could he get? Where could he go? The whole countryside was looking for downed pilots. There was no escape, no place to hide.

On the morning of John's fourth day in the cage, a Pathet Lao officer of high rank arrived in the village. When he heard they held a white man captive, he had the soldiers drag John from the cage and prop him up at attention in front of him. He spoke to John in French. John replied in Laotian saying he didn't speak French.

"You have identification; your passport," the office replied in Laotian. John could tell he was an educated man.

John explained that the soldiers had taken his camera bag which contained all his documents. The officer shouted to the soldiers and presently a soldier came running with the bag. The officer opened it, found John's passport and carefully checked it. Several times his eyes went from the photograph to John and then back again.

"You are an Australian," he said, but before John could respond he continued. "How do we know you are not a spy?"

Among the papers John carried in the bottom of his bag were press clippings, stories he had written with his photographs, denouncing the bombing. He asked the officer to look at the clippings.

The officer slowly read the first clipping, and then another. He studied the photographs. Finally, after carefully refolding the clippings he said, "You must excuse my solders; they do not understand these things." He immediately ordered the soldiers to release John, and turning to the people he explained that the man they had captured was neither a downed pilot nor an American spy. "He came to help us," he said to them.

That afternoon the villagers had a party, and John was the guest of honor. Tables appeared in the village square and were soon laden with food. Jars of rice wine were opened and glasses filled. The drinking began and soon in columns of twos the villagers began dancing around the tables in a kind of relentless shuffle. They sang as they danced, clapping their hands in rhythm. The drinking lasted until nightfall, and by then all the men, women and children old enough to drink were flat on their backs. John laughed when he retold the story. "I could have walked out of the village, but again, how far could I go? It was at least a week's march to Luang Prabang."

But there was no need to escape. John had won their favor, but he also realized he was still under suspicion. They were communist, well indoctrinated; most of them could recite the sayings of Chairman Mao by heart. They were also thirsty for information, information other than about the war and the bombings. Over the next few days, officers came to talk to him. Often until late at night they sat conversing and drinking rice wine.

"You mistook me for an American," John said one night to a couple of officers. "Don't you know what Americans look like?"

"We do know," one officer spoke up. "We saw captured American pilots in the villages."

Captured American pilots! These men knew something about the American MIAs. John had to get more information from them, but each time he tried they changed to another subject. It wasn't until much later that he was to learn the truth about captured American pilots.

The day finally arrived when orders came for John to be transferred. He was sent by truck to the Plain of Jars, a remote highland area that the Pathet Lao had turned into their headquarters. Here the high command confirmed through the Australian Embassy in Vientiane, the capital, that John was Australian, and, indeed, a journalist. He was free to return to Vientiane. After twenty-nine days of captivity, he was released and a few days later arrived back in the capital.

In Vientiane John continued to file dispatches about the American bombings of hilltribe villages in the north. The Pathet Laos were pleased with his reports, but with the foreigners in Vientiane, especially the Americans, he wasn't winning any new friends. "None of the foreigners liked what I was writing," he admitted, "and so they concluded that I was a communist. It didn't make sense. I was against the war and the bombings, not a communist."

John's strained relationship with Western authorities grew worse when he filed a report on undercover operations in Laos. He wrote about the growing American counterintelligence operations. He claimed U.S. military leadership, fearing that bombing Laos wasn't enough, had begun to form a special CIA-trained army to counter the growing influence of the Pathet Lao. This army of 10,000 was largely made up of Hmong tribesmen under the direct command of the Royal Lao Army General Vang Pao, himself a Hmong. These troops were trained for mountain warfare and were not, as has been claimed, mercenaries in the true sense of the term. Since the troops were U.S. trained and financed, covert American undercover agents posing as fertilizer salesmen and mining engineers were soon seen everywhere in Vientiane. They all knew John Everingham, the thorn in their sides, and they all disliked him. Something had to be done about John Everingham.

In a cover story that appeared in the *Washington Monthly*, John showed bombed out villages in northern Laos. The article shocked Americans, but it also deepened the rift between John and the other foreigners in Vientiane. "It got to the point where I couldn't go into a bar in town without threats of getting beat up," he said. Soon his fears were more than just getting beaten up; he began to fear for his life. He spent more and more time outside the capital.

He found his retreat in hiking the mountain trails around Vientiane and visiting the hilltribe villages. Often he would be gone for days. There were no roads, only trails, and in some distant villages he met people who had never seen a white man. Villagers would gather around him, touching his blond hair, feeling the hair on his arms; they giggled at the way this funny looking foreigner walked and the way he talked.

John was quick to pick up the languages and make friends, and he enjoyed the peace and quiet of the time he spent with them.

In his office in Vientiane, John had three assistants: a secretary, a young man to take care of photos and a full-time translator. "In every sense of the word a journalist is a spy," he admitted. "I had the man translate news clippings, decrees from the government, everything that

I might be able to use. I had enough material to write a book, which I intended to do."

John was certain he was under surveillance by both the Pathet Lao and the CIA. He was being followed and his every move was closely watched. But he thought there was one place they couldn't follow him—into the hills when he went hiking.

Except for his staff, John never told a soul when he was leaving for one of his mountain jaunts. Often he would simply grab his pack and camera bag and take off. His sudden and unexpected movements frustrated those who were watching him.

One afternoon while coming back from a mountain village he learned that even the mountains were no longer safe for him. "It wasn't an accident," he said. "That helicopter was after me." He had come around the side of a hill, to an open grassy slope that had been stripped for farming, when suddenly a helicopter came zooming around the side of the mountain, no more than two hundred feet above him. He could clearly see the pilot and two passengers in an open doorway. One was armed.

The pilot quickly did a sweeping turn and came back, this time with John directly in their gun sights. "You never saw anyone move so fast as I did when I slid down the side of that mountain," he said. He was able to find cover in the thick forest. Back in Vientiane John realized he could turn to no one. Who would believe that one of the Western powers had sent an armed helicopter to do him in?

Gradually the Pathet Lao tightened restrictions on foreigners in Laos and eventually they were all expelled—all except John. He became the last western journalist to remain in Laos. For nearly two years he had free reign and he could travel freely between Bangkok and Vientiane. His stories and photographs appeared in magazines like *Far East Economic Review* and *Newsweek*. He became a stringer for BBC and his voice was broadcast around the world.

"Everyone was interested in the MIAs and wanted any information I could give them," John said. "That was 1977, and I believe I had the best information available, but when it came to telling the truth, no one wanted to hear what I had to say. I didn't have to go looking for information; it came to me."

John had a big house at the edge of town and his doors were always open. "I could use the commissary at the U.S. Embassy, and I got booze cheap," he said. "Everyone stopped in, from Pathet Lao battalion commanders to minor officers. With a little Jack Daniels in them they always felt compelled to sound important, and so they talked."

John was particularly interested in the MIAs. "One time I came right out and asked a couple officers drinking with me what happened to all the American POWs. They told me very bluntly, that since the Americans would not recognize the Pathet Lao, they were not bound by the peace agreements that were signed in 1972. If America wasn't going to recognize the Pathet Lao they weren't going to release the prisoners."

John believed they kept prisoners in the beginning but when the war with Vietnam was coming to a close, they couldn't let the prisoners go, so they took them out and shot them. "They had to," John said. "After years of denouncing Americans, the greatest criminals in the world, it would make them look very weak and soft to release them."

John wrote the story about the fate of the MIAs for Associated Press but they didn't want it. "I met congressman Robert Dornan from California back then. He wanted to promote the idea that prisoners were still in captivity. He heard that I was imprisoned in Laos and phoned me when I was in Bangkok. He wanted me go to Washington and testify before the Senate. He would make all the arrangements, flights, hotels, expenses. I agreed to go, but told him that the information I had indicated that all MIAs were dead. He dropped me like a hot potato. I never heard from him again and I wasn't asked again to testify on MIAs. What I had to tell wasn't what people in America wanted to hear, nor would it win votes for ambitious politicians."

Except for *Newsweek,* John filed all his stories under his own name. "It's frustrating writing for New York publications," he explained. "You send in a dispatch and it's rewritten, from what they say are agency reports." The Laotian Foreign Ministry became suspicious that John was supplying spurious information to journalists outside the country. Twice he was called in, and each time it was harder for him to explain that he was not acting as an undercover source.

Meanwhile, John was becoming more and more disillusioned with the Pathet Lao government. With the entire country under their control, they had become oppressive, a complete about-face to how they had first appeared. John felt compelled to write the truth, however hard hitting. "In the beginning," he wrote, "the Laotians were thrilled when the Pathet Lao took over the reigns of government; they never considered them to be hard-line communists, only the patriotic troops of Prince Souphanouvong. Once victory was theirs, they dissolved all local governments and representation."

Still, life in Vientiane continued.

To entertain themselves, foreigners got together for private parties. At one of these functions in 1976, John met a lovely Laotian woman named Kao Sirisomphone. Under the most trying of circumstances, beneath the watchful eyes of the communist authorities, John and Kao fell in love.

About the same time that John met Kao, a new Russian intelligence officer arrived and began cracking down on foreigners. He started by monitoring the homes and offices of all foreigners, John's house included.

"Intelligence kept a detailed log of every person who entered my house," John said. "Even errand boys who brought coffee. It wasn't long and they thought they had enough to convict me."

John was arrested and brought to trial–a mock trial. He was thrown in jail where he remained for ten days. The chief of intelligence, a man named Petsamong, ran the case himself against John. The final decision: John Everingham was to be expelled from Laos as an undesirable.

The Pathet Lao government declared a public holiday the day he was expelled. His departure made headlines in every newspaper in the country. A convoy of vehicles from embassy cars to military Jeeps and trucks escorted him from the Australian Embassy to the river where he was put aboard a boat and sent to Thailand. Kao ran alongside the convoy until she was forced back. She stood on the bank and watched John leave, sobbing, wondering if she would ever see him again.

John returned to Thailand with only the clothes he wore. Gone were his film files, books, diaries, cameras and all his photographic equipment. Gone were ten years of work. Perhaps the worse part was the senseless destruction he saw when he was taken from the prison to his house after the trial. The contents of his filing cabinets, which included all his photographs, had been dumped on the floor. Soldiers with muddy boots had trampled over his collection of negatives, transparencies and prints. They were all ruined. Distraught, he dared not even look into the office when he left the house.

John's first order of duty after settling in Bangkok was to find a means of communicating with Kao. He discovered a Laotian underground that smuggled letters and messages back and forth regularly, for a price. He found a contact, wrote a brief letter and turned it over with the assurance that it would reach her. A week passed, two weeks, a month and no word came. He could not wait any longer. He had to return to Australia to visit his family and earn enough money to make a new start.

John was visiting his parents when a letter arrived from Kao. It was one of the happiest moments of his life. "What's so special about a letter from a girl in Laos," his mother and father asked.

"Don't laugh," John announced, waving the letter over his head, "this letter is from your future daughter-in-law."

"And how do you propose to marry a girl you can't even see?" they asked.

"I'll think of some way," he replied.

John returned to Bangkok and this time made contact with an underground organization that guaranteed they could get Kao out of Laos. A woman and her two children were scheduled to leave the following week and Kao could travel with them. According to the plan they would be trucked out of town at night to a spot downriver twenty kilometers south of Vientiane. The arrangements were made, but John felt uneasy. Dennis Gray, his close friend at Associated Press, had told him of reports AP had of atrocities that were taking place on the river. Dennis advised John not to attempt it. John cancelled the arrangements. He decided to wait a little longer until he was certain.

The woman and her two children never made it. A Pathet Lao boat patrolling the river opened fired on them and she and the children drowned. Kao could have been aboard the same boat.

Through friends at the wire services in Bangkok, John learned that the smugglers were as big a problem as the patrol boats. These profiteers knew the refugees carried valuables with them, both money and jewelry. Often the smugglers stopped their boats in mid-river and took the valuables from their helpless victims. Sometimes they even raped the women, and threw them into river.

John continued to search for someone he could trust, but all he met were shady characters promising the moon. After many endless, frustrating months of plotting and planning, it suddenly occurred to him that he was going about it all wrong. "Why was I going to risk her life with someone I couldn't trust? Why not do it myself?"

Then John devised a plan. Attempts made by refugees to swim the river had always failed because the swimmers were easy to detect on the open water. But what if one swam beneath the surface of the water with scuba gear? Then there was less chance of being detected.

At a prearranged time, Kao would be waiting on the other side. He would put a diving mask on her and pull her under the water before anyone could stop him. Once underwater they had a chance by swimming along the bottom to reach Thailand. They didn't have to swim all the distance underwater, just out of range of the guards. The river around Vientiane averages a mile wide.

The next day John borrowed a car from a friend and drove to the end of the road at Nakhorn Phanom, the last town in Thailand that faces Vientiane across the Mekong River. He sat on the river bank for hours studying the river. He drove a few kilometers downriver, and then a few more kilometers upriver. He surveyed the current and watched the movements of the water. In the shallows along the bank he saw the wrecks of smugglers' boats that hadn't made it. He gave thought to the route he would take. Every attempt to smuggle people out of Laos had been made either upriver or downriver, as far away from Vientiane as possible. Why not try the opposite, he thought. Why not make the attempt right under their noses, right in the middle of the day, right in the middle of the city? Everyone would be completely off guard. He could be half way across the river by the time the guards alerted a patrol boat.

He drove upriver once again and parked. He walked for a kilometer or two along the mud bank. Because of the debris floating downriver with the current, he could slip into the water and snorkel most of the distance before he had to go underwater. He would be hardly visible with only his snorkel and part of his face mask above-water. If he began far enough upriver the current would carry him to the other side with little effort.

It was wild and crazy but far less risky than entrusting Kao's life to someone else. At least he would be in control. He talked to a few diving experts in Bangkok. It was possible, they said, but only with the right training and preparation. Timing was important. Kao would have to be waiting on the river bank at the precise moment he came out of the water.

There was, however, one drawback that John didn't tell anyone. Kao couldn't swim. In fact, she was terrified of water. "Once you reach her, you will have only two or three minutes to instruct her on using scuba," an instructor said. "Think you can do it?"

"I have no choice—when do we start training?"

John began immediately, and in the meantime he got word to Kao not to give up hope. He told her he had a plan, though he dared not tell her what it was.

John joined a local dive club and in the weeks that followed he went on every dive the club had. To further get into shape he did hundreds of push-ups and sit-ups each day. He jogged and he cut out drinking. Except for his instructor, his only other confidant was Dennis Gray at AP.

He had to make the crossing in April when the river is at its lowest. During the monsoons it would be impossible.

John got his final letter off to Kao. The time was set for Sunday afternoon when everyone was off work and the beach would be most crowded. Kao was to come down to the river with a friend. John would be on the opposite bank on the Thai side. He would flick his headlights on and off twice. At this signal, Kao was to stand up and comb her hair, to let John know she was there.

Two friends drove with John to the river crossing. Things were working exactly as planned. He flashed his lights and Kao stood up and combed her hair. "That's her," his friend said putting down his binoculars. "Go for it!"

They quickly drove a kilometer up river and here John slipped into the water. His friends wished him luck. He let the current carry him downstream to the Laotian side. It was an easy crossing, and with little difficulty John reached the top end of the sandbank that marked the beach. He now let the current carry him slowly down river, about twenty meters off shore, to a point where he figured Kao and her friend sat. He moved in closer, remaining just beneath the surface. Slowly he rose until his mask was just above water. He was five meters from shore. He saw people sitting on the sand and quickly ducked down before anyone took notice of him. Kao had to be one of them sitting there. He had to act with speed for the current was still carrying him downriver. Without hesitation he shot for the surface, but something had gone wrong.

John came up not in open water but under a boat with its bow pulled up on the beach. Again he rose to the surface. In a fleeting second he could see that it was a patrol boat, and along the rail were armed soldiers in green fatigues. As he bolted for the bottom, the first thought that came to mind was hand grenades. He pictured a soldier lobbing a hand grenade into water. He reached the muddy bottom and made a zigzag course back across the bottom of the Mekong River to Thailand. He never did learn if the soldiers had actually seen him, but he was more concerned about Kao who he knew would be disappointed. He sent her another letter, telling her to not give up.

Weeks passed. May came and went, and letter followed letter. Finally a second attempt was planned for the first week in June, this time on a weekday. John knew now that he would have difficulty picking Kao out of a crowd and on a weekday the beach would be less crowded. Kao would have to take time out from the university where she was studying but this could be arranged. Again things went as planned. John arrived by car, flashed his lights and Kao stood up and combed her hair. This time there were only two people on the shore.

As before, John crossed the river and surfaced at the same sandbank. He drifted with the current, and when he came to where he thought Kao would be, he slowly rose to the surface. He slid back his face mask, and his heart missed a beat.

Kao was sitting there all right, with a friend, but now they had been joined by two men, and both men carried .45s on their sides. They were soldiers. Without making the slightest movement, John floated slowly past them downriver. He had missed his second attempt, but he nevertheless felt victorious. Kao had seen him and had kept the soldiers distracted.

"It was now getting into June," John told me, "and the river was rising. It was now or never."

At eight o'clock one morning he and his two friends arrived at the river for the third attempt. A mist lay over the water and they could hardly see the opposite bank, but sure enough, when they blinked their lights, Kao stood up and through the mist they could see her combing her hair. As planned, she was with someone else.

John entered the water at his usual spot upriver, but now with the rising water the current was much swifter than he expected. It took him thirty minutes, fighting every meter of the way to reach the other side, but even with all his effort he couldn't make it to the sandbank where Kao and her friend waited. All he could do was watch the bank pass by. But he could see Kao clearly; she was with her young cousin. Both had fishing poles. John swam back to the Thai side.

He found his two friends waiting on the Thai shore and announced that he was going to make another try. It was still morning. They went back upriver, much farther this time, and John began his fourth attempt. He was completely exhausted now.

When John came to the surface some twenty meters from shore, he saw Kao and her little cousin walking away towards a group of soldiers. He had to do something. He knew he might never have another chance. He closed the distance to the bank, felt his feet touch bottom and stood up in full view. "Kao, Kao," he shouted at the top of his voice. She heard his cries, and turned, and when she saw him she did exactly what she was not supposed to do. She dropped her fishing rod and ran straight for him. With all eyes upon her, her little cousin included, Kao stopped a few meters away from John and stood there looking at him, tears flooding her eyes. She was about to throw herself into his arms when her cousin let out a terrifying scream. The young girl had fallen back when she saw a masked man coming up from the muddy river with all kinds of strange equipment, bits of seaweed and river debris hanging from his body. She then turned and ran, still screaming at the top of her voice. Now everyone on the beach was staring at them—the soldiers, the guards, the people who had come down to the river to enjoy the early afternoon. Everyone was too startled to realize what was happening.

Taking advantage of the confusion, John pulled Kao into the water, waist deep and quickly put the mask on her. "Just close your eyes and breathe," he said. He was surprised by how calm she remained. She had put all her confidence and trust in him. He kissed her on the forehead, squeezed her in a love embrace and they slipped beneath the surface–as curious eyes watched.

"We reached the sand bottom at three or four meters," John said. "We were out about twenty meters when she panicked. She went wild. She fought and kicked and pulled off her mask and regulator. We had to get back to the surface."

When they reached the surface, Kao was coughing and choking, and John pounded on her back to get the water from her lungs. A full five minutes had passed and those on shore now crowded the water's edge. When they saw the two surface, in what appeared to be a struggle, they believed Kao was being abducted. She was struggling against this strange man who had appeared from out of nowhere and was beating her.

Fortunately for John the current was now carrying them quickly downriver but the situation was becoming more complicated. He had to keep Kao's head above water while trying to refit the mask and regulator, and all the while they were being washed toward a military bunker at the end of the sand bank.

John had no alternative but to pull Kao ashore, and here they sat on the sand and rested. Minutes passed and slowly she regained her confidence. John kept whispering, "We'll make it, Kao, believe me. We'll make it." He was aware that soon the soldiers would be down upon them.

He had to try a different approach. With her swimming beneath him face down, she was looking into a black void. What if she were face up? He unfastened his belt and used it to tie her to him, face up. They would float only inches below the surface, where she could see him and the light above. They slipped back into the water.

It worked. This time Kao didn't panic. They floated past the bunkers and soldiers at the end of the sand bank, no more than forty meters off shore.

Once past the end of the bank, John began to swim with all the energy he had left. He was exhausted but still he couldn't stop. He had to fight not only the current but debris floating down river along with them. And he could hear beneath the water the sound of engines, boat engines. He was certain they were after him, and no doubt dropping charges.

But he also knew they were getting closer and closer to Thailand. Finally he reached the point where he had no strength remaining. He rose to the surface and pulled Kao's head above the water. He gave a shout of joy. They had drifted several kilometers down river, but that didn't matter. They were alive, and they were more than half-way across the Mekong River, well within Thai waters.

A Thai patrol boat working its way upriver saw them and pulled them on board. They radioed their report and within hours the news was flashing around the world. Dennis Gray in Bangkok was the first to put the story on the Associated Press wire service. The governor of the province even invited John and Kao to a gala lunch. That afternoon Kao had to be taken to the hospital to recover from the ordeal.

The next day, the governor who had wined and dined John, sadly informed him that he had to put him into jail. Kao was taken from the hospital and sent to a refugee camp. The Thai immigration authorities in Bangkok considered both John and Kao illegal immigrants. John was further charged with bringing an illegal immigrant into the country. He faced expulsion from Thailand and possibly a heavy fine. Kao would have to remain in a refugee camp until the authorities could decide what to do with her. John was given five minutes with Kao and then taken away to jail.

John hadn't considered that such a thing would happen to them. To complicate matters, he was broke. He didn't have five baht to his name. For all those months while he planned and trained for the rescue, he had not been able to work. Without cameras and equipment he couldn't continue with his photography. The next day he was transferred from the province to the immigration jail in Bangkok. He was not permitted to see Kao before being moved.

In Bangkok it appeared he would be deported back to Australia. He decided that once he was home and able to raise money he would arrange somehow to get Kao out of detention. He was planning his next move when a guard slid the bolt back on the door and called his name. He was told he had a long-distance telephone call. His parents must have tracked him down, he thought.

"My name is Hal Bartlett," the voice at other end of the line said and waited for a comment.

"Am I supposed to know you?" John asked.

"I'm calling from Los Angeles," the man replied. "I'm a movie producer." The first thought that came to John's mind was that this was a hoax.

"Yeah, yeah," John replied. The man from Los Angeles went on. In a very serious voice he explained why he had called.

"I read about you in the newspaper," he continued, "and I'd like to talk to you about doing a movie based on your adventures in Laos."

"I don't want any publicity," John said. The publicity, John figured, was doing him harm. Immigration would have dropped the case had not the press and other media made it such an issue. More publicity could be adverse, that he was convinced. The Thai press had been unmerciful. One news story stated: "Laotian girl in hospital after five nights of love-making with foreigner."

"I can arrange a ticket for you," Bartlett said. "You can fly here to Los Angeles and we can talk."

An air ticket to Los Angeles! John was all ears. This could be the solution he was looking for. He was aware that once he was out of Thailand he could re-enter the country legally and then secure Kao's release.

Thai immigration was satisfied with the proposal. Bartlett sent the air ticket and booked him a room at the Holiday Inn in Los Angeles.

John arrived in Los Angeles late at night; Bartlett was there to meet him, contract in hand. "It's that easy," he said. "Just need your signature."

John was skeptical. He didn't want to be rushed into something he wasn't sure about. He wasn't keen about a movie. Kao was still in detention. What effect would this have on getting her out? He had to think. He told Bartlett he couldn't sign such an important contract until he had a good night's sleep.

The next morning Bartlett met John at his hotel for breakfast. "Okay," Bartlett began over coffee, "I've rewritten your contract. I gathered from yesterday you didn't like the terms." John remained mum. It wasn't the terms that disturbed him; it was the movie and the publicity. Bartlett continued: "Aside from more money for your story, we'll hire you and Kao as advisors. You'll both be paid while we're filming. Accommodations, travel, everything paid for."

John signed and caught the next flight to Bangkok. With

money, and worldwide publicity, he was able to get Kao out of the refugee camp. They were married soon after.

At a later press conference Bartlett explained why he wanted the story: "I liked the idea of doing something different, and I liked the John Everingham role, and the man when I finally met him. He's a hero, not an antihero; a nice guy, a good guy. I think people need more good people to look up to and to follow. I don't mean that everybody should swim the Mekong River, as my character does in *Comeback*. But Everingham is a decent human being, who loved someone deeply. I think one of the alarming things in the world today is that people, men and women, are afraid to love."

Twentieth Century-Fox set the filming schedule. They would shoot three months in Thailand, and another month in Florida, for the underwater scenes. John was delighted. This was his chance to tell the story of the bombing of the villages in Laos, and he could inform the world about the fate of the MIAs. For hours he and Kao sat in front of tape recorders and told their story. John was thrilled when he learned Michael Landon, from the television series "Bonanza" and "The Little House on the Prairie," would be playing his part. He knew Michael was sympathetic to the causes of justice and righteousness.

Kao would be played by Moira Chen. John's instructor and advisor was the British actor Edward Woodward, and the Russian officer in Vientiane would be played by a new German actor, Jurgen Prochnow. In the movie John had an American girlfriend. Her part was to be played by Priscilla Presley, the wife of the late Elvis Presley.

"On paper it looked good," John said. "In reality it was quite a bomb." Prochnow was established in Germany but had never done a film in English. Moira Chen was a model living in Rome at the time and had played only small roles in unimportant Italian movies. And Priscilla Presley had very little experience as an actress."

Once the filming began, John and Kao were ignored by both the producer and director. They had no say in the direction, costumes, the dialogue, or anything else.

"They wanted to embellish the story in their own way," John said. "The story was much better in reality. It could have shown depth, conflicts of minds between East and West and so many things."

At once it was obvious to John that Michael Landon was just a swaggering cowboy, not a freewheeling Australian expat covering a war in Indochina. He was out of place and didn't fit into the Asian scene.

"I liked him," John said, "but he had his own ideas. We got along, but he wasn't interested in facts, the truth. Hollywood wanted their own bang-bang movie, and that's what they got. I was not even invited to the opening."

John has yet to see the movie and refuses to talk about it publicly. But, he admits, the money did offer him a new start.

With some of the money he received for his story line, John did a crazy thing that he wouldn't normally have done. It came from his love for food, Asian food, and particularly Indian food. He always said if he had the money, he'd start his own restaurant, hire the best Indian chef money could buy, and then create a menu with all the dishes he favored. When the movie was finally completed, John remembered his friend, Cha Cha, a famous Bengali who had been the personal chef for Lord Mountbatten. Cha Cha had been working in Laos before the revolution and had made a name for himself with the expats there. John contacted Cha Cha and together they opened the Himali Cha Cha, a chic little restaurant behind the Trocadero off New Road in Bangkok. John designed the decor.

With the movie over and the war winding down in

Vietnam Today

A weapon yesterday becomes a toy today

Southeast Asia, John returned to photography, his first
love. He set up a studio and began his own publishing
business in Bangkok. But he is still adamant about the
MIAs and the way it is being handled. "All you need do to
get elected in America is say you can get inside information
on MIAs. Look at your Senate Select Committee on POW
Affairs; they couldn't answer the big question. They had a
budget of $1.9 million a year of research time, unlimited
travel, access to top-secret records and a staff of
experienced investigators. But they still couldn't answer
the big question. Are U.S. POWs alive in Southeast Asia?"

John is outspoken about the MIAs. "You know damn
well that they couldn't take everyone off the embassy roof
top when they were evacuating Saigon. You know damn
well some Americans were left behind and became
prisoners when the United States withdrew its troops
from Vietnam in 1973," he continued.

At a press conference when he was released from Laos,
a reporter asked him the question: "Why would they keep
prisoners all these years?"

John answered without hesitation: "There is no possible
reason for them to do so. It's against their own interests,
and if they didn't shoot them long ago they would be
foolish, more reason for them to shoot them now than to
let them go. To do so now would make themselves look
like liars, fools."

John remains angry about the whole MIA business.

I first got to know John many years ago when he was a
correspondent in Vietnam. I used to listen to him brag,
as many Australians do, about how his early ancestors came
to Australia aboard a prison ship from England. History
tells us that Sydney was founded as a British penal colony.
"On the very first ship, in fact," John would say. We all
listened but few of us really believed it. And even if it were
true, it would be a difficult thing to prove. *National*

Geographic didn't think so. In February, 1988, the magazine devoted an entire issue to Australia, and in one section called "Children of the First Fleet" John's story appears. It begins: "Banished to the farthest corner of the Earth, a cargo of British convicts inaugurated a nation when they landed at Sydney on January 26, 1788. One of those aboard the infamous First Fleet was Matthew Everingham, transported for stealing two law books... Photojournalist John Everingham here recounts his ancestor's story and visits with many of his Australian relatives." There were many red faces when that issue came out.

John is a successful businessman, but first and foremost he's still an adventurer. He takes his camera to the far reaches of Asia and the South Pacific. He has trekked the high Himalayas and explored the depths of the Oriental jungles. He has dived on every reef worth diving on in Southeast Asia, and his collection of photographs of the Thai Royal Family is probably more complete than that of any other foreign photographer in Thailand. He dines with heads-of-state and drinks with *samlor* drivers. He is in touch with the pulse beat of Asia. A short while back, he asked me to accompany him on an expedition across the Australian Outback to look for lost Aboriginal cave petroglyphs. The safari took us to the Kimberly Range. John thrives on action. We met drovers driving cattle by helicopter. John asked if we could fly with them, and then asked the pilot to remove the doors so that he could get better photographs. My knuckles turned purple holding myself in when we did banks and sharp turns. John hung far out the side like the old pro that he is. That same afternoon he went waist deep into a crocodile-infested river to get the shot he wanted.

"There's crocodile in there," I exclaimed.

"Safer than V.C.s," he replied.

John and Kao have two lovely children, both boys, and

they live in a grand house with a beautiful lotus pool at the edge of Bangkok. But chances are you won't find John at home. He'll be somewhere where the action is.

A young Hans Hoefer poses.

Hoefer today with family.

Chapter 2

HANS HOEFER
From Rugs to Riches

The first time I saw Hans Hoefer was on Bali in the Fall of 1969. He and his attractive assistant, writer Star Black, were staying at the newly opened Bali Beach Hotel. The story I heard was that Hans and Star were preparing a guidebook on Bali, jointly sponsored by the hotel where they were staying and the tourist association.

I knew Star's mother, Cobby Black. She had a gossip column in the *Bangkok World* and when she heard I was traveling to Bali she had asked that I look up her daughter. One afternoon at the Bali Beach I gave Star a call in her room and invited her down to the lobby for a drink. Tall and blond, in her early twenties, and with the flair of an American college student, Star was cordial, but it was obvious she had joined me out of a sense of obligation. She said she was terribly busy, and before we parted I caught a glimpse of Hans. He was impatiently standing at the desk, waiting for Star to join him. "We're going on a shoot," she said. We shook hands and as she rushed off, I got a second look at Hans while he and Star were leaving the hotel. He was thin, very tall, well over six feet, and had a crop of unruly hair. Not much older than Star, he was dressed in the fashion of most young men of the day— bell-bottom trousers, a baggy-sleeved shirt and wide belt with a big buckle. Instead of boots, however, he wore sandals. Star helped him with his camera bags.

I didn't give much more thought to Hans or Star. There was talk about them on the island, and about their project. Everyone agreed that Bali did need a good guidebook. The enchanted island was on the verge of opening up to international tourism. Blue prints for a dozen new hotels were approved and the landing strip at the airport was being extended to accommodate super jets flying directly from overseas. Thai Airways International was launching the first international service, and I was there to report on their inaugural flight. The extension was not yet completed when the flight was due to arrive, but that did not stop Thai Airways. When the Caravelle jet dropped out of the blue sky and touched down at the end of the tarmac, a parachute suddenly popped out from its tail and brought the aircraft to a halt. It was exciting for all of us at the airport to watch, and equally exciting for us to witness a new era coming to an island of old traditions.

Guide to Bali was published a year later, and in a very short time it appeared on news stands in every city in Asia. It was an immediate success. The first edition had a print run of 20,000 copies and was sold out within months. It won awards from *Popular Photography* and the American Society of Travel Agents for its use of photographic illustration.

Hans was hailed as a bright new star in the publishing business. His photographs, everyone declared, were supreme. The guide, the critics said, was a new approach to guidebooks, with its historical background, and an interplay on the customs and culture of the Balinese.

Other honors were to follow, and among them was a special award by the top professionals of the New York Art Directors Club for Hans' original concept, creative ideas, and handsome results. Hans immediately set out to produce two more books in a series, one on Singapore and another on Malaysia. The question everyone now asked was could Hans make a repeat performance?

He did, and his success was phenomenal. He began a publishing empire with a single book and within twenty years Apa Productions, the name of his company, was

publishing more than two hundred titles, printed in eight
languages. More awards and recognition followed. His
highest accolade came when Singapore's Nanyang
University presented him with the Entrepreneurship
Excellence Award for Man of the Year.

How was it possible that a man who came to Asia with a
pack on his back could in twenty years become one of the
biggest and most successful guidebook publishers in the
world, and a millionaire several times over? More than
two and a half million copies of Apa guides are sold each
year, with a turnover of more than twenty million dollars.
How did he do it? To give you the answer, I must go back
to Singapore and the second time I saw Hans Hoefer.

This time we were formally introduced. The Singapore
book was nearing completion and now it was Star. who
contacted me. Hans wanted to see me, she said, and
arranged for us to meet in a little Chinese coffee shop in
town. Hans was pleasant, filled with smiles. He announced
he had an offer to make me. He asked if I would write the
Malaysian guide. "It will take at least a year," he explained.
"We'll cover every inch of Malaysia, every town, every back
road, the beaches, the rivers, the mountains. We'll explore
the jungles. We'll come up with something no one has
ever seen."

Han's enthusiasm was infectious. But I was uncertain. I
liked Hans from the start, but I hardly knew anything about
him, and to commit myself for a year was more than I
wanted to do. I had been toying with the idea for the past
few years of building a sailing schooner in Singapore and
outfitting it for an extended South Seas voyage. I also
had my own travel column to write every week for the
Bangkok World.

"You'll have time of your own," Hans insisted. "You can
do your column. *The Straits Times* has agreed to provide
us a house in Kuala Lumpur where you can live. You can

have a cook, a secretary, a part-time researcher. You'll have time for your other projects too."

The more he talked the more interesting his proposal became. His voice became mingled with my own thoughts. I could put off building the schooner for another year, I reasoned. And while traveling around Malaysia I could gather material for my column. He said we'd explore the jungles. I had done some jungle "bashing" and always wanted to go back. We would travel to the offshore islands and go diving on the reefs. This would help me later when I had my schooner. We would go spelunking in the caves in Borneo, climb Southeast Asia's highest mountain, interview sultans and get to know ministers and curators of museums. We would do everything I always wanted to do, and more. Hans was a master at his trade. He could wheedle anyone into doing what he wanted them to do. I found myself asking when we would start.

Within a week I was settled into a house in Kuala Lumpur. Hans kept his promise. He had at the house waiting for my arrival a wonderful *baba* Chinese cook who introduced me to all kinds of new *nonya* dishes, a Chinese woman on loan from *The Straits Times* who would be my secretary, and a young Tamil student from the University of Malaysia who would work as my part-time researcher. The only thing missing was a butler.

Our first order of business was a call on Mohammed Khan, the Chief Game Warden of Malaysia. I had met him several times before and now wanted to talk to him about further jungle explorations.

It's exciting just going to Mohammed's office. The offices of the Game Department are housed in two-story wooden buildings at the outskirts of Kuala Lumpur. Rangers in khaki uniforms parade through the buildings, and the hallways are usually crowded with equipment, some new and shiny heading out on an expedition, others battered and mud-covered returning from a jungle trip. In the reception room to Mohammed's office are a pair of elephant tusks taken from a poacher, and piles of bones and animal skulls. I was immediately reminded of the first time I had met Mohammed. He was assistant game warden then, and the Game Department was in Seremban, some fifty miles from K.L. Mohammed was not in his office when I arrived. He was sitting in a barn-like shed, surrounded by heaps of bleached-white elephant bones, all neatly marked and labeled. For several years he had been collecting bones and was working out a theory how he could determine an elephant's age by its foot size.

Hans and I found Mohammed seated behind a spacious desk cluttered with paperwork, for which he apologized. "I'd rather be in the jungle," he commented. At one side of his desk was the Malaysian national colors, and on the wall behind him was a huge relief map of the Malay Peninsula. Under Mohammed's supervision and guidance is one of the largest and oldest jungles in the world, with dozens of animals that are on the endangered species list, the Asian elephant included.

Mohammed shook hands with Hans and me, bid us to take a seat and ordered coffee. "Lucky you didn't wait," he said after we explained why we had come. "I'm leaving next week and will be gone a month." He then rose from his chair and stood next to the map. He started talking about elephants, about a herd that was reported in the northern reaches of the National Park. I remembered that first meeting with Mohammed when I interviewed him about his method for determining the age of elephants in the wild. Saving the wild elephants was Mohammed's main interest. "We're setting out to see if we can track down this herd," he said, pointing to the map.

"Will it take long?" I asked, looking at Hans. I think Hans

and I had the same idea.

"Three weeks, maybe a month."

"Who's all going?" Hans asked this time.

"I handpicked three rangers, four negrito porters, two guides, ten in all," he said, and by now he knew what was on our minds. "It's going to be rough. We plan to follow the Tembeling River to its source, cross over the peninsula through unexplored jungle and try to locate the source of the Liber River, a tributary of the Pahang. We then build bamboo rafts and float downriver. We'll be fighting rapids all the way."

I don't know how but we convinced Mohammed to take us with him. The expedition took a month and gave us enough material for a book chapter which we called "The Green Heart," and enough material for me to do dozens of newspaper and magazine articles. And it gave me the chance to get to know Hans better. There's something very intimate about the jungle, when after a hard day

Hans Hoefer resting on a log mid-stream in the Malay jungle.

you've bathed in the river, had dinner by the camp fire and tucked yourself in under a mosquito net for a night's needed sleep. It's then, when you are at peace with the world, that thoughts come to you, clear thoughts, and you talk without inhibitions.

Hans told how he had never known his father. "He died when I was two years old," he said. He brightened up when he said he was raised near Stuttgart. "I think that's why I like to travel," he said. "Stuttgart is home of the Mercedes. As a kid the test drivers used to feel sorry for me and they'd take me for drives. When I was a little older they took me on trips."

These were the dreadful war years. Hans' father had been an art teacher in northern Germany. When World War II began he was given a commission in the home forces and assigned to an anti-aircraft unit which took him and his family to southern Germany. In the winter of 1945, Hans' father was transferred to the Russian front. Hans never saw his father again. He and his mother, along with his brother and his sister, were stranded in a little village in southern Germany. It was there that Hans grew up.

The Hoefers lived away from the rest of their relatives. Hans and his sister Helga were very close. Helga was blind and Hans had to take care of her.

At the age of seventeen, and the war being over, Hans went to Dusseldorf, "back to my basic roots," as he puts it, to study printing. "Not just to study a trade or craft," he explained, "but to become a real apprentice in the old-fashioned sense of learning everything I possibly could about the subject."

Next it was art school for a diploma in graphic design, then a masters degree in printing. He was among the last students to graduate from what was called the traditional "Bauhaus School."

"It has changed since my days there," he said, "when

certain groups of designers could trace associations back to the Middle Ages. With printing, it went all the way back to Gutenberg's invention of the press in the late 1400s."

Every now and then the sounds of the jungle night would come to an abrupt stop, and we would halt our conversation, expecting elephants to come crashing down upon us. Gradually the sounds returned and Hans picked up where he left off.

Parallel with his interest in graphics was a devotion to satisfying his wanderlust. His travels began when he was in his teens with bicycle tours of Europe and North Africa. The same year the printing apprenticeship commenced he spent his summer holidays hiking and biking around Morocco. Later he was able to support his studies by working as a part-time tour guide.

"In the late fifties and early sixties train travel was in vogue, and every weekend I'd take a long trip looking after a train carriage of holidaymakers," he explained, swatting a mosquito that had gotten inside his net, "and it gave me enough money to go to school and study design."

The jungle trip began our close association. Hans had his office in Singapore and whenever we planned a trip he'd come flying up to K.L. and off we'd go traipsing on new adventures. As he said in the beginning, we would leave no corner of Malaysia untouched. We turned up some amazing discoveries about Malaysia. During the week I would spend hours in the basement of the National Museum and other library archives, researching every rumor, legend, and modicum of anthropological and historical data I and my researcher could find. When we uncovered something that might prove interesting, Hans and I would use the weekend to investigate, by whatever means appropriate: Land Rover, plane, Avis, riverboat or shanks' mare. We followed trail after trail on what at times appeared to be wild-goose chases through remote jungles, lonely islands, forgotten villages and isolated hill stations. We found a Buddhist monk living in one cave, and a hermit in another. We located an abandoned and forgotten European castle in the jungle, built by a mad English rubber planter named Kellie-Smith. It's now on the tourist map. We explored caves and traveled with Tunku Mohammed Archibald to Tioman Island on the East Coast. Archibald was looking for a place to build a tourist resort, and when we passed Rawa Island, Hans pointed it out and said, "There's your island." Rawa today is a popular resort.

Hans enlisted the help of Tan Sri Mubin Sheppard, an Englishman who joined the colonial Malayan civil service in 1928. Promoted to district officer, he was interned by the Japanese during the war and tortured when they found that he was running a secret postal service between two camps. The war ended and in the 1950s he became the British adviser of Kelantan and Negri Sembilan. He helped set up the National Archives and founded the National Museum. After Independence in 1957, he elected to stay in Malaysia and became a citizen.

Mubin Sheppard willingly shared with us his knowledge of the Malaysian culture. He led us to the East Coast, and told us how when there were no roads he got about by cycling along the beach at low tide. He took us to the palace of the Sultan of Perak so that Hans could photograph the Sultan's treasures—krises made of gold and crowns studded with jewels. At Kuala Kangsar he pointed out a knurled and twisted tree. Nearly a hundred years old, it was the first rubber tree that Henry Ridley, aptly nicknamed "Rubber Ridley," had planted in Malaya. Ridley's hope was that one day coffee planters would turn to the cultivation of rubber. He was scoffed by the planters until John Dunlop invented the bicycle tire and Henry Ford put the automobile on the assembly line. After that the planters couldn't get rubber saplings fast enough.

Every time I thought I had gotten to know Hans, I would find out something new about him. He had little secrets that he never talked about, but which came out when you least expected them. Early one morning we were photographing on the Langkawi Islands when we came upon a group of men practicing martial arts on a deserted beach. Their instructor, who called himself Killer Kong, drilled them in the defensive art of tae kwon do. He kicked out a leg, and his students kicked out a leg; he did a twist and a twirl, and his students did a twist and a twirl. They looked impressive in their linen white trousers and open jackets, held in place with bright sashes.

Killer Kong saw us standing in the back and motioned for us to come forth. "You know tae kwon do?" he asked Hans. Hans said he was only familiar with judo. "Good," Killer Kong said, "but do you know tae kwon do is superior to judo?" Hans gave him a smile. The master then beckoned for Hans to come closer. "Here," he said to Hans, placing a hand on Hans' shoulder, "let's see you throw me." Hans started to back away. "Come on, come on," the man insisted. Hans just stood there looking at him. "You can't throw Killer Kong," he said, tapping his chest. The expression on Hans' face changed.

It was so quick I hardly saw it happen, but in the next moment Killer Kong lay flat on his back looking up at the sky. He quickly jumped to his feet, dusted himself off, and smilingly said in a loud voice for his students to hear, "See, that's what I have been telling you. You must be prepared at all times. I had to show you what happens when you are not prepared." He turned to face Hans, his open hands extended like he was ready to smash a stack of bricks. "Come, let me see you do it again."

Hans threw him again. He threw him down hard on the sand, and then gave a hand to help him up.

"You, you are a black belt?" Killer Kong said sheepishly. Hans bowed, from the waist.

"Yes," he replied. "You must forgive me. I should have said something."

"I never knew you were a champion black belt," I said to Hans when we were out of hearing range.

"I'm not," he said. "I'm only a brown belt." I didn't know until then that Hans had studied judo.

A similar thing happened one day when we were walking down the beach at Batu Ferringhi in Penang. Star was with us. A trainer came by riding a spirited horse and leading another. I surmised they were racehorses from the track in Penang. Star asked the trainer if she could ride. He dismounted but was reluctant to turn over the reins to her. Instead, Hans leaped on the horse's back and went thundering down the beach. His legs were too long to fit in the stirrups but that didn't seem to bother him at all. There was no doubt he had much riding experience. "Where did you learn to ride?" I asked him after he dismounted. "I've always been a frustrated cowboy," he replied.

Hans became fascinated with scuba diving. He had never dived in his life but after one lesson he was doing deep dives on our trips to the islands off the East Coast. I remember one incident where I was on the bottom at about thirty feet when I noticed I was alone. Then Hans appeared and with slow movements he motioned for me to follow him to the surface. I hadn't noticed but a huge shark had been circling a few feet above me. Hans had come to my rescue.

On all our trips, whether it was trekking in the jungles or island exploring, I carried my own cameras with me. I was keen on taking pictures and worked hard at getting good shots. I could stand with Hans looking at a scene, and with the same lens and same exposure point my camera in the same direction he did, but when we had the films developed, there was no comparison. Hans could see a picture no one else could. It took a while and I finally figured out what it was. It was training. Hans had training. In every sense of the word he had an eye for photographs. He had mentioned that his sister Helga was blind, and that he had to take care of her when they were youngsters in Germany. Through Hans, Helga got to know the world. This was a very important factor in Hans' life, walking around as he did in his youth, looking after a blind sister. "I provided the eyes," he said. "The whole intensity of living came through me, and the experience taught me to see the world with a different perspective." Hans in turn became the camera's eye, and as he had showed his sister the world through his eyes, now he takes photographs so that other people can see the world with his unique perception.

Hans loves to drive, and once he took over the wheel it was impossible to get it back. He revealed the secret of why he liked to drive one evening when we were sitting at the Titik Inn on the East Coast, talking to Brian Hughes, the owner. Brian is a British expat who came to the East as a conscripted soldier to fight communist insurgents hiding out in the Malay jungle during the Emergency, and in the wildest, most romantic story you could ever imagine, fell in love with a beautiful princess. She was Malay, and a real honest-to-goodness princess. Her name was Tunku Zahara. She too fell in love with Brian. They ran off and got married, and as all fairy tale prophecies, they were living happily ever after in their garden paradise when I met them. Their paradise in this case was the inn which they built. They lived their dream world, and if customers never came to the inn, so much the better. In fact, we had a hard time arousing them when we arrived. And so over drinks at the bar, before the dinner that

Princess Zahara was preparing, Hans told us about his early driving experiences.

Hans financed his studies and early travels by driving second-hand Mercedes to Iran during school holidays, trading them for carpets, and then selling the carpets back in Germany. About this time he also began writing for his hometown newspaper, gaining recognition locally.

"All this driving gave me the itch for travel," he said. He got his diploma at art school in Krefeld graphic design, and unlike other graduating students who went to work for agencies, Hans bought a Volkswagen van, teamed up with a, friend, and decided to drive to Nepal. He arrived at the end of 1968 and there decided not to return to Germany.

Hans can recall the exact spot where he made his decision. "I went to a place in the hills outside of Kathmandu with a 360-degree view of the Himalayas," he said, "and there, among all that beauty, and absolute freedom, I thought it over. I didn't want to stop here. I wanted to go on, forever, down through Southeast Asia, all the way to Australia. I wrote home telling them the news. It wasn't an easy thing to do."

After Hans sold the van, he traveled by bus and train down through India to Madras and from there caught a banana boat to Penang in Malaysia. He began wandering, wherever his fancy took him, through Thailand to Laos, and then to the Khmer ruins at Angkor Wat in Cambodia. Back down through Malaysia to Singapore, and from there by trading boat through the Indonesian archipelago to Bali. He arrived in Bali at the end of 1969.

Like all those before him, all the artists, writers, poets and travelers who had ever visited Bali, he too became bewitched by the island. Along the road to Bali he befriended another German graphic designer, Werner Hahn, and together they wandered around the island, living in different villages, sketching and painting. "I painted, when I felt creative," he said, "and I loafed when I felt lazy. I let the island's beauty work on me. It began to have its effect. Gradually I realized I wanted to start building my establishment here in Southeast Asia."

Hans became good friends with the Dutch artist Han Snel who had been living on the island since the end of the Second World War.

Hans recalls that Bali was going through the nightmare of opening the Bali Beach Hotel. Built by Japanese repatriation money, it was the biggest and most luxurious hotel on the island. But business was not good. There were few tourists going to Indonesia in the early years. The year Hans and Star were there, the hotel had sixteen guests, and fourteen hundred employees. "The hotel needs advertising," Han Snel said to Hans and introduced him to the German manager, Siegfried Beil. Together they hatched a plan. To attract tourists, Bali needed an attractive guidebook. Hans put his mind to work.

The foundation stone, as he saw it, was a paperback book—The Book, he called it—on the enchantment of the island. It had to include a comprehensive text and enough superb color photographs to give even armchair travelers a true picture of Bali's beauty and artistry. The idea was no more than a photojournalist's pipe dream, but Hans had the very solid background of printing and graphics training to put it together. Star Black arrived with an introduction from her mother to Seigfried and became the writer/editor for the project.

Financial support came from the Bali Beach Hotel, where Siegfried Beil's imaginative management was willing to take the unusual step–for a hotel–of going into publishing. "Not as a giveaway, or a write-off," said Hans, "but as a profit-making venture." Beil knew that a fine book on Bali would upgrade tourism, and his young partner in the enterprise knew how it should be done.

"I had it pictured perfectly in my mind before the first words were written and the first photographs taken," Hans admitted. He and Werner Hahn went to work taking photographs. The book's two hundred photographs were selected from more than two thousand they took. The text grew to 100,000 words.

Finally, after painstaking editing and re-editing, adding and replacing selected photos, the entire package was taken to Singapore for printing. The book was on sale by May, 1970, and turned a profit before the end of the calendar year.

The rest is history.

Hans turned his house in Singapore into a miniature Bali. He and Star brought back collections of masks, paintings and artifacts that adorned their walls and gardens. Hans longed to go back to Bali but now he had new directions he wanted to go. A year came and went and still we hadn't finished the Malaysian book. Hans was a perfectionist and everything had to be just right. When he had trouble with the labs that developed his photographs, he began his own. When a photograph didn't suit his satisfaction, he went out and shot another. And if he didn't like a section of the book, we rewrote it. All this took time.

In the meanwhile, the plans for my schooner arrived, and I was anxious to begin construction. I even found a yard in Singapore where I could begin building.

But Hans had other ideas. In his publishing agreement with *The Strait Times*, he would have full publishing rights starting with the second edition, which was the Singapore book. Star completed the text, and Mort Rosenblum, a mutual close friend, wrote the introduction. Mort was at the time the bureau chief for all of Southeast Asia for the Associated Press.

What Hans had in mind now was to start his own publishing company. He envisioned a series of guidebooks similar to his guides to Bali, Singapore and Malaysia. He thought of them as a "family of books."

"They wouldn't look alike," he said, "but they would have a continuity of style that makes them recognizable." To make sure the first book was just as planned, he recalls standing and watching at the side of the Singapore printers, supervising every step.

The format was faithfully carried out with the Singapore and Malaysia guides, even to his business arrangements with *The Straits Times*. Now Hans was ready to move. When the Malaysian book was completed, making it the third in the series, Hans had a proposition for Mort and me.

"Join my team," he said, "and we'll make it together." He sounded convincing, but we were concerned that oftentimes Hans was too rash when precaution was necessary. We were worried about his spending. He didn't care about costs when it came to getting a book published. He didn't care if it took two dozen rolls of film to get the right photograph, or if he had to hire a helicopter at hundreds of dollars an hour. Mort and I pondered over a solution, and we came up with the idea of hiring a business manager. If we could convince Hans to do this, to hire someone who would be an arbitrator and whose decisions would be final, then we would join the team. Hans, to our surprise, agreed. He would look for a sharp business manager immediately.

In spite of the hot, sticky weather that's so common in Singapore during the monsoons, Mort and I were elated that late afternoon as we walked down the narrow lane from Hans' house and headed to Bukit Timah to catch a taxi into town.

Mort had made a difficult decision, more so than any of us. He was giving up his position as bureau chief for

Associated Press in Southeast Asia. I went back to
California to wind up my affairs and Mort and his wife
Randi headed to Vietnam on an assignment. A month
later we received cables from Hans. He had hired a
business manager, a sharp attorney, he said, who had been
defending G.I.s in Vietnam. Our first meeting was called.
Mort and I returned to Singapore, and there we met
Henry Aronson.

"Aronson, the new business manager for Apa," he said
holding out a hand when we were introduced. He was
slight of build with kinky hair, and married to a very pretty
New Yorker. She came into the conference room with me.
Mort and Randi were nowhere around.

Without waiting for Mort to arrive, Henry began.
"Stephens," he said when I was seated, "I believe we all agree
to the terms. In the new company, Apa International, I am
to serve as business manager, and I understand from you
and Mort, that you two want me to be the sole arbitrator."

I nodded.

"Then I must tell you," he continued, "my word will be
final." He paused. I knew instantly he had something up
his sleeve. I could feel the tension. "I find, after careful
consideration of the matter, that the services of one Harold
Stephens and one Mort Rosenblum are no longer needed.
You have little to contribute to Apa, except your writing,
and we can always hire writers. In other words, Apa doesn't
need you."

That was my first and last meeting with Henry Aronson.
I hadn't know it, but Mort had already walked out. When
he and Randi had arrived at the office that morning, Randi
walked into the lab, and according to Mort, Henry said to
her, nastily:"Only staff is allowed back here. You'll have to
leave." Right then and there Mort decided not to leave
the Associated Press to join Hans and his rude lawyer pal.
In 1973, Mort was tranferred to Argentina to head the

South American operation, and a year after that became the Editor-in-Chief of the Paris *International Herald Tribune*. I went on to build my schooner in Singapore, sailed it to Bangkok where I outfitted it and spent the next dozen years sailing the South China Seas and the South Pacific. Hans went on to become the biggest guidebook publisher in Asia and the millionaire that he predicted he would become by the time he was thirty-five.

My meetings with Hans after that were sporadic. I'm sure he worked with his writers and photographers much the same way as we had done on the Malaysian book. There were, as can be expected, troubles in his organization from time to time. Business manager Henry Aronson didn't last long. Mort and I thought by hiring him we could keep expenses down. Henry took a business trip around the world to see buyers, and Hans got the bill. Hans in turn fired him. Star went to Thailand to do the Thai book, and soon after that left the company to return to the U.S. Today she is an editor and photographer with United Press International in New York. Another business partner came and went.

Hans' rise to the top wasn't easy. "In ten years I had produced only nine books," he said. "I was winning awards, getting a name, but no money was coming in; I mean money to expand. I was making a nice living but that wasn't want I wanted. I had to do something. I had no outside financing. Banks wouldn't even give me an overdraft."

Hans explained that in the beginning when Apa Productions was first formed, it cost US$50,000 to produce a book. Now, he claimed, it cost US$100,000. The cheapest place in the world to print was Singapore, and by keeping a small staff without writers and photographers on his pay roll he could do it. There were times when another person would have given in, but Hans never even considered it. Few people agreed with him, and, in fact, more were against him than with him. "People are leery about anything new, something that was never tried before," he said. His concept for his books was new and original. "And life here in Asia, if you have to suffer through life you might as well do it in Asian conditions," he lamented. "Living in Asia, doing what I wanted to do with people I liked, that was important. My philosophy was if something didn't work, try it another way. I did this all the time. Doing it is most important, and once it's done, forget it instantly and go on to the next thing."

In the beginning Hans had endless disagreements with printers, mostly over how things should be done. To solve the problem, he bought printing presses and started his own printing business. Then when book publishing became high-tech, he computerized his operations.

Hans' real success came when he went to the Frankfurt book fair in 1980. For the fair he had some of his books translated, and once there he got people interested in his product. It took him ten years to produce his first nine titles. In the next ten years he produced two hundred titles.

Apa doesn't hire or use the services of big name photographers. Hans prefers to find prospective, aspiring photographers, mostly local talent, and then hire them for relatively little cost. They work for recognition. Hans is the main motivator and driving force. In his twenty years in the business, and having had hundreds of people on his team, Hans has given people the chance to make names for themselves after leaving Apa. Hans has given them the start they needed.

Apa Publications today has three editorial directors, one in London, one in Munich and another in Singapore. Each director has at least four managing editors below him, all employed staff. Each editor can manage five or six books at one time. From an office at home with a staff of three, Hoefer Communications and Hoefer Press now employ over a hundred people and operate out of Hans' own factory premises in Singapore's industrial estate in Jurong with direct editorial links to his offices in London and Munich.

Hans has gone beyond publishing only guidebooks. Apa's *Insight Guides* also publish wildlife books that include the Amazon, Africa, Southeast Asia and India. There are others like *Crossing America, Marine Life in the South China Seas* and *Waterways of Europe*. Established books are coming out in new languages, and new books are being printed in several languages. *Eater of the Winds* is a book about Bugis traders. Bali is obviously Hans' great love and he has several books on the island that include *Stoned Images*, about the island's carvings, and *Hall of Justice*, which Hans describes as a " Bali Divine Comedy."

Hans guarantees photographers who sign up with him another advantage. Apa is also a picture bank, a repository of thousands of some of the best photographs ever taken in the Asia/Pacific region. Apa produces and organizes regional photo exhibitions for major corporations and Apa photographers undertake special assignments for international publications. Apa encourages its photographers to bank their photographs with the agency.

The company also has co-publishing arrangements with other leading companies around the world—European, American and Australian publishers—with lines that include travel, art and photography books.

Hans had to become a sort of jack-of-all-trades in publishing. "This business takes patience, faith in the outcome, and money in the beginning," he explained. "I had plenty of faith, and some patience, but very little money. I was fortunate to find good partners for those first three books."

"The time it takes to assemble words and pictures, edit, print, and distribute is endless," said Hans. "It seems

Hans Hoefer, founder of *Insight Guides,* poses behind some of the two hundred titles that his company now publishes.

forever before the profits start to come in." But eventually they do, each and every time around, which is a record few publishers anywhere in the world can equal.

Hans normally spends half the year "in harness" in the office and half the year traveling to sell, consolidate deals, or to photograph. But, as he told me when he was showing me around his factory, he'd like to spend more time in the field photographing.

Hans is happy in Singapore. He is a Singapore permanent resident, has a lovely Singaporean wife and two children, an 80-foot schooner which he had built in Turkey, and a great colonial house filled with treasures. He has come a very long way since he first arrived in Singapore, with a pack on his back, wondering where to go next.

Della Butcher—A heart for the arts.

Chapter 3

DELLA BUTCHER
Singapore's Grand Dame of the Arts

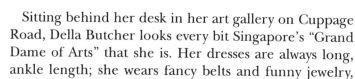

Sitting behind her desk in her art gallery on Cuppage Road, Della Butcher looks every bit Singapore's "Grand Dame of Arts" that she is. Her dresses are always long, ankle length; she wears fancy belts and funny jewelry, jewelry which could include anything from seeds to wood chips; and her red hair is loosely tied up in a bun.

There's usually an artist or two in the shop. The phone rings and her assistant passes the phone to her. "Yes, darling, you must stop by." Della's accent is English. Still on the phone, she gets up to address a customer who is about to depart. "Wait, wait, don't go," she says, "I want to hear more about what you're doing."

Talk to anyone in Singapore, and they will tell you what a great woman Della is. She is great, and she's not only interested in art; she's interested in people. Everyone. Her friends are oilmen from offshore rigs, jungle trekkers, filmmakers, actors and actresses, poets, writers, treasure hunters and the man and woman on the street. Some people bring home stray animals; Della brings home stray people, many of them destitute. She is one person who believes everyone is truly worth a book. "Just by their being alive makes it so," she says.

There's another side to Della, that debonair lady sitting behind the desk, with her reading glasses on a gold chain around her neck. She's an adventurer, with a bit of the devil in her soul. But then, if she wasn't, she wouldn't be living in Singapore nurturing budding artists. Let me tell you about the first time I met her.

That was back in the mid 1970s, and I have to admit, it

wasn't under the best conditions. I was standing at the boat landing far up the Tembeling River in Malaysia's National Park, waiting for the riverboat to bring up a group of passengers that I was to lead into the jungle on a weekend safari. I did a double take when the boat arrived and the passengers began to disembark. At that moment I wished I hadn't accepted the job.

First off was a Chinese gentleman, a Mr. Chan Tek, and his middle-aged wife who was wearing tight silk pajamas. The boatman whispered that he was an important banker in Kuala Lumpur. Then came a businessman in bright fluorescent-green Bermuda shorts whose ten-year-old son wore glasses so thick they looked like the bottoms of Coke bottles. I found out later he was the manager of Singer Sewing Machine Company in Southeast Asia and had an office in Singapore. Other assorted people disembarked, mostly in the travel business, and all dressed in motley outfits. Last came Della, dressed in a Saks Fifth Avenue safari outfit, with high boots and a solar topee with a mosquito net dangling down the back. She was, I must say, the only one who looked the part.

I should explain the circumstances that brought us all together.

A big and progressive Singapore tour company—I won't mention the name—had the idea that they might be able to sell jungle safaris to their clients in Europe and America, and they asked if I would lead a film crew into the Malay jungles to produce a promotional film for their foreign tourist market. "We'd like to air it in every country in Europe and America," the director said. Shortly before this, I had made a lengthy expedition deep into the Malay jungle with Hans Hoefer and Malaysia's chief game warden. We had some good press coverage and now the manager thought this was the time to cash in on all the publicity.

The offer was a challenge that I couldn't turn down.

What I didn't know when I agreed to lead the group was that it would be made up of people who had never stepped into the wild before. The director thought it might add something to the film to have people register their excitement when they experienced the jungle in the raw, and he invited a cosmopolitan group at company expense. "Get them face to face with a python or a tiger," he said. "Get their expressions when a tiger roars."

The chances of seeing a python or hearing a tiger roar are almost nil in the Malay jungle. The rain forest is dense, so dense in fact that you can lose sight of someone walking a dozen meters in front of you. Even sounds become muffled. But don't misunderstand, the animals are there, not to mention insects and leaches. Insects are rampant. They make dreadful humming noises, and when they bite they leave their mark. Then there are the leaches, which seem to leap out at you from the trees. You don't know you've been attacked until you see the blood, and then it's too late. You have to burn the little buggers off with a cigarette butt, and it's hard to stop the bleeding.

Dark little aboriginal people called the Orang Asli also live in the rain forests. You see whole families of them coming out of the bush; unwashed, fly covered, the kids with swollen stomachs. Photographs of them will not likely entice tourists to come to the jungle.

Our plan, after a good night's sleep at the rest house, was to spend the first day wandering around Park Headquarters, taking short walks, hiking to one of the observation platforms, called "tree hides" in Malaysia. The next day we would venture further afield. The cameraman wanted to film some shots right from the guidebook— "Boating through swirling rapids, fishing for giant carp, shooting game with a camera, watching birds, exploring caves, swimming in placid river waters" and so forth.

Like the others, he too knew nothing about the Malay jungle.

Headquarters does have a fine, modern rest house and here we spent the first night. I knew when I heard the night sounds of the jungle—the shrill cries of white-handed gibbons frolicking in the trees across the river, and an Argus pheasant calling to its mate—that some of our intrepid explorers might change their minds. I even thought it might be Della. On the contrary. The next morning she was up before everyone and anxiously waiting in the restaurant for the rest of us to arrive. When the banker and his wife came in, he announced that he had completely forgotten about an important engagement he had in K.L. and he had to get back as quickly as possible. He asked if I could arrange a boat to get him and his wife back downriver. That made two down.

Five minutes down the trail toward the tree hide, the first leach struck, right through Della's long trousers. I saw the blood and had to call it to her attention. "Well, what do you know," she said calmly. "I never did like these little devils. Anyone have a cigarette?"

The Singer Sewing Machine manager's son reached out to touch the creature, causing his father to panic. "Don't do that," he cried, "you wanta get bitten?"

"Leaches don't have teeth," the ranger explained, while the cameraman hovered about looking for an angle.

"But they might be poisonous," the father said, pulling his son away. They returned to headquarters by themselves and had left the park before we returned.

Another couple dropped out the next morning, not wanting to go upriver in the heat. We were down to a young Chinese Singaporean, who was a tour director, and his girlfriend. I think he might have wanted to leave too, but earlier in the day I heard his girlfriend tell him she thought he was very brave. And then there was Della. No way was she going to give up.

We caught no giant carp fish, and didn't go boating down swirling rapids, but we did swim in placid river waters and explore some caves. Della was a sport and loved every minute, and the cameraman thought he got some good footage. Della did everything he asked.

It was difficult for me to believe, after watching Della bounce around the jungle, that she was a lady of the arts. I asked her about it when we were coming downriver, returning to the rail station at Tembeling Halt. She said she had actually studied painting at the Royal Academy of Fine Arts in London where she was born. After graduating from the Academy in 1939, she joined the Reigate division of the British police in which she served throughout the Second World War.

When the war ended, Della admitted to herself that she lacked the talent for painting. Instead she indulged her creative inclination by working as a fashion designer in one of London's most prestigious houses, Drury Lane. "I quit when I discovered they were using my designs in shows and giving credit to the fashion house. It happens, of course, but I couldn't accept that."

Della went from one extreme to the other.

"I guess I was a little wild back then," she said. "No one will believe it, but I briefly took up race car driving." That wasn't it either. "A bit too exhilarating, perhaps," she mused. She now had the urge to travel and she joined Hunting Clan Airline as a flight stewardess. The job took her to Africa and various European countries. She was most fond of Africa. "I liked every single thing about Africa—the glow of the light at sunset, the sounds of the animals, the smell of burning wood. One time, feeling brave, I separated myself from the rest of the tour, and went on a mini-safari by myself. It was beautiful."

On one flight she met an exciting archaeologist who

was doing field work in Cyprus. She left the airlines and for the next several years worked as his assistant. "It was dusty, tedious work, but I loved it." She also fell in love with the archaeologist, but he was being promoted to assistant curator in London and she could not see herself working in the basement of the London Museum for the rest of her life.

Della then went to Beirut where she worked with the American University Alumni Association in the field of public relations. Beirut was an exciting city and Della enjoyed every minute she was there. Perhaps she would have remained contented in the Lebanese capital except once again the call to adventure presented itself. She met a lady who had a boutique in a town called Jesselton on the island of Borneo. The lady said good workers were hard to come by and she needed a reliable assistant. She asked the right lady when she asked Della if she wanted the job.

Just the name Borneo was enough to send chills up the spine of any true armchair traveler, but to actually go there was more than Della could have hoped for. Borneo! She reveled at the thought. At last she was on her way to Asia. It was the early 1950s.

Della's journey took her through Singapore. Instantly she became fascinated with this bustling seaport where East and West meet. Great sailing junks and Bugis trading schooners anchored alongside freighters and rusted tramp steamers. Sampans and flat bottom scows weaved their way in and around the ships, carrying cargo to and from the godowns along the busy Singapore River. Here was Asia at its best, she thought.

In Singapore, Della booked passage aboard the Strait Steamship *Raja Brooke* for Borneo. She found herself steaming up the Rajang River to Kuching, the capital of Sarawak, and finally sailing into the harbor at Jesselton, which is Kota Kinabalu today and the capital of Sabah. Della was living a dream, a Conradesque world coming to life. Jesselton in the early fifties was a frontier logging town where near-naked tribesmen, with tattooed bodies, elongated ear lobes and carrying blowpipes, came out of the jungles to buy tobacco and bolts of colored calico. Here in Sabah with Mount Kinabalu, the highest mountain in Southeast Asia looming in the distance, Della got her first taste of a tropical rain forest. When she wasn't at the shop ,she was bouncing up and down in Land Rovers with expat loggers wanting to show her their bush camps.

Della also became fascinated with the arts of the Ibans and the Kenyahs—their handwoven cloth, their belts and jewelry made of intricate silver filigree and the unusual carvings. The tragedy was that the people had no outlet for their creations. Jesselton had few visitors and fewer tourists. Della began thinking, perhaps Singapore was the place to market the arts of Southeast Asia. Singapore was certainly the crossroads of Asia, with ships flying the colors of every nation in the world.

Back in Singapore Della studied the art scene. The only gallery of any merit she could find was Donald Moore's gallery, but it was for artifacts mainly. "After some searching I found the Straits Commercial Art Shop, suppliers of artists materials," she said. "They told me of an area in Princess Elizabeth Walk, which is today The Esplanade, where artists displayed their work, rather like the area in Greenpark, London. There I saw paintings by Cheong Soo Pieng, Chen Wen Hsi, Lee Man Fong, Thomas Yeo, Y.B. Pang, just to mention just a few. I was very impressed by their standard of work and subject matter and more than surprised that there was nowhere else for them to display their work. I made a promise that I would open an art gallery if I had the chance."

Soon Della opened the Myer Gallery, next door to the

old Robinson's Department Store in Raffles Place in downtown Singapore. Robinson's in the fifties was Singapore's main shopping area. Once she settled in, Della set out to befriend local artists and was soon exhibiting their work in her gallery, along with art from Sabah and Sarawak. "I held a solo exhibition every two weeks, just to get known," she said.

Tragedy struck when a devastating fire completely gutted Robinson's. Her gallery was flooded, causing much damage. But the setback didn't deter Della from opening a new gallery. She found space in Raffles Hotel on Beach Road. Before long she was traveling overseas setting up exhibitions to promote Singaporean art.

She began to make frequent trips to England, Bahrain, Australia and the United States. To support herself and the arts, she renovated and furnished flats and then rented them out, which to this day helps finance her galleries.

"I hate to admit but there is very little money to be made in supporting artists," she said. "Everyone thinks I'm so successful, but the truth is I'm lucky if I just break even."

Money has never ceased to be a problem with Della but the lack of it doesn't seem to stop her from doing what she wants. Aside from running the gallery, she has tried her hand at a number of different jobs which included everything from organizing film documentaries for foreign companies to designing uniforms for Saber Air— thirty-three uniforms in three weeks.

Over the years whenever I was in town I would stop and visit with Della at her gallery. A few years back she moved into a splendid colonial house that sits on a wooded rise with a lovely vista of a green sprawling valley. All about the house are paintings, sculptures, carvings and all sorts of relics and *objets d'art* collected from her travels. Here artists are free to come and go. Several may live and study while others might stay over for a night or two while passing through Singapore. Della is always there to assist struggling artists who have cash flow problems.

What I like most about Della's house is her Sunday brunches. She will have the most interesting people in Singapore come dine with her on Sunday mornings—writers, artists, poets, diplomats and maybe even a down-and-out back-packer she met the day before on Orchard Road.

Della has a knack for collecting people that's uncanny at times. I must tell you about two characters she introduced me to who were right out of Robert Louis Stevenson's *Treasure Island*. There were no wooden legs or eye patches but there were plenty of tattoos and missing teeth. And even a treasure map of sorts.

It happened when Della invited me to dinner one evening, before she moved into the house I mentioned. She had a small but very neat flat on Outram Road, and she insisted that I come early. "There's someone I want you to meet," she said but refused to tell me more.

I was living at the time aboard my schooner at the Singapore Yacht Club on Sungei Pandang. I had, in fact, just completed construction of the vessel and was preparing to go cruising. I knew Della loved the sea and I thought she might be angling her way into joining us for a short voyage. But it wasn't for this that she invited me.

I arrived at her house just after dark. The table was set for four, with candles and her best dishes set out. This has to be someone important, I thought. "I invited you before the others came because I want to talk to you first," she said, handing me a drink and pointing me toward the sofa.

"You are going to meet two men," she said. She spoke in a hushed voice. "What they have to tell may startle you, but I promise you they are legitimate."

"Why me?" I asked.

"You will see," she replied.

Presently the two men arrived. They immediately went to the bar and helped themselves to drinks; apparently they were not newcomers to the flat. We were introduced. They had British accents, Welsh to be exact, which I found difficult to understand. I felt that I was missing half the conversation.

The men were out of place in the surroundings. They had gruff manners and spoke harshly. The older of the two, a man perhaps in his mid-forties, was heavily tattooed on both arms. The other man had several teeth missing. When we sat down to dinner I had the feeling that I had seen them somewhere before.

The suspense was too much. Before the first course was served, I asked directly: "Why is it that we are all invited here together?"

The man with the tattoos, without faltering, answered by asking me a question. "How would you like to make a million dollars," he said. It was more a statement than a question.

Here we go again, I thought. Another get-rich-quick scheme. No doubt they had a story in mind. Quite often when I meet people and they hear that I am a writer, they will say: "I have a great story for you. I'll tell you what, you write it and we'll split the profits down the middle. We'll both get rich."

My three dinner partners sensed my skepticism. Della spoke up. "They have been out to the shipyard and they've seen your boat," she said.

Now I knew where I had seen them. On more than one occasion I noted them lurking in the background, watching the building operation. I had not given them a second thought. Lots of people hung around when I was building my schooner.

"You have just the boat we need," they interjected, and in the next hour revealed the most unlikely story I had ever heard. It seemed the two men sitting before me had located a sunken World War II submarine off the west coast of Malaysia, near Penang. They were careful not to give me the exact location, thinking, no doubt, that the information might be useful to me. The submarine, they explained, was German and had a cargo of mercury, some sixteen to eighteen tons, worth millions on the open market. They had already brought up two tons but when they took it into Penang the authorities had confiscated it.

They now wanted to make a clandestine dive on the wreck, using my schooner. They explained the operation. The fact that I had not yet put ballast in my schooner, some ten tons of lead keel, made it easy. Instead of permanent ballast I would carry removable ballast, which we would unload at the site and replace with mercury. We would even jettison the salvage equipment used to raise the cargo and then sail for Turkey. There would only be three of us, the two divers and me.

"What do we do with the cargo?" I asked, out of curiosity.

"We have all that worked out," they explained. "We scuttle the schooner on a deserted beach, salvage the mercury and we're all set pretty for life."

Scuttle my schooner! They had to be joking. I was certain they were half mad, or drunk, or both. It was most likely, I reasoned, they had only an inkling about the submarine and to tempt me further added the bit about having already salvaged two tons of mercury. No doubt, they did not have enough money to fit out a ship on their own. I was glad to get away from that dinner party.

I never saw the two men after that night, but I did read about them in the newspapers several months later. They had made headlines. They had, indeed, found a sunken

German submarine, and it did have, the papers stated, a rich treasure of mercury. It seems that after they had salvaged another six tons, all operations stopped. Three Governments laid claim to the wreck. The Germans said it was theirs; the Japanese insisted the cargo was intended for them; and the Malays claimed it was sunk in their waters. The men did not receive a cent.

Della celebrated her seventieth birthday in Singapore in grand style, and in an interview in the *Singapore Tatler*, she said that looking back at her life, she has no regrets. "I am a great believer in positive thinking – regrets on the other hand are destructive."

Now in later life she does admit to a sense of urgency, as she believes there is more to accomplish in her life. "When you are twenty years old, your life expectancy is another fifty years, but when you are seventy years old, you cannot expect to live another fifty years – surely not a good fifty years."

But Della, far from taking a backseat, plans to do more for local artists. "I am dedicated to Singapore's artists," she says. "I think they are of great worth and of a high standard. They are my family. I've watched them grow up and marry and I have watched their children grow up. They have experienced no rougher deals, no easier deals, than artists of any other nation.

"The poorer the nation, the poorer the artist, but when it comes to a developing nation like Singapore, I think artists are inclined to be neglected, to be left behind in the country's development, unless there are people out there to pull them along," she says. Della is a puller.

Best of all, Della likes to stage exhibitions whether or not they are financially profitable. It's the constant challenge that she enjoys. "You never know whether an exhibition is going to be a success or not," she says. But Della's devotion to the arts has led to her steady rise to

DELLA BUTCHER

Della Butcher on an expedition in the Malay Jungles in 1966.

Della Butcher in 1995 poses with group of artists she once helped support.

become Singapore's leading patroness. That no one can deny.

To pay tribute to Della on her seventieth birthday, a group of established artists staged an exhibition and, as a token of appreciation, each presented her with one of their own paintings.

Nothing can keep Della away from the opening of any of her exhibitions. Not even a fall. She turned up at one exhibition in 1988 in a wheelchair, thus earning herself the headline "Indomitable Della" in the *Business Times*. And when it was less than a month away from her seventieth birthday exhibition, she had another accident, and was hobbling on a swollen foot as she organized material for the show.

It isn't only in her own gallery that she organizes shows for Singapore artists. She arranges exhibits in many other locations, ranging from the Long Bar in the Tiffin Room at the old Raffles Hotel to the lobby of the new Oriental-Mandarin Hotel. Between 1981 and 1982 she staged exhibitions at Changi International Airport, and she has even "exported" Singapore art by taking the paintings of thirty artists on board the *Princess Mashsuri* in 1984. In the seventies she organized some fifteen overseas exhibitions in London, Bahrain, Hong Kong, Sydney, New York and elsewhere. There was even a phase when her Gallery of Fine Art operated from her living room of her Winchester Park home. For the past several years Della has been happily settled in the Della Butcher Gallery in the fashionable Cuppage Terrace off Orchard Road. The location suits her well.

Della Butcher hadn't changed since the first time we met many years ago on the river in the National Park. She has the same enthusiasm and the youthful spark that she had when she arrived in Singapore the first time. Since that time, how many hundreds of artists has she fostered and helped? Probably there is no other individual who has done more than she has to promote the arts and local artists, and that's not only in Singapore but in all Southeast Asia as well.

Art to Della is something very special, but certainly not a means to making money. "But there's more to life than making money," she laughed as we strolled through her gallery the last time I talked to her. "I'm an extremely privileged person. Though I don't have money, I've had the pleasure of meeting and befriending many beautiful people, artists and those who promote the arts." She stopped to admire a copper plaque. "Furthermore," she continued, "I like to think that there is nothing political in an artist, or at least in his presentation. He paints what he sees, he sees what he paints and his is a world which is often apart from reality, which I like because I like to dream in that world as well."

I asked her about some of the named artists she helped get started over the years. "Don't misquote me," she said. "I can help make an artist, but I cannot help make his skill and talent. That's a gift. But what I can do is encourage him, work with him and give him moral support. I can even give him shelter." She is very critical about those artists who paint solely for money. "There's a lot of talent in Singapore, but I'm afraid the driving force with many artists today seems to be the mighty dollar. This is something I want to express to today's artists: they should not give predominant emphasis to money."

Della Butcher is from another era. Her kind is rare nowadays. Her lifestyle and values reveal a true artistic, cultured and refined woman who has spent her time, energies and money promoting artists and their art in Southeast Asia. The art world is indebted to her.

Robin Dannhorn arrives in Bangkok.

Years later posing with young women in Bhutan.

Chapter 4

ROBIN DANNHORN
Breaking Barriers

Everything that I heard about Robin Dannhorn was confirmed the moment I laid eyes on him. We were in Bangkok, the hottest time of the year, and there he stood in a dark suit and narrow tie. At a time when men were wearing their hair long, his was clipped short. And when it was in fashion to wear wire-rimmed glasses, like Raybans, he wore dark horn-rims.

Aside from appearance, what surprised me most about Robin was his age. I was expecting someone much older. He couldn't have been more than twenty-seven or twenty-eight years old.

"So nice of you to come," he said in his BBC English. It can't be, I thought. This is the man I will have to work with? Willy was right after all.

Robin had been hired as a public relations consultant with Thai Airways International's advertising agency. The airline was beginning to expand its international routes and Robin was brought in to build up the company's worldwide image.

I was the airline's travel correspondent, and the arrangement I had with them suited me well. All I had to do was to produce weekly travel articles to appear in the English-language *Bangkok World* newspaper. Beyond that, I had always been able to do pretty much as I pleased. Now, I was told, it would be Robin's duty to keep tabs on the airline's writers and photographers.

"He's demanding," Willy Mettler, a photographer friend, had warned me. "You might have a hard time." It was under these circumstances that I first met Robin Dannhorn in his office.

We discussed my duties only briefly and the conversation drifted to other things, the weather in Bangkok, his search for a house for his wife and two small children. I was hearing him talk but my mind was elsewhere. I wasn't quite sure what to make of him. I left the office after that first meeting very uncertain. I really didn't know what I could expect from Robin Dannhorn.

I have always prided myself with being a rather good judge of character, yet with Robin it was different. He was obviously ambitious, and according to Mrs. Chitdee, the PR Director of the airline, he was determined to do well in his consultant job for Thai Airways International. But the truth was he was a newcomer to Asia, enthusiastic but inexperienced, and with the big disadvantage of having a wife and two kids in an alien environment. The odds were certainly not in his favor. He also appeared overly conservative in that "hard-to-know" way the English have. He seemed rather cold and I could not really imagine him taking up a new life in the Orient. I remembered Willy saying, "Give him six months and he'll be out of here." I was much more optimistic. I gave him a year.

But I completely misjudged Robin Dannhorn.

Never would I have guessed that in the coming years Robin would not only stay on in Asia but would do things that only youths dream about. Who could ever have imagined that this man sitting behind the desk in Thai International's office with his horn-rimmed glasses, his dark suit and tie, would one day dive beneath the murky waters of a jungle lake in Malaysia to look for a lost city, hitchhike his way aboard a smuggler's boat going from the southern Philippines across the pirate-infested Sulu Sea to Borneo, explore lost ruins in Laos and be taken captive for a while by Pathet Lao guerillas, drive an open Jeep alone overland from Singapore to London, visit forbidden Buddhist monasteries in far-off Bhutan, trek the high Himalayas with a pack on his back, sail the South Seas as crew aboard a lusty trading schooner, restore a ruined stone farm house in Spain, and do a thousand other things a young man coming from London might dream about but never do. Robin did all these things, and much more.

For the first six months he was in Bangkok my association with him was casual, although he did have me to his home for dinner one evening, and on several occasions we had lunch together. He was always pleasant and was keen to know what I was doing, and he took an interest in my writing. He even edited a collection of my short travel stories that were published in a book called *Discover the Orient* which the airline sponsored.

In spite of my early misgivings about Robin, he seemed happy with his challenging work in Bangkok, and when I left to spend some time in Sarawak, he was helping the airline plan their new international route to Kathmandu. I posted my weekly articles to the newspaper and things went as smoothly as I could want.

When I next returned to Bangkok, Thai International had moved to new offices on Phaholyothin Road. No sooner had I entered the public relations office when Mrs. Chitdee told me that Robin was having problems.

A dozen thoughts flashed through my mind. Had he given up and gone back to England? Had Asia been too much for him? "What happened?" I asked Mrs. Chitdee.

She pulled me aside. "He's separated from his wife," she said. "He's really depressed."

Robin separated from his wife! He and Jan seemed so content when I had seen them at their home. She even said she liked Bangkok and would rather be here than in cold, dreary London.

Before I could ask Chitdee more, Robin came into the office. I could see at once he was distraught. I knew the symptoms. I had suffered somewhat the same fate, a failed marriage, and I could tell he was suffering. I wanted to ask him about it, why the marriage had failed and what he intended to do, but I knew in time he would tell what he wanted, and no more.

In the weeks that followed, Robin seemed to find some satisfaction in my words, in my sophistry perhaps, and we became better friends. We often had lunch together, and sometimes we met in the evening. We enjoyed mostly going to the small coffee shops along the Chao Phraya River, those that can only be reached by ferry. Over cups of strong Thai coffee, we idled away our hours talking. We talked about all matter of things, about writers and travel, and about our pasts. The river does this to you; it creates a mood. Under its spell, Robin told how he came to Bangkok. "It was more than just a job," he reminisced. "I came to find myself." Slowly I was learning the truth about Robin; he was still suffering from aspirations.

Robin was born in 1938 when the British Empire was at its highest peak, when one-third of the globe and half of its population were under the crown. The inspiring books he read as a youth were about the Empire, about the Boer War and the Northwest Frontier and battling Fuzzy-Wuzzis in the Sudan. He read every book he could find on exploring the Amazon, traveling in Tibet and wandering through the remote parts of the Orient. He lived in his own fantasy world of romance. He believed in all things good and all things honorable. He believed secretly that such a world was out there, somewhere. But during Robin's teens England was suffering her worse crisis. England had won the war but lost the Empire. He had an ordinary childhood, went to ordinary schools, and took up an ordinary job. He married young, which then was the ordinary thing to do, and he became an ordinary husband and an ordinary father.

In every sense of the word, Robin Dannhorn was doomed to mediocrity for the remainder of his days, except for one thing. He had his dreams. Try as he did, he couldn't escape his dreams.

"I longed to travel but in those days young people didn't travel," he said as we sat by the river watching a string of rice barges being towed up stream. "I started work at eighteen for a London newspaper as an advertising clerk, typing schedules. I left school on Friday and on Monday morning I was working." He remembers well walking up the concrete steps to the newspaper, thinking this was the end. He'd never be able to travel once he entered those doors. "I was about to be locked in, but some element in me rebelled."

Robin wondered as he typed up schedules if he might not be romanticizing the world. Maybe traveling was not for him. Maybe he was not made from the same stuff as adventurers and explorers. He decided the only way to find out was to put himself through a test. He managed to save a few pounds from his earnings and the first summer he had free he set out.

He found a third class berth aboard a cargo-passenger boat sailing from London to northern Spain, a voyage lasting four days. Without knowing a word of Spanish, he traveled by local buses along the north coast of Spain to France, took a train to Paris and from there the boat-train to London. He was elated; he proved to himself that he could do it. That was in 1957. Three years later he married, moved into an ordinary suburban house and started a family. He was told he had to put aside his nomad dreams. He did, but they were not lost.

The story of Robin Dannhorn might have stopped here had he not, on a cold, snowy January day in London, posted a letter. That single act changed his life forever.

The year was 1967. He was now working for one of those big advertising agencies in London. The pay was good and he had a promising future. Then one afternoon, while scanning through the *Times,* he read that a hotel chain was seeking a senior public relations executive who would be willing to travel. Out of curiosity, he typed up his resumé and posted it. A week later he was called for an interview.

Robin never got that job, but the recruitment officer, feeling sorry for him, subsequently wrote saying that the director of an advertising company in Bangkok was looking for someone to work in their office. He suggested that Robin give a call to a Mr. Mike Brierly who was staying at the Hilton.

"Can you come over right away?" Mike Brierly asked when Robin phoned. An hour later Robin was sitting with him at the Hilton.

"I can see that this job means a lot to you," Brierly said.

"It means everything," Robin replied and held his breath. He felt he had a loaded pistol pointing at his chest.

Brierly poured them another coffee. "Okay," he said, choosing every word carefully, "I'll tell you what. I'll cable Bangkok. You'll have to fly there for an interview. It's routine. Now tell me"—he leaned back in his chair—"think you'll like Bangkok?"

Out in the street the snow had turned to slush; wind whipped down Park Lane with such fury it sent everyone scurrying for cover. But Robin was unaware of the slush and cold. He didn't even stop to button up his overcoat. Anyone seeing him that afternoon, his coat flapping open in the wind, oblivious to the world around him, might have thought he was crazy, or drunk. In a sense he was drunk, drunk with life. He was going to Bangkok.

Instead of returning to the office he found his way to the Thames, and when he looked out upon the river there came to mind a passage from Conrad: "It was the capital of an Eastern Kingdom, lying up a river as might be London lies up this old Thames of ours." He was going to this same Eastern Kingdom. He was going to Bangkok, far up a river called the Chao Phraya.

Robin got the job and within a month had moved his family to Thailand. Bangkok was everything he expected an Oriental city to be. He thrilled at the sights from his taxi window as he drove from the airport into town. It was early morning, and mist hung over a canal that closely followed the roadway. Monks in yellow robes and with shaven heads walked in single lines along narrow footpaths, and through the mist a crimson sunrise set the sky all ablaze behind golden temples with carved serpents and upturned roofs. It was all too dazzling to believe, a flow of joyous emotion.

The noise, the cacophony of sounds, the sights and smells, they were like music to Robin's ears. He loved Asia from the very start.

And so, in bits and pieces, I found how Robin came to Bangkok. About his marriage, he was more reticent. He was still very depressed and found it difficult to talk about. But gradually it all came out.

He surmised, and perhaps justly so, that he had deluded himself into believing his marriage had been a firm and happy one. "How naive I had been," he said. "I came out East thinking I knew everything. I thought I knew my marriage. I thought I knew public relations. Asia taught me that I know nothing."

From what he said it was clear his marriage was doomed. Within a few months Robin and Jan separated, and later divorced. This made Robin even more depressed. What could I do to help?

"You've got to change your lifestyle," I said to Robin one day. "Let yourself go. Let your hair grow long! Grow a beard! Throw away those dreadful glasses!"

He stared hard at me as if wondering what ailed me. I had never given him advice before, but now I felt compelled to do so. Yet I couldn't tell if I was helping or making matters worse. I continued, for what it was worth: "It's no good to pine away with regrets. You wanted to do things you couldn't when you were married, so what's holding you back now? Make new friends. Meet some girls.", He just sat there, nodding, taking it all in. "Look," I said, "have an affair."

I guess I never really thought Robin Dannhorn would take my advice seriously. And I never thought he would go to the extremes he did to find himself.

Months passed before I saw him again, as I was away researching a new book. He had moved into the Grand Hotel and wrote to suggest that I stay there when I returned to Bangkok.

The Grand Hotel was not what I expected. Taxis jammed the entrance and from the sidewalk I could hear loud music coming from somewhere inside. I had to push my way through the front door to reach the lobby which was as crowded as a bus station at evening rush hour.

Robin's hotel turned out to be an R&R hotel for G.I.s from Vietnam, not at all the type of place I associated with a respectable Englishman.

The desk clerk connected me to Robin's room. "I'll be right down," he said jubilantly. "Meet you in the lobby." Then as an after thought, he added, "I have a surprise."

What more of a surprise could he possibly have?

I could hardly recognize Robin when he stepped from the elevator. Gone were the horn-rimmed glasses and dark suit. He wore light colored slacks and a high-neck Thai silk shirt. His hair was long, covering his ears, and he sported the beginnings of a beard.

I shook my head in disbelief. "I booked a room for you,"

he sang. Even his voice had changed. Then looking around, he announced. "I followed your advice. There she is!" He waved a hand and a Thai girl with a beaming smile came bounding forth like a rubber ball and threw herself into his arms, almost knocking him over. He lifted her completely off her feet and spun her around. "Meet Pensee," he cried.

"You," she said, smirking, "you have big eyes." It was evident Pensee didn't miss a thing. She had noticed me ogling at her while waiting for Robin.

"What a fantastic hotel," Robin exclaimed, leading Pensee by the arm and pushing me before him to the South Seas Bar in the basement. "You'll like it. We have three nightclubs, and they're all open all night."

The South Seas Bar was a tiny narrow place with portholes that looked into the swimming pool. There wasn't enough room for a floor show, but about four in the morning, Robin explained, a couple of naked girls provided the entertainment by jumping into the pool.

Robin and Pensee danced until the early hours of morning. How long I don't know, for I retired long before they did and went to bed.

It was a Friday night that I checked into the Grand, and Pensee remained at Robin's side until he went to work on Monday morning. She was uninhibited. She obviously cared for Robin, and he was fond of her, and together they were outrageous. On Sunday Robin asked if I would like to join them for a day at Pattaya Beach, a two-hour drive from Bangkok. We set out in a French Citroen that Robin had bought a short time before. He took delight in revving the engine, at which command, like a praying mantis, the vehicle reared up about half a meter and prepared to charge. And charge it did, each time Robin put the machine into motion. To announce he was coming, he lay on the horn, which in this case was a truck

AT HOME IN ASIA

horn he had added to the vehicle when he purchased it.
The horn seemed to blast openings through the traffic.

Pensee sat close beside him in the front seat, and like
two teenagers they pinched and tickled one another and
fell into uncontrollable laughter at the slightest
provocation. We were nearing Pattaya when we shot over
a hill, and there across a stretch of empty sand loomed
the blue Gulf of Thailand. Robin stepped on the brakes,
swerved off the main road and turned down a sand track
toward the beach. "Let's go," he shouted, "let's go for a
swim."

He didn't wait for my reply. He and Pensee dashed
toward the beach, and as they ran they began peeling off
their clothing piece by piece until they were both naked,
still running and laughing all the way to the water. Without
stopping they dove into the surf. "Come join us," Robin
shouted. "What are you waiting for?"

I was thankful no one was around to see them, although
I'm sure it wouldn't have bothered either Robin or Pensee.
I sat on the beach and waited for the frolicking to come
to an end, and sitting there I couldn't help remembering
the framed picture that was once displayed in Robin's
office, the family picture with him in a dark suit.

Eventually Robin told me all there was to tell about
Pensee. She came from a village in the north, but he was
never able to ascertain which one, for Pensee would
change her stories, or invent new ones, to suit the occasion.
"She picked me up at the Grand," he said plaintively. "I
must have looked dreadful. I know I was feeling very sorry
for myself. Before I knew what had happened she had
taken over. I wasn't really interested but she is a very, very
persuasive woman."

Robin was finding it hard to explain. "Look," he finally
said, "Pensee is one of the best things that has happened
to me. She gave me back my manhood. She taught me to

love again. I followed your advice." I decided then I'd be more careful about offering him advice in the future.

Robin's position with Thai International enabled him to travel widely around Asia. On one of his trips to Kathmandu he asked if I would join him. We spent a week in that delightful capital, and when it came time to return we decided that rather than fly we would travel overland via the mountainous road out of Nepal and then by train to Calcutta. In Calcutta we could pick up our flight to Bangkok. This overland Kathmandu to Calcutta adventure would be the first of many I would experience over the years with Robin. We left no part of Asia uncovered. Robin was at his happiest when he was rumbling in a broken down bus through the Khyber Pass or bouncing up and down on a train through central Malaysia. Nothing could equal the fullness, the complete emotional experience, he got from travel. And those who traveled with him found his enthusiasm catching.

The Raj Path, the first road to Nepal completed in 1956, winds down towards the India border. Heavily loaded trucks and over-loaded buses, with ferocious Sikh drivers, thunder madly downhill at reckless speeds. Along with seventy-two other passengers crowded into a bus with forty-eight seats, Robin and I joined the race. The unpaved, dusty mountain road twisted and turned and snaked back upon itself, looking down upon sheer drops. Miraculously we reached the hot humid plains of India.

Dust-covered and weary, we had to walk, toting all our luggage across the border from Nepal into India where we boarded the Calcutta Mail Train for Calcutta.

Our carriage, with doors that opened to the outside, had seats for six. Names of the occupants were posted outside. Our fellow passengers were seating themselves when we arrived. Reluctantly they opened the door—but only after we had showed our tickets—and then quickly swung the bolt closed, locking us in. It seemed rather rude, to lock us in as they did, but presently we discovered their motive. In short time the railway platform was jammed with people shoving and pushing and clamoring to get inside. A group of unruly students massed outside our door. "Open up! Open up!" they demanded, pounding on the door and waving their fists. "Let us in!"

Robin would hear none of this. While the Indian passengers in the compartment slithered into the background, he stood up to his full height, brushed down his shirt and in a very loud voice—and in his proper Queen's English—he cried, "What is the meaning of this!" The students jumped back. "Behave yourselves," he said boldly, then turned and sat down. The students backed off. To the Indians in the compartment he said, "That's all we need, a little discipline." He was in every sense of the word the British Raj reincarnated.

Soon we were rolling across an endless, barren Indian landscape, with Robin saying over and over, "God, I love this country."

In a secondhand bookstore in Kathmandu, Robin had found a copy of John Masters' *Night Runners of Bengal*, about the Indian mutiny of 1857 in which Indian sepoys revolted and laid siege of Lucknow. Aboard the Calcutta Mail, he began reading the book and became so absorbed he couldn't put it down. "You have to read this," he said and began tearing out the pages he had already read. Soon I too was reliving the glorious days of the British Raj. We were traveling the same rail line, perhaps aboard the same carriage the empire builders had built and used, and when I looked out the window the view certainly had to be the same—the vast dusty plains of India.

We reached Calcutta, with thoughts of *Night Runners of Bengal* still with us, and had hardly dropped our bags in the old colonial Great Eastern Hotel when Robin dragged me off again. "Where to?" I asked.

"St. John's Church," he answered.

"We come to Calcutta to go to a church?" I protested.

"No," he replied, "to go witness history."

St. John's Church was the British garrison church. It's a tall white Gothic building that was consecrated in 1847, ten years before the Indian Mutiny. Rows of fans hang from a wooden ceiling, and the stalls and pews are made of heavy wood. Stained-glass windows cast an eerie light into the interior. From one of the vaults the sound of an organ filtered through the halls and seemed to permeate the very walls, where, when our eyes adjusted to the dimness, we saw row upon row of commemorative tablets memorializing the British killed during the Mutiny and various other frontier battles. It was to these tablets that Robin led me, and slowly, in his deep resounding voice, he read. "Sacred to the memory of Henrietta, aged thirty years, the beloved wife of Captain R.P. Anderson, Twenty-fifth Regiment Bengal Native Infantry, who departed this life on the seventeenth August 1857 during the sad and disastrous siege of Lucknow. Also to the memory of Hilda Mary, aged seven months, who died three days later."

Another, for George Thomas Gowan who "fell on the evening of nineteenth June 1857 at the head of his gallant regiment, the Fifth Royal Lancers."

We left St. John's, with a feeling of despair, walked across the Maidan and approached the Victoria Memorial, a massive domed building of white marble from Rajasthan, inaugurated in 1921 by the Prince of Wales. In front of the monument stands the statues of Queen Victoria, Lord Curzon and other gallant figures of the Raj.

But Robin didn't stop to admire the statues; instead he led me to the top of the main stairway landing; and here in a side gallery, covering the entire wall, appeared a portrait by Lady Butler—"The Remnant of an Army." It portrays Dr. Bryden, the sole survivor of sixteen thousand of the British Forces, arriving exhausted at the gate of Jellalabad on July 13, 1842, during the First Afghan War.

We walked back to the Great Eastern, had tiffin in the grand dining room and that afternoon went to Mantons, the Calcutta branch of the famous British gun smith and manufacturer. Robin was in his absolute glory. "I saw this place when I was a kid," he said, and then added, "In my mind, of course."

We inspected fine handguns, sporting rifles that once belonged to the maharajahs, and massive bore elephant guns of forgotten viceroys. Robin introduced himself to the manager, Mr. Greengrass, an English gentleman born in Calcutta. His father, an engineer, had been called out from the UK before the First World War to build Dumdum Airport. Greengrass retired from the prison service, where he claimed he once had Mahatma Gandhi under his charge, and became manager of Mantons. He had fallen on hard times and hadn't been to England since 1936, but, he assured us, he would return one day to live with his granddaughter. He never did. On one of my subsequent visits to Calcutta, I learned that Mr. Greengrass had passed away.

An Anglo-Indian ex-police chief entered Mantons and took a seat beside Robin and me at a great oak table. As he served tea, Mr. Greengrass made the introduction. "Mr. Parker here," he said. We shook hands. Mr. Greengrass continued. "Mr. Parker is one of the last big game hunters in India." The mood was set. For the next few hours, like kids listening to ghost stories, we became enthralled by Mr. Parker's tales of daring big game hunts. He hunted tigers with a 400-Express using a solid bullet. He still hunts elephants and tigers, but only when called upon to rid a village of a menace. The problem he faces is that he can no longer find cartridges for his 400-Express. "They don't make them anymore," he explained, and then he told how he corresponds with gun dealers and collectors around the world who will occasionally find him "a bullet or two." Then, sullenly he added, "You are never quite sure they will fire."

Out in the street, with the Indian Mutiny forgotten and thoughts now about stalking tigers and elephants, we strolled down Chowringhee, the wide arcaded street where thousands of Calcutta's homeless live. We were instantly besieged by panhandlers, beggar kids and pimps.

Not all our travels went without mishap. In Laos once we got more than we bargained for. It happened quite innocently.

From Bangkok we flew to Vientiane and checked into the Lan Xang Hotel, considered to be the best in town but a bit seedy, dating from French colonial times.

The lobby had a strong scent of cigar smoke mixed with the smell of insect spray. The sound of French music from the forties came from hidden speakers in the ceiling, and on a rack near the front desk were French newspapers. The signs at the desk were in French.

The Lan Xang was very much like walking onto a Hollywood movie set. This was 1971, a time when conflicting powers vied for control in Laos. Sitting around in the lobby, with VISIT THE USSR posters on one wall and SAN FRANCISCO AWAITS YOU on another, were the actors, a few neatly dressed Asians, but mostly Americans, Frenchmen and Russians. There were no smiles, no laughter, no happy faces. Anyone who entered the Lan Xang Hotel was scrutinized by the whole lot.

We arranged a trip to Pakse in the south. Robin was interested in visiting some Khmer ruins near Champasak.

We arrived in the southern capital and were walking in town when a big American car pulled up. The driver explained in broken English that he was there to pick us up. It seemed strange, but we climbed into the backseat and before we could ask any questions the driver shot through town at a reckless, shattering speed, not stopping until we reached the outskirts of town. The driver opened the door. We stood in front of a large concrete shell of a building under construction. The roof was finished, and four concrete floors were in place, but missing were the interior walls and outside facade. We were soon to discover this was the unfinished palace of Prince Boun Oom.

What could a Laotian prince want with us? "Please be seated," the Prince said, and then offered us drinks. In front of us was a table lined with bottles of imported spirits —American and Scotch whiskey, Russian vodka, Spanish brandies and sherries, French wines and cognacs, German schnapps, Puerto Rican rum and a dozen other varieties of alcohol. Stacked to one side were crates of soft drinks piled as high as a man can reach. "Qu'est-ce que nous boire?" he asked. What would we like to drink?

Then came the food—corn on the cob, thin slices of sugar-dried pork, rice cooked in bamboo, grapes and sliced oranges. Attentive servants were there to fill our glasses and answer our needs. Throughout the meal the Prince didn't stop talking, except when he coughed, which was frequent. He spoke in French, which at times was hard to follow.

When the meal was finished, Prince Boun Oom clapped his hands. Finally, we figured, we would learn why we had been invited. Not quite. A servant appeared carrying a violin. We couldn't believe it. The Prince began to play for us, though we were unable to determine whether he was attempting Bach or Grand Old Opry.

When he finished he again clapped his hands, the violin disappeared and he announced that a Land Rover was waiting for us out front. He would see us later. Robin and I were more puzzled than ever.

The driver took us to another part of town, and now we stopped at what appeared to be a row of garages, all with the doors securely locked. The driver produced a key, opened one of the doors and bid us enter. Inside we were startled to find a treasure trove of magnificent Khmer carvings. Entire sections of temple ruins, from lintels to eaves, were lined up in neat rows, each piece carefully marked with white chalk. There were literally a hundred or more pieces, some small, others that would require a dozen men to lift.

What was the meaning of this? Why was the Prince's driver showing this to us?

Our answer came very shortly. The Prince had mistaken us for someone else. He thought we were French and that we had come to buy stone carvings from Khmer ruins he had stripped from somewhere in the jungles. We had, in fact, met a French couple on the plane from Bangkok, antique dealers from Paris, they said, and they were carrying a vast amount of French francs in two briefcases. We had seen the money when custom officers checked their luggage.

It all came clear, like a curtain opening on a stage, when the French couple rushed up to the garage in a taxi, shouting and screaming and waving their arms. Robin and I bowed out of the picture and quickly disappeared. Later we heard talk that the Prince was mysteriously receiving money to build his palace from an unknown source. Robin and I knew the source, and it wasn't, as some speculated, all from his wife who ran a gambling casino in Vientiane.

We wanted more than ever now to go visit the Khmer temples at Champasak, before another prince or general carved them up and sold them to dealers in Paris. The only transportation we could find to reach the site was an overcrowded bus. Rather than squeeze inside we sat on top in the open, in the wind and dust. Robin sat cross-legged atop the bus and sang out in his baritone voice arias from "The Barber of Seville" and "Rigoletto" while he pounded out the rhythms on the tin roof, making those sandwiched below, I'm sure, wish we would quickly reach our destinations.

The Khmer temples at Champasak were everything we expected, another Angkor Wat but on a much smaller scale. We returned to Vientiane and then flew up to Luang Prabang, a fascinating small town in the north.

In town that night we visited an opium den, with little old men lying on wooden pallets while another withered old man fixed their pipes. Did we want to smoke? We hedged. Six pipes full of opium for less than the price of a Coca Cola. "Too expensive," we said and left. We settled for a bottle of rice whiskey back in our hotel.

Before leaving Luang Prabang we wanted to take a river trip along the mighty Mekong River. We found a ferry boat going downriver and bought passage. The river was low, and the weather surprisingly cold. To keep warm we huddled under blankets.

The ferry was required to stop at various checkpoints along the way. While the captain waited, with the bow nosed into the shore, a young boy with the boat's papers ran up the bank where armed soldiers waited. At villages passengers disembarked and others came aboard. The garrison at one village was celebrating and all the soldiers were drunk. They fired rifles and pistols into the air. We were beginning to become unnerved.

We felt safe on the river. Great sand dunes, like the north African desert, rose up from the riverbanks, and in the far background the hills diminished into shades of blue. In places, sand dunes gave way to bare-faced rocks worn with age. Soon there were more checkpoints, and more soldiers with automatic rifles. It was nearing noon and still the sun had not burned away the morning fog. At one bend we were startled to find a group of elephants half-submerged in the river. Their mahouts were splashing them with water.

We came to one checkpoint that appeared different from others we had seen. We drew closer. Soldiers came down from the fort, with rifles at port arms. Even their uniforms differed. They wore black. Then I noticed their rifles were not American made; they were AK-47s. We had unwillingly arrived at a Pathet Lao outpost. A patrol of soldiers swarmed aboard.

Our lives now rested in the hands of a half dozen boy soldiers. Their leader couldn't have been more than seventeen or eighteen years old. Seeing that Robin and I were foreigners, unmistakably white men, he instructed us sit in the open at the bow. We then continued down-river.

We discovered that the Pathet Lao had overrun the checkpoint that very morning. They were now traveling to villages along the way in an attempt to convince royal government forces to surrender. With both Robin and me positioned on the bow in plain view, they could avert possible gunfights. We stopped at several villages while the young officer went ashore. He would converse with the people for a few minutes and then return.

As we came chugging around one bend in the river, the boy leader began waving and pointing toward the beach. He instructed the boat captain to head toward the shore. It was a sandy, desolate area without person or building in sight. This was it, we thought. No more new sunrises for us; no more horizons to conquer. But to our surprise, instead of ordering us ashore as we thought they would, the soldiers themselves disembarked. They waved goodbye, and when Robin motioned that he would like to take their picture, they stood at rigid attention. The boat continued downriver to its destination, and from there we traveled overland to Vientiane. We were fortunate, for had the soldiers been seasoned veterans we may not have lived to see another day.

Robin needed a place in Bangkok he could call home, a place to store his books, where he could write. He was tiring of the Grand Hotel, and besides, Pensee had long since departed. She had married, with his blessing, and was living in America. Robin found what he was looking for in a beautiful Thai house next to the famous Jim Thompson house. Jim Thompson made a fortune in Thai silk—they called him the Thai Silk King—and one Easter Sunday mysteriously vanished while visiting friends in the Cameron Highlands in Malaysia. He has never been seen or heard from since.

Robin's new house was a classical Thai dwelling with a high sloping roof, and with tiny bells that tinkled with the breeze. It was built on the bank of a canal or *klong*, where in the early morning women with lampshade hats paddled their tiny sampans carrying vegetables and fruit to the market. Robin had monks come bless the house before he moved in, and soon he was giving dinner parties that became the talk of the town. His cook was undoubtedly the finest in Bangkok. He got her from his old friend, Paul Rice Chapman, who was an international food columnist and had trained her himself. Paul went back to Australia and Robin got the cook. Her name was Som.

After Robin moved into his Thai house, I enjoyed more than ever visiting him, for he had an air-conditioned guest room and I was always welcome to stay. Every morning when I awoke Som would have a breakfast of fresh, chilled fruit and steaming Thai coffee waiting for me on the veranda. Robin would join me and we always had much to talk about, often jabbering so long he would be late for the office. One morning he didn't go at all. He became intrigued by a rumor I casually mentioned. I had just returned from a fishing trip on the Endau River in the Malay jungle. It had been successful. We caught dozens of carp and saw some beautiful pristine rain forests. We had put up one night in an Orang Asli village far upriver and in the evening I had listened to the tales the villagers had to tell. They spoke of a mysterious lake farther to the north, and said in its depths lived a huge dragon. It sounded like Asia's version of the Loch Ness monster. Before I left Malaysia I stopped at the National Museum in Kuala Lumpur and checked with the curator. Did he know anything about a lake monster? He led me to the library in the basement. Sure enough there was a sighting which was documented in a book by Stewart Wavell called *The Lost World of the East*. But there was more than just a monster of the deep. Another book, *History of Pahang*, by Dr. Linehan, a former Director of Museums in the Federation of Malaya, had another story to tell. He wrote of Lake Chini, forty miles inland from the east coast along the Pahang River. In my notebook I jotted down what he had written, and now showed it to Robin. "It is possible," Linehan wrote, "that the lake did not always exist in its present form and that it covers the site of an ancient city. Only when the jungle gives up its secrets will the truth be known."

I didn't have to say another word to Robin. We spent the rest of the day planning our expedition to Lake Chini. Two weeks later we were motoring up the Pahang River in a longboat, looking for the hidden entrance to the lake. Aboard with us was Bill Mathers, an ex-U.S. Navy diver with experience in these things. We had in addition to scuba equipment underwater cameras.

With some difficulty, we located the canal that led to the lake and there left our longboats. We inflated rubber dinghies and poled our way up the narrow, ten-kilometer-long watercourse. The canal ran a straight course and the walls appeared to have been dug by hand.

We reached the lake and found it was far more vast than we had expected. The water was murky and from the dark depths branches of trees, long-dead and covered with green slime, protruded above the water. We set up camp and at dusk an eerie fog rose from the still waters, giving the place a macabre appearance. We would not have been surprised had the monster of Lake Chini risen from the mist at that very moment.

We began our diving the next day, with assurance from the Orang Asli who lived in a village along the lake that the dragon, which they call *naga*, wouldn't harm us, nor would the crocodiles bother us. We were told they were sacred.

The very thought of diving in the lake, with crocodiles swimming about and a Loch Ness monster coming up from the deep to check us out, was not a happy one, but once we began diving we were more concerned about becoming tangled in tree limbs and debris than encountering living creatures in the deep. Our first objective was to probe the bottom of the lake and investigate some sacred stones the Orang Asli told us about. Our visibility in the murky water was only centimeters. We did locate the stones, but we were unable to photograph them. The slightest movement of our fins stirred up fine sediment causing the camera flashes to bounce back. The stones, however, appeared to be monoliths standing upright.

The entire floor of the lake was composed of soft alluvial mud. We probed down six meters but still did not touch solid footing. The mud layer could be twenty or thirty meters thick. We determined that unless the lake were drained, it would require a drill to be put down through the ooze to determine the lake's past history.

We did find laterite bricks and a number of pieces of unglazed pottery with strange cord markings. That was the closest we came to finding our lost city in the Malay jungle. We both concluded that if the ancient inhabitants deliberately flooded their city when invasion was threatened, as some archaeologists theorized, then redraining the lake is feasible. But until then, as Dr. Linehan said, the jungle of Malaysia will hold on to its secret.

Robin's time as consultant to Thai International was running out. He wanted something more out of life than working in an office. It was time, he thought, that he lived by his wits. He would travel and take photographs and then write about it. He would become a travel writer. He resigned and began traveling in earnest. He journeyed from one end of Asia to the other. There were some places that he favored more than others. One such place was Zamboanga, a rambunctious untamed seaport at the southern tip of Mindanao facing the wicked Sulu Sea. Here was adventure even Hollywood couldn't invent. Anchored in the roads, rusted freighters stood side by side with sea-going outrigger canoes and barter trading boats from the forbidden isles of the Sulu Sea.

Robin imagined himself living in Zamboanga. He gave thought to buying a house there, and perhaps a coconut plantation. He thought about this as he walked through the streets and along the waterfront. He checked the freight schedule and the passenger loading times; he went to the warehouse and studied the price of copra. He watched the Bugis sailors come in from the Sulu and he strolled through the barter trading area enclosed behind barbed wire. A few short years before, back in England, he dreamed about traveling to such exotic places as Zamboanga; now he was considering living there.

Then as he watched the trading boats come in, he fixed

upon an idea that one might say bordered on lunacy. He wanted to travel to Borneo through the islands of the Sulu Sea. In those days under President Marco's Marshal Law, the only way to enter the Philippines, or exit, was from Manila. Ships were not permitted to sail to Borneo from Zamboanga. Those that did were barter traders without papers. The route they sailed was risky.

Robin had little difficulty finding a trading boat that would carry him to Jolo, the capital of the Sulu Islands, but from there it would be touch and go. He was disappointed to find that the Philippine navy had bombed and destroyed much of the town. "It was upsetting to see such a beautiful place in ruins," he said. From Jolo he found a much smaller boat to take him to Bongao Island where the inhabitants lived in bamboo houses with grass roofs built on stilts out over the water.

"It was the most beautiful island I had ever seen," he said, "but one that was outside the law." Bongao was controlled by smugglers, pirates and renegades who had fled from the north. There were no hotels and the only room Robin could find was in a bordello. For the next two days he walked up and down the plank sidewalks looking for a boat to carry him across the border into Borneo. He spread word everywhere he went that he was looking for passage.

He was sitting in a coffee shop when a Muslim approached him and said, "I hear you want to go across to Borneo." Robin nodded. "It will cost you ten dollars."

The boat was little more than a skiff. It was open, with a canvas awning, and carried forty people. They said it would make the crossing to Sandakan in Sabah in thirty hours. It took four days.

"Everything went wrong," Robin said. "The engine kept breaking down, the steering broke and the pump gave out." Navigating was done with a pocket compass. When the captain wanted to see what direction they were headed, he took the compass from his pocket. They ran over shoals only inches below the surface, shoals that could have torn the bottom out of the boat. A boy standing on top of the roof pointed out the way, often through driving rain.

Most of the passengers were illegal immigrants, and there were so many there was only space to sit upright. Fortunately every night they stopped at an island, where the captain knew everyone ashore.

A few times they were forced to continue after dark, and then the cockroaches came out in droves. Some measured four inches long. They swarmed across everyone's bodies; they got into their clothing. On the evening of the fourth day they arrived in Sandakan, a port on the north coast of Borneo. Robin had made it across the Sulu Sea, but he still had a long way to go. From Sandakan he hitched a ride aboard a cargo ship that carried him along the northern coast of Borneo. From Kuching he booked passage aboard a Straits Steamship to Singapore.

Robin and I hatched dreams while sitting on the veranda of his Thai house, drinking coffee served up by Som, watching the sampans wending their way up and down the *klong*.

We did not always confine our journeys to Asia. One year we did the length of the Baja Peninsula in Mexico, traveling by rickety buses, dining on tacos and drinking tequila in cantinas with swinging doors, and sleeping in haciendas that had rooms to rent. But Robin's biggest dream, and mine too, was to go to sea, as Herman Melville had done, not as a passenger but as a simple sailor, right before the mast. Ever since I had read Jack London's *Cruise of the Snark* I wanted to build my own boat and sail the South Seas.

The most ambitious dream that Robin and I had was to build a sailing ship, not an ordinary sailing ship, mind you, but a full-rigged barquentine. She was to measure a hundred feet long, with three masts. We named her *Argo*. Soon it became a dream that was taking on reality. We began seriously to lay out our plans. I convinced a yacht designing firm in Vancouver, Canada, to design our ship in exchange for publicity in a book we would write and publish. Robin found us sponsors: sail makers, a diesel engine manufacturer and various other nautical outfitters. The method of construction we decided upon was new. Called ferro-cement, it had been successfully developed in New Zealand. Robin convinced the Siam Cement Company to furnish the material and let us build the hull at their yard on a small *klong* north of Bangkok. But in the end the project was too grand, and the ship too large to build far up a river in Thailand. It was one dream we had to put aside.

But I could build a smaller vessel. I spent the next year in Malaysia, researching and writing an *Insight Guide* on Malaysia, and then began looking around for a place to build my seventy-foot schooner.

In the meantime Robin hatched a wild idea of driving overland from Southeast Asia to London. "Make the trip with me," he said.

"I'll tell you what," I replied. "Help me build my boat and I'll drive with you to London." We shook hands.

I found a yard in Singapore, rented a house near the yard, bought my first supplies and couldn't wait until I told Robin. Then, unexpectedly, he phoned. He was in town. What a surprise. I had been waiting for him. I was about to tell him over the phone that my plans had arrived and I was starting construction, but I thought it best to wait until he arrived at the house to show him the plans. He was certain to be surprised. He could help me begin construction. I laid the plans out on the living room floor, and there came a knock on the door. Robin stood there.

"Come in," I said. "I have something to show you."

"No," he insisted, "you come out first. I have something to show you."

We bantered back and forth, and finally I relented and stepped outside. As I did Robin waved a hand, a gesture like an actor introducing a star performer, and pointed to a shiny new vehicle in the drive. It was a Minimoke with a canvas roof. "Surprise!" he shouted gleefully. "Now we can drive to Europe."

I couldn't drive to Europe, not with my boat building project started, and Robin couldn't remain behind to help me build my schooner. But still, we encouraged one another, and like two kids, we exalted in our new toys. He tinkered with his engine; I went over my plans. He studied his road maps; I read my instruction booklets. I talked about being able to beat into the wind; he talked about tires that could carry him across the Dash-i-Kavir Desert. I went to the yard early one morning and Robin took off for Penang. There he put his Minimoke aboard a freighter bound for Madras.

Postcards came from Robin. They were brief notes but with messages that spelled out his journey. The vessel that carried him and his Minimoke from Penang to Madras also carried over a thousand Tamil deck passengers. It took six days for the leaking ship to reach its destination. He then began his drive. From Madras he drove down to Sri Lanka and then up through the middle of India to Calcutta. From Calcutta he retraced our steps over the Raj Path to Kathmandu. He had drinks with Boris and his wife Inger at the Chimney Bar and dined with Barbara Adams who was running the Third Eye Travel Agency. At the Third Eye he met Lisa Van Gruisen, an energetic English woman who came for a two-week trek and decided to stay. She won the favor of Colonel Jimmy Roberts and he hired her to help run Tiger Tops Resort in the Royal

Chitwan National Park.

From Kathmandu he headed back down to Patna, then ferried across the Ganges, drove the Grand Trunk route to New Delhi, drove up to Simla, Kashmir, Amritsar, into Pakistan, the Khyber Pass to Kabul, the capital of Afghanistan, north over Hindu Kush to Mazar-i-Sharif and back to Kabul. From Kabul he continued on to Kandahar to Iran, along the Caspian Sea to Teheran, from there to Turkey, across to Istanbul, by ferry to Greece, Yugoslavia, across the Alps up to West Germany and finally France.

Not until he drove off the ferry in England did Robin realize the magnitude of what he had accomplished. He had driven some twenty thousand miles alone over some of the world's toughest terrain, from Singapore all the way to London. Elated, he bought a bottle of champagne and went to visit his father whom he hadn't seen in several years. He had it all planned. He'd walk up the drive, knock on the door; the housekeeper would open the door and he would announce, "Well, here I am. I've done it." He felt like Captain Livingston. He had been rehearsing the role for days. The day came and he drove up to his father's house. With a bottle of champagne in hand, he knocked on the door. The door opened and the housekeeper appeared, just as he imagined she would. "Well, here I am. I did it," he said proudly. A horror stricken look came to the poor lady's face.

"You haven't heard?" she said, reaching out for Robin. "You didn't get our letter."

"No, what letter?" Robin replied.

"I'm afraid your father died two months ago."

Robin came back to Asia with a vengeance. Soon his stories and travel articles began to appear in dozens of magazines throughout Asia. He sent out travel trade news stories to newspapers all around the world. He developed a column in a syndicated travel trade press. He wrote on aviation and tourism development. When ASEAN, the Association of Southeast Asian Nations, was formed he went around to each of the five countries as an official representative for Thailand and often hosted their meetings. He gave lectures and talks to clubs, he wrote speeches and he continued to do technical writing— brochures and company profiles—for Thai International. He wrote videos, TV scripts and commercials. He assisted PATA, the Pacific Area Travel Association, every year and put out their newsletter. He did part-time public relations for several large Bangkok hotels. I was with him when he gave an impromptu speech at the Adventurers' Club in Los Angeles.

With the money he made from writing and his other activities, Robin started to invest. When the market was low, he bought a group of shops on Magnetic Island north of Queensland in Australia, and he sold them when the market was high. Next came a row of shophouses near the airport in London, and then an apartment house in London. At forty-five years of age, Robin could easily have retired, but retirement wasn't a word in his vocabulary.

There was a period of two or three years that I had been out of contact with Robin. I had completed my schooner and was sailing the South Pacific, and every now and then word reached me about Robin. He was either in India or Bhutan, or else trekking in the Himalayas. He had gone up to Namchebazar, and to places like Dingboche and Pangboche. Then one day when I was anchored in Papeete on Tahiti, a cable arrived from Robin. He heard that I was sailing from Tahiti to Honolulu and wanted to know if he could sign on as crew. Could he! I cabled him back that same day.

A few weeks later I was asleep in my cabin. We were tied up stern-to along the quay, with a gangplank from the aft of the ship to the dock. Dawn was beginning to break when a knock came at the door. "Captain," the voice of one of the crew called, "Captain, you had better come have a look."

I couldn't understand why I was being awakened to have a look at something, but fearing it might be of some grave importance, I dashed up on deck.

"Over there," the crew said, pointing to the dock. "He's just been sitting there like a statue, since it got light, looking at the boat."

It took me but seconds to get my thoughts together. I knew the moment I looked down the quay and saw a man sitting cross legged atop a bollard that it was Robin. But then, could I be wrong? This man had a shaven head that shined even in the pale light. And in his left ear was a large gold earring. He sported a Vandyke beard. Then he saw me and stood up, and I knew immediately it was Robin.

"Didn't want to wake you," he said as he came up the gangplank. "The plane landed at 4:30 and I just wanted to sit here and look at her." He cocked his head to one side. "Ahoy, so good to see you, mate." He said it like Robert Newton who played Long John Silver in *Treasure Island* on the silver screen.

I shook my head in disbelief. This couldn't be the same man I met fifteen years before in Bangkok. But it was.

The next two months would bring us new adventures. We survived the Tahitian Fete, with its wild dancing competitions, to the beat of shark-skin drums. They took place on the waterfront right before us. We then sailed off to Moorea, reputed by many to be the most beautiful island in the world, and continued on to beautiful Bora Bora, also reputed to be the most beautiful island in the world, with stops en route at such islands as Huahine, Raiatea and Taha. At Bora Bora we hiked the hills looking for World War II cannons. Then we sailed to Rarotonga in the Cook Islands where we climbed over the wreck of

Irving Johnson's famous brigantine *Yankee*. And through wild tossing seas we sailed northward towards Hawaii. We put into Tongareva where islanders swam out to the schooner to greet us, and where Robin traded for pearls.

"Rubbish," I warned him. "You're wasting your time." Nevertheless, he carried away a box filled with pearls. Later when he was in Bangkok he wrote to tell me he had two pearls mounted, and the jeweler valued the pair at fourteen hundred dollars.

Those who don't know Robin might wonder if he is ever serious. He can turn dour moments into humorous ones, like the time he was doing PR at the Hyatt Rama when Axel Goerlach was the manager. Robin invited me to join him for breakfast one morning in the coffee shop, but when we arrived it was jam-packed with Japanese tourists. There was not one empty seat. We didn't feel like waiting, and there was no other place to go. Then Robin saw on the desk next to the cashier an armband, a whistle and a small flag on a stick. The Japanese tour leader had left it there. Without a further word, Robin put on the armband, blew the whistle and waved the flag. He then marched to the front door. The restaurant emptied out, with the Japanese tourists in close pursuit behind Robin. He led them out into the street and returned to the restaurant, alone. We sat down to breakfast. Robin asked that I not mention the incident to the manager, Axel Goerlach. I have kept my promise.

Or there was the time at the Oriental Hotel. Manager Kurt Wachtveitl was hosting the opening of a restaurant in the new Tower Wing called Lord Jim's. In keeping with a Joseph Conrad theme, it was decorated to look like the aft deck of an Edwardian yacht. Invitations went out—a champagne reception followed by a formal dinner. Guests were requested to attend in nautical attire. Robin felt very honored to be invited, as the guest list included diplomats, bankers, ranking members of the various military missions, owners of trading companies and many of the elite of Thai society.

Robin readily accepted, but he didn't have naval attire. What could he wear?.

In true Robin Dannhorn fashion, if you do something at all, do it in grand style. He found a tailor and designed his own naval military uniform. It was spotless white, with a high collar and gold anchor buttons down the front. Robin was aware that he could offend the Thais so he avoided gold braid around the sleeves. Still, the uniform needed something. Maybe epaulets, he thought. But he couldn't impersonate the Thai military; it had to be something different. He searched around town and in a little shop found some old black velvet epaulets with wonderful gold designs. They didn't look like anything a naval officer would wear so he bought them. Little did Robin know, but the epaulets had once been worn by a Thai cabinet minister. The moment he stepped through the door at Lord Jim's he created a sensation. With his shaven head, his gold earring, his dashing white uniform with a red sash and red cummerbund, he looked the part of an Eastern foreign dignitary. But which one? From what country? The naval attaché from the American Embassy was there, with his gold tassels and medals across his chest.

"He kept looking at me very strangely," Robin said. "He tried to get close to me, and each time he did I'd move away. You could see it on his face, he figured I had to be someone important and he should meet me. Why hadn't his intelligence people informed him? I never did learn if he ever found out that I was simply a travel writer. I certainly never told him."

Robin continues to be grateful to Pensee who long since has married and now lives in southern California with her husband. But Pensee wasn't Robin's only flame. He had a string of flamboyant women who followed him across Asia, but none could keep up with him. He did finally meet his match, a German woman working with Neckermann Tours. He met Maren in Bangkok and they fell in love. When Maren was transferred to Mallorca, to head the office there, Robin found himself traveling back and forth from Asia to Spain. On one trip he saw the ruins of a 400-year-old farmhouse which hadn't been occupied for more than twenty years. The roof was falling in and some of the sides had collapsed. As Maren and Robin drove up the drive, the car had to push through brambles. "It was so overgrown we could hardly see through the windscreen," Robin said. At the end of the driveway they came to the ruined farmhouse. "Anyone in their right mind would have turned around and gone back," he said, "but then I'm not anyone." Robin bought the ruin.

Maren and Robin married in 1980 and together they began restoring the ruin. Today it is a showpiece. The house has become a repository for their art and the antiques they have collected around the world.

The house in Spain hasn't curtailed Robin's spirit for adventure. With our good friend Axel Goerlach we have ventured to Bhutan, the most remote kingdom in the high Himalayas, and most recently Robin and I traveled by river-boat far up the Jamuna River to the Brahmaputra in Bangladesh. And I know one day the phone will ring, or a letter will arrive, and the message will be from Robin, spieling out Kipling—" 'An' the dawn comes up like thunder outer China 'crost the Bay!' When's the last time you've been to Burma? It's time!" And off we'll go again.

Han Snel at home with wife.

Chapter 5

HAN SNEL
Life Among the Gods

Islands possess us; they become obsessions. In his novel *Moby Dick*, Herman Melville compares islands to the "soul of man" and that in each of us, he says, lies "an insular Tahiti, full of peace and joy."

In that dream we all long to find that perfect island, and so we search, in mind if not in reality. Sometimes we find it, but then the agony, the real agony, begins, for we know we cannot remain there forever. We have other duties to perform, other tasks to fulfill back home. And so we push off from that isle, perhaps better for having known it, maybe worse. Still, we can't help wondering—what if, what if we could remain there forever.

Few souls ever do. There are, nevertheless, exceptions. Han Snel, a graying Dutchman, is one of them, and the island that he chose is that magic island—Bali. And so we ask the question, what is it like to spend the rest of your life on your dream island, never having to return to a place you once called home? How is it to live perpetually in so-called "paradise?" How is it, really? Honestly? We have to ask Han for the answer. He went to Bali as a very young man and with the exception of a few short visits abroad, he has lived there ever since. If anyone has the answer, Han does.

In 1969, the year Thai International opened up Bali to international air travel, I met Han the first time. He had been on the island twenty years by then, and he lived in a hand-carved stone house that stood out above all others.

The house was located down a quiet lane in the village of Ubud, and so magnificent was the place that everyone who went to Bali in those days went to see Han Snel's house. It would seem that all Han had to do was entertain guests, but back in 1969 there weren't too many tourists visiting the island.

The house looked more like a Balinese temple than a private residence. It was built of carved stone with a tiled roof and eaves of magnificent designs. There was a lovely lotus pool in the garden, with stepping-stones that led across the water to Han's art studio and private gallery.

There was another walkway that led down to a ledge below the house, and here on the open terrace in the cool of evening, Han and his lovely Balinese wife Siti entertained guests at dinner. There are incidents in our lives, happenings we can call them, that we never forget. I remember one such evening, an evening when Han and Siti invited me to dinner to their house in Ubud.

The meal was, of course, traditional Balinese, with suckling pig roasted whole, basted with strange but delicious herbs and spices. Before dinner we had rum punches made with tropical fruit, and with the meal we drank Balinese wine. Dim lights – wicks dipped in coconut oil which filled the night air with a most delightful fragrant scent – flickered and danced in all the corners. And somewhere off in the background came the sound of a *gamelan* orchestra playing ever so softly. You couldn't see musicians but they were there in the shadows. The conversation, like the wine, flowed, and it was about Bali, the old Bali that Han knew. Han talked about his coming to the island, and meeting and working with artists like Le Mayeur, Rudolf Bonnet, Theo Meier, Donald Friend, Mario Blanco, Arie Smit and others.

It was a superb night, more dream than real. There are times like these in the tropics when you awake the next morning and wonder if it had happened at all.

That was many years ago when I first dined with Han

and his wife. Every time I return to Bali I visit them, and sometimes I stay in their bungalow, and always, when I awake the next morning, I wonder again if it is all real. But it's no dream with Han Snel. His life may seem like a fantasy to us, but to him it is very real. He is a first-class foreign artist who has continuously lived on Bali longer than any other foreign artist there today.

Times certainly have changed on the islands since I made that first drive up to Ubud. There were few art and gift shops along the drive then, nothing outstanding; today along the same route you can see hundreds of impressive, stone-carved buildings, art galleries mostly, much like the house that Han Snel had built. And Ubud was no more than a little village where painters lived. Today it's a thriving, pulsating community with restaurants, shops, art galleries and hotels. Doors do no longer close when the sun goes down.

The narrow lane that leads to Han Snel's house is still there. And when I enter through the stone-carved gate that leads to his house, I could be walking back through time, except now Han and his wife Siti have grown daughters, and the house has been expanded. And they have also added a restaurant. Han jokes about the restaurant. It wasn't that he was going commercial, he said, but after tourism came to Bali in the 1970s, their house attracted an increasing number of admirers from abroad. While entertaining these visitors, Han and Siti found themselves regarded as masters of Balinese and Indonesian cuisine. "The restaurant was a necessity," Han said. Siti took over the supervision, and a few years later she opened six Balinese style chalets in their compound. "Gives her something to do while I'm painting, and after I'm gone," Han remarked.

I always enjoy my visits with Han and Siti, and now when I considered writing about him and his lifestyle for *At Home in Asia,* I went to see him specifically for that reason. I had known him all these years, but there were dark areas I knew nothing about. For example, it was rumored that he fought the Japanese while he was in the Dutch army, but when the war ended they say he refused to fight the Indonesians in their war for independence from the Dutch. They say he deserted and became a hunted man. Bali was his hideout and he learned to paint only as a cover up. It was also said that Swiss artist Theo Meier took Han under his wing and taught him everything he knows about art. And there was the question about his wife Siti. They said he had actually kidnapped and run off with her into the hills, with her family after him in hot pursuit, ready to kill him. Han had to pay off the family.

I wondered if Han would answer these questions.

There is so much more to Han's life than simply living on a beautiful island and painting for the rest of his days. His life is a storybook of intrigue as well as romance, of incredible deprivation during the war in Europe, of Indonesia's struggle for independence from the Dutch, and of his own struggle to remain in the islands when independence did come. His is a story of the countless people he met, the rich and famous, and the not so rich and the not so famous artists who lingered on in paradise, also struggling for survival and recognition.

My problem was that I found it hard to get Han alone long enough to talk to him. If we met him at his restaurant, there were always others around vying for his attention. Many in the art circles gather at the restaurant for lunch and drinks, and everyone wants to talk to Han when they see him. If it isn't a reporter or travel writer who wants to interview him, he is playing like a godfather, giving advice, telling people what they want to know. And if he's not in Ubud he is fishing. Han likes to fish, or so he claims, and he has built a fishing bungalow on the north coast somewhere. I suspect the bungalow is more his escape haven than anything else. It's easier for Siti to say Han is out at sea fishing rather than sitting in his studio where he can be disturbed. At sea they can't track him down.

Finally one afternoon I was able to get him alone. We sat in a small pavilion, away from the others, drinking strong Balinese coffee. He was in the mood to talk, and he had Siti bring out all their photo albums, stacks of them. There were also scrapbooks, with news clippings in a dozen languages from around the world. I began asking him the questions everyone wants to know. He laughed.

"Rumors, all rumors," he said with a grin on his face. "There's nothing mysterious about my life. I wanted to paint, and I came to Bali. I married a Balinese girl and we have three grown daughters and a couple grandchildren. What else is there to tell?"

There was plenty to tell.

Han admitted he went to Indonesia against his will, as a conscript soldier. I asked him about the rumor that he was a deserter from the Dutch army.

Han chuckled and poured another coffee. "No, I hate to ruin a good rumor, but I didn't fight the Japanese," he said. "In fact, I didn't come to Indonesia until 1946, after the war, and it wasn't the case of my deserting the Dutch army. I wanted to stay when my time was up, but the Dutch government insisted that soldiers return home after their tour of duty was up."

When Han first arrived in Indonesia, the country was in turmoil. In 1945, President Sukarno had declared Indonesia a free nation, but it wasn't until 1949 that all of Indonesia was officially declared independent. Han recalls that many unfortunate Indonesians were starving and poverty was frightful. "People were dying in the streets and there seemed to be no relief," he said. Han arrived in Jakarta aboard a troop ship from Holland and was sent to

Bandung where he found some respite from the damages of war, even though much of the city had been burned down. "It was a bit more prosperous there," he said. "Still, I couldn't help feeling sorry for the Indonesians, for the suffering they had endured during the war."

I was curious about Han's youth, his growing up in Holland and leaving the country of his birth for a foreign land, never to return. Did he have regrets? Did he ever long to go back?

"Holland left me with some bad memories," he said. "Remember, I was born on July 16, 1925, and when I was still in my teens, my country was overrun by the Nazis. The war years were not very pleasant."

Prior to the war, his father had run a printing office. Han went to primary school like all normal kids did then, and when he graduated he entered a commercial art school where he remained for two years. He dabbled in painting and desperately wanted to go to the Academy and study art, but with a war spreading across Europe that was impossible. "So you see," he said, "I didn't become an artist simply because I wanted to remain on Bali. I was always interested in painting, as long as I can remember."

But Han never went to art school and the Germans went on their march. Within weeks they had overrun Holland and the Low Countries and Han's fate was sealed.

Han, with melancholy and sadness in his voice, remembered the cold, miserable winters, when the only thing his family had to eat was sauerkraut. "I hate the stuff to this day," he said. "Just mention it and I want to throw up." He was a little more fortunate than his older brother and two younger sisters. He landed a job as a cook in a small restaurant. "At first I knew nothing about cooking," he said. "I managed to convince them that I did know. I would go home at night and my mother would tell me how to cook and what to do. The next morning I would go back to the restaurant and practice what she taught me. It worked and we pulled it off. I still like to cook."

The war ended and Han never gave up the thought of studying art, but now the army had different plans for him. Although Holland was liberated, the war for the Dutch was hardly over. They had their vast colonial possessions around the world that had to be maintained, at a time when colonies were clamoring for independence. Han was conscripted into the Dutch army, given a uniform and sent to what was then called the Dutch East Indies. Ironically, he did not want to go to the Far East. All he wanted to do was remain home in Holland and paint.

But once he arrived, Han immediately fell in love with the tropics, and he sympathized with the plight of the helpless Indonesians. But as a soldier, there was little he could do to help them. Distasteful as they were, he had his soldierly duties to perform. When Indonesia did declare independence and the Dutch slowly began to pull out, Han didn't want to go back to Holland. According to the letters he received from back home, Holland still suffered from the war. He made up his mind; he would remain in the islands. "At least here in Indonesia there were palm trees and I was warm," he explained.

The question was how could he stay? It was evident that all of Indonesia would eventually be liberated, and for certain the Dutch would be expelled.

There was a possibility. Han had heard that if when discharged soldiers could find employment, and the companies who hired them would guarantee their repatriation when their contracts were up, they were sometimes granted government permission to remain behind. With his background as a cook, Han found a German bakery in Bandung who would hire him, and he immediately began to work. He intended to report to the military once he was established but the military came looking for him first. They gave him twenty-four hours to report to the high command in Jakarta where he was told he would be sent back to Holland aboard the next available ship.

Han gave up hope. He had no choice but to go back to Holland. But before he could leave he had to settle his affairs. While he was in the army he had kept up with his sketching and painting, even while employed at the bakery. He had left all his works, dozens of paintings and countless sketches, in Bandung. He convinced his commanding officer to grant him two weeks' leave to try to sell his possessions. "You aren't going to try to run away?" the C.O. asked.

"Not at all," Han said in earnest.

On the road back to Bandung, the C.O.'s words kept pounding away at this thoughts—run away, run away. "And do you know," he said to me, "the thought never entered my mind until the C.O. mentioned it. I had no intention of escaping, until then. I didn't have a plan, not until I got to Bandung."

Han knew a painter in Bandung and went to him to ask about selling his sketches and paintings. He mentioned to the painter that he was being shipped back to Holland against his will. Han explained to the man that he would rather remain, and even become an Indonesian citizen. "In the land of art and beauty, you too want to become an artist," the painter said. "Well, then, here's my advice to you. Don't go back to Holland."

The artist suggested that Han get himself to Yogyakarta in central Java. "The place has already been handed over to the Indonesian government and declared itself independent," the painter explained. And then he advised, "If you go, go now. Don't wait."

Han followed his advice. He sold what he could and with only what he could carry in one small handbag he headed to the train station in Bandung. Once there he discovered he had to clear through a military checkpoint before boarding the train to Yogyakarta, and, of course, he didn't have the authorization. "The guards pointed out the train for me to take to Jakarta," he said, "but I played stupid and in all the confusion I got on the wrong train, the one to Yogyakarta. Once I was aboard no one questioned me. Not one person. The next morning I was in liberated Yogyakarta."

When he reported to the newly proclaimed independent Indonesian authorities, he expected to be received with open arms. "But it never happened that way," he said. "They had never heard of a Dutch citizen who wanted to become an Indonesian. It made them suspicious. They didn't believe me."

Instead of accepting him, the Indonesians took him to be a spy working for the Dutch. He was arrested and locked up behind bars. Every day, without fail, he was repeatedly screened by military police who threatened to send him back to Jakarta where he certainly would have to face a Dutch military trial. He pleaded his case. "I want to be an Indonesian," he insisted. "I want to live here and paint." Finally, after a month of intense questioning, his wish was granted. He was given a letter stating he had applied for citizenship and was free to go. He left immediately for Bali. For the sake of easy pronunciation, he dropped the letter "s" from Hans and the extra "l" from Snell. He now became Han Snel.

"I literally burned all my bridges behind me," he said. "There was no turning back. My father wrote to me. Surprisingly, he had no objection to my remaining in Asia, but he asked that I do not disappoint him nor my mother. They had suffered too much and I guess he understood. My brother had already emigrated to Canada."

"But why Bali?" I asked. "Why this island among thirteen thousand others in Indonesia?"

"Being Dutch," he replied, "Bali was not alien to me. None of Indonesia was, except we called it the Dutch East Indies. It was our colony and we had been taught a lot about it in school. We studied places like Sumatra, Flores and Timor. Names of islands and towns in the East Indies were household words to every Dutch boy. Everyone knew about Bali. And for aspiring artists, we were familiar with names like Walter Spies and Le Mayeur, and we envied them. When I got to Bali, Walter Spies was dead. He was German and had died at sea when the ship he was on was torpedoed. All were lost. But Belgium painter Le Mayeur was still here."

Han went on to tell me about Le Mayeur, who, among others, inspired him to go to Bali. Back in the 1930s, Le Mayeur Merpres was the most famous and most talked about artist living on Bali. People from all over the world and from all walks of life went to Bali with a single purpose in mind, to visit this noted European painter. The very first colored photographs ever to be published in the *National Geographic* were taken of Le Mayeur and all his lovely, bare-breasted Balinese models. Before long he had established a remarkable reputation for himself that soon became synonymous with the island.

Even more so than it is today, the 1930s was an era of adventure for artists from Europe and America, and the East held a particular attraction for them. It conjured up images of exotica, of a world where the fruits of nature were bountiful and the mystery of dark skin and simple lifestyles were alluring. More than anything else, the women attracted the artist's attention. Le Mayeur found his model, and his love, in a beautiful *legong* dancer named Ni Pollok.

It wasn't only artists who went to the island. Writer and musician Colin McPhee was drawn to the unusual music of the *gamelan,* while scientist Margaret Mead came to study and write about the "primitive" people. They helped to create the island's mystique and lasting fame.

And so Han Snel went off to Bali to become a painter.

From the ferry landing at Gilimanuk at the western end of Bali, Han and a Dutchman he had befriended—he called him a "real" deserter—caught a bus to Denpasar. His friend was also an aspiring painter. It took them a whole day to reach the town. "It was a big sleeping island then," Han said. "It truly was paradise."

But he did have to admit, Denpasar was a bit of a disappointment. "We arrived in the early evening, and already the streets were dark and empty. Not a soul was around. It was like a ghost town. We had little money and looked for the cheapest room in town where we could spend the night. We couldn't waste money on a hotel room."

They found a room and the very next morning the two travelers set out to find Le Mayeur. They had heard that he had a house along the beach at Sanur. They found the house without much trouble, as every Balinesean they met knew who he was and where he lived. The famous artist greeted them warmly. Le Mayeur was then in his fifties. He was extremely thin, almost emaciated, but very tanned from sitting on the beach every day. "So you want to live on Bali and become artists," he said and led them into his studio. His wife, Ni Pollok, appeared and offered them tea. "She was still very beautiful," Han remembered, "and at the time perhaps the most painted woman in Asia."

When she left the room Le Mayeur told how in the early days he would go to Denpasar to collect Ni Pollok and another model, Ni Ketut Reneng, in a horse-drawn carriage. In those days the streets were quiet and the half hour that it took to reach the beach at Sanur was marked by the clipclop of their buggy.

During the early morning at Le Mayeur's studio the two girls held poses while the artist painted them. In the afternoon when the sun became unbearably hot, he would take them down to the beach and teach them to write by drawing letters in the sand for them to copy.

Ni Pollok was sixteen years old at the time, and Le Mayeur fell in love with her. They eventually married. Their wedding celebration was in Balinese style. "Half the island attended," Le Mayeur said. "But remember, something like this didn't happen every day."

Le Mayeur told the two men how he took Ni Pollok to Singapore with him for his first overseas exhibition. The opening ceremony of the show included Balinese *legong* dances, and Ni Pollok was the star. The exhibition was well received and both the name Le Mayeur and his beautiful *legong* dancer wife became known the world over. Other exhibitions followed, from Singapore to Japan. Ni Pollok accompanied him wherever he went. With the money he was now making, he was able to expand his house in Sanur and vastly improve his lifestyle. "Pick the right woman," Le Mayeur said, and then suggested that they go to Ubud to live. "It's an art colony, where all the painters live." And then what came as a surprise, Le Mayeur told them that he had just completed building a house in Ubud and the two men were welcome to stay there until they found a place to live. This was the break they needed. Le Mayeur gave them many other tips, about buying art supplies and how to find models, and then sent them on their way.

The two young men took their work seriously and started to paint immediately. They made drawings and sketches and took them to the Bali Hotel in Denpasar to sell to the tourists. A little money began to come in, enough so that they were able to rent a small house in Ubud for five hundred rupiahs. The exchange rate then was twelve rupiahs to the dollar. Han accepted an offer to teach drawing in the local school. Before long the Bali Hotel let Han hang his paintings in the lobby. He soon was commanding a thousand rupiahs a painting. That was close to a hundred dollars. His next step was to buy his own house. He found one he liked near Goa Gajah, the famous Elephant Cave, founded by the Majapahit conquerors in 1365. His Dutch friend remained behind in Ubud, leaving Han to shift for himself.

Han befriended other painters living on Bali. He remained friendly with Le Mayeur but he had little to learn from the artist. Le Mayeur was helpful but Han thought he had become very commercial. "He was more interested in selling himself than his art," Han said.

Two painters who did more than anyone else to influence Balinese painting styles were men that Han had never met. They were Walter Spies and Rudolf Bonnet. Until they arrived in the late 1920s, Balinese painting was little developed as an art form. Mythological scenes were almost the only subject and these were painted to decorate shrines and religious calendars. Walter Spies and Rudolf Bonnet soon had the island's younger artists turning to new subjects, new forms, new materials and new techniques. They were careful, however, not to influence their ideas nor to introduce subjects foreign to them.

Balinese painting now took on a new meaning. In the old manner people were only painted in profile, and to a large extent its subjects were religious and mythological, but now the young painters began to paint themes from everyday life. The new style was highly decorative. Despite the inherent weaknesses of composition, the simplicity and decorative naivete of the paintings carried them off. Ubud became an art center. "The young Balinese artists were anxious to learn from the foreign artist, and we in turn learned something from them," Han said. "It was an exciting world, with so many people interested in painting. It was stimulating, and competitive. But it was healthy competition. You strived to create something that was new but still very Balinese. Painting in the early days became a real challenge."

Australian artist Donald Friend made an appearance in the early fifties when Han was starting to find success. He remained for many years and had a great influence on Balinese artists by teaching them individualism.

Another post war newcomer was Jim Pandy, partly Dutch, partly Chinese. He too settled in Bali and became friends with Han. Pandy and others like him started Balinese schools of art at Ubud and Mas.

From Manila came Filipino painter Antonio Blanco. He took a Balinese wife and became a painter, self-acclaimed poet and *bonvivant* who enjoyed entertaining tourists with his tales of self-achievement as much as he enjoyed painting. His subject matter was, and still is, nude women.

Arie Smit was another Dutch artist who settled on Bali. Although he had been in Indonesia for eighteen years, three of which had been as a prisoner of war under the Japanese, he didn't reach Bali until 1956. He was a recognized painter by then.

And then there was Theo Meier. From what Han had been telling me, it was obvious that Theo hadn't taught him to paint, as many thought. "No, he didn't teach me," said Han, "but he gave me some good ideas."

Han was on Bali painting for ten years when at last he met the woman he wanted to marry. She was young and pretty, and her name was Siti. During our conversation, Han had laughed off most of the rumors I asked him about, but when I questioned him about his kidnapping his wife he at once became very serious. "Well, if the truth be known, I did kidnap her," he admitted. "But there's more to it than just that." And then he gave me a big smile.

"It's a Balinese custom."

The custom of elopement, he explained, is called *ngrorod.* It's an accepted practice on Bali. On a specific date declared auspicious by a Hindu priest, the bride is forcibly taken by her suitor to the house of his friend, generally a long distance from her village. The parents are then informed of the event, and they feign horror. The matter, of course, has been prearranged. The marriage ceremony takes place in a gay atmosphere in the friend's village. Han did it just that way in 1958, and the friend's house was that of the Swiss artist, Theo Meier, in East Bali.

When Han and Siti decided they wanted to marry, they went to see Theo Meier's ex-wife, Peggie. She agreed to help them, after much persuasion on the part of Siti, but she informed Han that he must tell no one. Peggie then arranged everything. She found a taxi that would take them to Iseh in East Bali. The house had belonged to Walter Spies, but when they sent him away at the beginning of the war, Theo Meier took over the place. Being Swiss, Theo was permitted to remain in Indonesia under the Japanese occupation.

"I couldn't understand it," Han said, "but the taxi driver went into a fit when he saw me and a young Balinese girl running off to East Bali, especially when he learned why we were going. Peggie got him calmed down, but then Siti kept hiding on the floor. She didn't want anyone to see her. It was only a game. What was the difference?"

At the village two headmen came out to the taxi and wanted to look at Siti. One asked her if she was willing to marry this foreigner. Siti was very shy and for a long time didn't say a thing. The man looked at Han and then at her. "Do you want to marry him?" he repeated. This time she said she did. The headman then turned to the other one, and asked, "Do you think she is old enough?" He agreed with a nod.

The marriage ceremony was performed, with the traditional filing of her teeth, and for five days Han and Siti stayed at Theo's house in the hills in Iseh. Finally Siti's mother discovered where they were hiding out and came running. She was furious. Han hadn't realized but his kidnapping had been real and not merely a staged act as custom dictated. Siti's mother had her daughter betrothed to a medical student in Jakarta and they were to marry when he graduated. There was little her mother could do now and the young married couple returned to Ubud. It took Siti's mother a few years before she got over her anger, but she eventually did when she realized that Han would remain forever on Bali.

Bali had its time of troubles too. President Sukarno, who had been a friend of the artists, suddenly insisted that all Dutch, whether artists or not, leave Bali. Han and Arie Smit were ordered to leave the island immediately. Theo, who had a close relationship with Sukarno, became very disturbed by Sukarno's sudden change of heart. He went to Jakarta to see if he could talk to Sukarno. He was granted an audience with the president.

Supposedly, Sukarno told Theo this was political and Theo and the other artists should not get mixed up in politics. He advised Theo to return with Arie and Han to Bali and take up where they left off. Arie and Han did return, but Theo Meier decided he would leave Bali. He moved to Chiang Mai in northern Thailand and there remained until his death in 1983. Theo and his Thai wife made yearly pilgrimages to Bali, but he never remained longer than a month or two at a time.

In 1965, Sukarno's attractive wife, Dewi, the highly-talented Japanese bar girl whom he had met in Tokyo, arranged for an art exhibition for Han in the Japanese capital, and from there Han decided he would return to

Holland for a visit. It would be his first time back since he left. He also decided to take Siti with him. There was one problem. She didn't have a passport. Anywhere but on Bali it would have been a simple task. First, there was no registry of her birth, and second, no one, not even her mother, knew exactly when she was born. But she needed a birth date on her passport. Her mother determined she was born when the Japanese came to Bali. That must have been 1942. What was her favorite month of the year. She said May. The birth was set in May. Now the day. The officer at the court house in Denpasar tore 31 pieces of paper and numbered each one. He had Siti choose. She picked 23. Her birth date was established as May 23, 1942. The problem was still not solved. Han had to present the letter he received in Yogyakarta stating he had applied for citizenship. It took months and finally when he received his Indonesian passport he was informed his marriage to Siti also had to be validated. They had to remarry in a civil ceremony. At last they were able to depart for Tokyo and then Holland.

It was a sad home coming for Han. Most of his friends and members of his family had long since passed away. Deep inside Han felt that his father would have been proud, for as his father had asked him not to disappoint him nor his mother. They were happy to return to Bali and their house in Ubud.

Over the years Han and Siti have charmed countless personalities from six continents—writers, actors and actresses, photographers, dignitaries, curious tourists, all who have passed through Bali. Han talks about people like Ingrid Bergman and James Michener as one would talk about family members. Then he laughs. "When Theo Meier knew someone important was coming to visit me, he would suddenly appear, and would do everything he could to whisk them off. I should have been angry but I never was."

Han has been a great help to those who came to Bali for both business and pleasure. He has arranged feasts, dances and theatrical performances, staged cremations, made introductions, found locations for filming, has been advisor and guide, and assisted writers, photographers and musicians.

In 1969, Hans Hoefer came knocking at his door and soon they became fast friends. "Hans was interested in painting," Han said, "and he reminded me much of myself when I first came to Bali. I remembered so well how Le Mayeur helped me and I wanted to help Hoefer the same way. He did have one thing in his favor that I didn't. The tourist boom was about to begin. Hans talked to me about a picture guidebook on Bali that he had on his mind. He wanted to produce one. The only true guide we had at the time was Covarrubias' *Island of Bali*. It was our bible."

Han helped Hans Hoefer to convince Siegfried Beil, the German manager of the Bali Beach Hotel at Sanur, that he should commission Hans to produce a full-length guidebook rather than a brochure that he originally wanted. A business deal was made and the *Guide to Bali* became a reality.

After our coffee in the pavilion that afternoon, Han led me across the stepping-stones to his studio. Most of the paintings on display were part of his museum collection. Others were for sale. The Neka Museum in Ubud also has a generous collection of Han's oils and sketches.

Han loves to play with colors in his paintings. Darks against lights, long shadows, delicate lines superimposed. In one series of oils hanging on the south wall you can see the development of his style from impressionism to cubism. "I am still experimenting," he said. "If we don't experiment, if we don't try to develop new ideas, new techniques, then we are only craftsmen and certainly not artists."

No need for that. Han will always be the artist and the legend that he is.

Before leaving Han and Siti that day, I had one final question to ask Han. "Does it ever get boring?" I asked.

"Does what?" he asked.

"Living an entire lifetime on an island paradise."

"Tell me," he replied, "does it ever get boring eating, drinking, making love."

"Well, no, not really," I replied.

"That's your answer," he said and we shook hands.

Darkness had fallen and I drove in silence back to my hotel in Sanur. New artists may come to Bali, as they surely will, and they may spend a lifetime there, doing what Han Snel has done, but none will ever be able to lead a life as he had. Han Snel followed in the exotic footsteps of other expatriate painters who found their muse on Bali. But Han is a vanishing breed, like Covarrubias, Spies, Bonnet, Meier and others. His generation too is passing.

Hans and Siti in 1966.

Inger Lissonevitch—Destiny, Nepal.

Chapter 6

INGER LISSONEVITCH
Mrs. Boris of Kathmandu

⤳

This chapter, about Inger Lissonevitch, and the two that follow, are about three women of Nepal. They are three remarkable women, all expatriates, living a fairy tale come true. But to understand these women, we must know something about Nepal, not the Nepal of today but the Nepal they found when they arrived. Kathmandu, the capital, is on the tourist map; it wasn't then. Today hundreds of thousands of visitors arrive each year; when they do it is like stepping back four centuries in time. The kingdom had been tucked away and left in isolation throughout the years, and only in the 1960s did it begin to emerge out of the past.

Each of these three women, Danish, American and English, played a role in the making of a new Nepal, although if you ask them, they will think not.

If you haven't been to Nepal, try to imagine it. Try to imagine what these women encountered when they first went there. It was not until 1951, actually, that the King opened the doors to the outside world.

"The country of Nepal", wrote Marco Polo in the fourteenth century, "is little visited by strangers, whose visits are discouraged by the King." The blame has been placed upon the King, but in truth it was the ruling aristocratic Rana family who did the

discouraging. They treated all of Nepal as a sort of personal estate, and they managed to keep each king confined to his palace. With few exceptions, visitors were forbidden to enter the country, and the mountain terrain made it easy to enforce the ban.

It was only when India achieved her independence after World War II that the King's supporters were able to secure aid from the sympathetic Indian Government. The revolution came and the Rana Prime Minister resigned. In 1951 King Tribhuvana regained power, to be succeeded later by his son, Mahendra, in 1955. The Rana family still plays an important role in the Nepalese political scene, although somewhat indirectly. King Mahendra married a Rana, and on February 27, 1970, his son, the Crown Prince Birendra Bir Bikram Shah Deva who is the heir to the world's only Hindu throne, also married a Rana. She is Princess Aishwarya Rajya Laxmi Devi Rana.

Although Nepal did open her doors to foreigners in 1951, it was not until as late as 1956 that the first road connecting Kathmandu, the capital, with India was completed. Prior to this, supplies had to be carted on muleback or by rope line over the mountains.

The first impetus to tourist promotion was the converting of a Rana palace into the Hotel Royal under the guidance of Boris the Russian. This is where our stories begin.

At eighteen, Inger Scott was the belle of Calcutta. She was a true Danish beauty, tall and slender, with flashing blue eyes and lovely wavy blond hair. The war had ended and having completed her schooling in England, she went to Calcutta to live with her mother and stepfather, a Scotsman named Charles Scott.

Back then, when she first arrived in Calcutta, had someone told her that one day she would marry Boris Lissonevitch, a White Russian barkeeper in Calcutta, she would have thought they were teasing her. And if these same people had suggested that she would bear him three sons, she certainly would have believed they were carrying the joke too far. For one thing, Boris was twenty-five years her senior, and married. Second, she was under the strict guidance of her mother and stepfather, and not at liberty to choose and pick her male friends at will. Third, she wanted more than anything to get out of Calcutta, not to continue to live there the rest of her life. And last, she didn't even like Boris. "Oh, he was popular," she said. "Everyone in Calcutta knew him, and talked about him. But I wasn't in the least drawn to him when I met him. In fact, I even thought he looked an awful lot like that movie villain Peter Lorrie."

That was in 1947, just after the war, and Boris was, indeed, the talk about town in Calcutta. He was the leading entrepreneur of social life for all the colonials and expats in the city. He was by birth an aristocrat, and a colorful *bonvivant* who had fled Russia with a ballet troupe after the Bolshevik Revolution and eventually made his way to Calcutta where he opened the posh 300 Club. He was a friend of everyone, from very rich playboy maharajahs, reigning royalty, sultans, heads-of-state, foreign diplomats, actors and actresses, political leaders, and political agitators as well.

One of his closest friends was the Maharajah of Cooch

Behar. They were forever in the news, cavorting in Paris one week and hunting at the maharajah's estate in Bengal the next. It was the maharajah who informed Boris that there were three beautiful women living in Calcutta, and it was Boris' duty to throw a big party and invite them.

Boris gave the gala party as the Maharajah of Cooch Behar had bid, and he invited the three beautiful women. Inger, of course, was one of them. "I was shy and naive and so very nervous about going," she said as we sat in the garden of her son's restaurant in Kathmandu. "I was just out of school, and not very experienced. Anyway, Boris was much too busy to pay attention to anyone in particular at the party. It was just a fun time and nothing happened."

But things did happen. Boris had an eye on Inger, although it wasn't obvious at the time. One evening a few months later, when Inger was having dinner at the club with friends, Boris came up to her table and shocked everyone there by asking her if he could take her to a movie. "I was absolutely stunned," she confided. "He was like a school boy, asking me to go to the movies with him. I thought it was flattering, that the great and important Boris wanted to take me to the movies."

Inger was certain Boris would withdraw his invitation after she warned him that her stepfather would not approve. "Never mind," Boris said. "Come to the club and we can leave from there." Inger liked his boldness. She accepted and they set a date.

Inger arrived at the club as planned, nervous and a bit apprehensive, but to her dismay Boris was nowhere around. He had stood her up. Seeing her disappointment, Harry Waters, the club manager, took her to the movies instead. It wasn't until a few days later that she learned Boris had simply forgotten their date.

"That was Boris," she said, "and the truth was it really didn't matter. I wasn't chasing after him, and I knew not to take him seriously." Inger recalls it wasn't long after that Boris was off on another of his antics; this time to what he called his Hollywood expedition. "He actually left wearing gum boots, a safari bush jacket and a solar topee, with everything but a rifle," she mused. He was going to Hollywood to live it up with his maharajah friends.

Boris came back to Calcutta, as always, with stories that kept the club in laughter for weeks on end. Inger didn't see much of him during this period. He was continuously occupied while entertaining and playing host, forever surrounded by people hungry for his attention. Then one evening, again without warning, when Inger was at the club for dinner, Boris appeared at the table and asked if she would like to dance. As before, she was flattered, until she discovered Boris was not asking for a dance for himself but for the Pan Am pilot who had flown him and the maharajahs back from California.

"I guess any other girl would have been annoyed, or even angered," she said, "but I wasn't. I thought it was all rather amusing. I liked the attention, and the pilot was a good dancer."

Weeks passed before Boris made his next move. This time it was a special invitation. He invited Inger to a private dinner party.

"A dinner hosted by Boris was always something special," Inger said. "When Boris traveled he always wore a heavy overcoat which was lined with pockets on the inside. These he filled with smoked salmon, black caviar, red caviar, herring and all those delicacies we couldn't get in Calcutta. He could hardly walk he was so weighed down."

That first dinner was more or less the beginning of Boris' courtship of Inger. After that they went to parties together and were seen at the races. Hardly an important social function passed that Inger wasn't at Boris' side. "Boris was always the perfect gentleman," Inger said. "I found myself falling in love with him, but I never suspected that he had anything but admiration for me." Inger was so wrong.

Inger Scott was not a newcomer to Asia. She was born in Denmark but when she was nine she went to live in Singapore with her mother and father. The year was 1936. Her father was a Danish ship captain, who like a character from a Conrad novel ran cargo and passengers between the port of Singapore and Bangkok. Life with a sea captain can be difficult, and eventually Inger's mother and father separated. War had just broken out and Inger and her mother were forced to flee aboard the last boat from war-torn Asia to Scotland. There her mother met her husband-to-be, Charles Scott. In time they married and after the war moved to Calcutta. Inger remained behind, finished her schooling and joined them two years later. Charles Scott was a civil engineer, employed to work in the jute industry with his headquarters in Calcutta. He was a stern man who believed in Christian ethics, especially when it came to bringing up a young daughter.

All did not go well when Inger became friendly with Boris. The more she saw him, the more estranged became her relationship with her stepfather. Finally the situation reached a crisis. Inger's father forbade her to see Boris altogether. "I felt that was none of his business," Inger said. "My mother didn't mind so why should he?" But it did bother Charles Scott. Boris was actually much older than he, a married man and was dating his stepdaughter, which didn't help his image in Calcutta. He called Boris "that Russian pimp."

"When I told Boris what my father had said, I thought he would do something," Inger said. "But he only laughed. Boris was always very forgiving."

Their meetings now had to be clandestine.

"My stepfather was unreasonably strict," she said. "I was nineteen now and still on weekdays I had to be home by ten; at twelve on Saturday nights. Eventually it got so bad that when I did break one of his rules, he gave me a written notice to leave the house within twenty-four hours. I had no other choice but to move into a hostel for women. There wasn't much my mother could do, for he was very nasty to her if I didn't listen. I guess I was too young to realize what was happening. My father always wanted me to go along when he took my mother out dining or dancing. If I didn't go, he wouldn't take her. It became very unpleasant. I couldn't see what was happening, being so young, but my mother could. My stepfather was infatuated with me. And here was Boris, older than him, and dating me. That didn't set very well with him. My stepfather was jealous. Still, I was very naive. He did funny things, like putting nasty notes on my bed. Finally my mother had to send me back to Denmark to get me away from my stepfather. And then, dear Boris, he began to take my mother out, to lunches and tea. This must have infuriated my stepfather even more."

Boris at the time was a married man, which he never attempted to conceal from anyone, including Inger. His wife, Kirita, also White Russian, had been his dancing partner. Together they had performed in every club and theater in Asia, from Shanghai to Singapore. To this day, a poster of them hangs in the lobby of the old E&O Hotel in Penang in Malaysia. When they could no longer fill the bill as a dancing team, and Boris opened the 300 Club in Calcutta, Kirita wanted to move on. She had become disillusioned with Asia, but Boris had found his niche in Calcutta. Kirita went to visit friends in California and never returned.

Despite Boris being the *bonvivant* that he was, or appeared to be, life for him was difficult and uncertain. He had suffered greatly from the revolution and could never completely escape his past. Being stateless, a man without a country, he had to make the most of whatever opportunity presented itself. He had to establish a residence somewhere, and he had chosen Calcutta. For him there was no retreat, no going back. He missed Inger terribly when she left Calcutta.

Inger had been in Denmark barely six months when a knock came at her door. She opened it and found herself speechless. Boris was there, kneeling on bended knee, with a bouquet of flowers. She was both shocked and pleased to see him. He had been constantly in her thoughts ever since she left Calcutta. Life without Boris had become dull and colorless. And now he was at her door.

"I came to ask you to be my wife," he said, and before she could answer he went on. "There's a Russian church here in town and we can get married immediately and then return to Calcutta." Inger was too overwhelmed to refuse.

"Like most girls I had dreamed of a white wedding," she said, "but with Boris there was no preparing. Everything he did was spontaneous." The very same day that Boris appeared at her doorstep they went to the Russian church to get married.

"But we had no papers, nothing," she said. "Boris didn't have his divorce papers. The Russian church refused to marry us."

"Never mind," Boris said unperturbed. "We will get married in Brussels on the way back to Calcutta."

"So we arrived in Brussels," Inger said, "and I'm still naive and believed him, and the same thing happened. No papers, no marriage. And I thought so what, never mind, and we continued on to Calcutta."

Back in Calcutta Inger and Boris moved into their own quarters at the club. "Everyone assumed we were married," Inger said. "Being Danish, and liberal, it didn't matter to me. I don't think my stepfather ever knew." Time went by and still the divorce hadn't become final.

Quartered above the 300 Club as they were, their life was a perpetual round of parties that alternated with visits to the maharajah's palace in Cooch Behar. Inger admits she didn't like public life but went along with whatever Boris wanted to do. "I knew three months after we were in Calcutta that living with Boris wouldn't be easy, but by then I was pregnant. In any case, I loved Boris. The problem was I couldn't ever get him to myself. He had to have people around him all the time. The more the better. Eventually I began to get a complex. I began to think maybe I was boring. Whenever I told Boris this he would laugh and tell me to be patient."

On Boris' birthday, Inger gave birth to their first son, Mikhail, nicknamed Mishka. Five months after Mishka was born, Boris collected his small family and set out for Cooch Behar on an invitation from the maharajah.

After the partition of India and the formation of East Pakistan, Cooch Behar was cut off from direct rail or road contact with Calcutta, and the maharajah needed equipment for an ambitious farm project he was developing. Boris offered to personally transport to the maharajah's estate all the equipment that was waiting on the docks in Calcutta. To accomplish this, Boris had to journey with Inger and their young son over dirt trails and along cart tracks. Their biggest obstacle in reaching Cooch Behar was crossing the Ganges; even today there is but one bridge across the Eastern part of the mighty sacred river of India. The only way for them to cross was by barge. After finding a suitable barge and negotiating the price, Boris loaded aboard Jeeps, tractors and other equipment, along with his wife, his infant son, and a few Indian helpers to drive the motor vehicles. As there was no road on the opposite side of the Ganges for the barge to unload, they had to sail some thirty miles downriver to reach a possible landing point where they could disembark and continue their journey overland.

All might have gone well except that a second barge, filled with scrap metal and attached to their own heavily laden craft, began to founder in mid-river. The panicked crew of the sinking barge jumped onto the heavily laden one on which Boris and his family and his Jeeps and equipment were precariously balanced. As the frantic passengers piled aboard, the clumsy barge listed perilously, shipping dirty water into the bilges. Somehow Boris managed to get the frightened Indians away from the low side of the barge and got the boat on an even keel. Their time of peril was still not over. The muddy river water was nearly up to the rail. Grabbing a couple of buckets, Boris passed them to the crew and with shoves and blows finally got them to start bailing out the water. Gradually the freeboard of their overloaded craft rose a few inches and they reached shore.

The trip was supposed to have lasted four days; it took nearly a week. But in true Boris fashion, the hardships were soon forgotten when they reached the maharajah's palace. Caviar came out and the champagne bottles popped. They celebrated for two weeks without stop.

Finally after three years of living with Boris, after producing one son, Mishka, and with their second, Alexander, kicking to come out, Boris and Inger got married. His divorce from Kirita finally came through. Their wedding, however, wasn't what one might call typical. They were married on the terrace of the 300 Club by a Bengali Babu clad in a dhoti . "It was hardly romantic, and such a farce," Inger laughed. "I didn't know whether to laugh or cry. It certainly was not the white wedding I envisioned, but it was official."

Among the maharajahs and royalty who visited the 300 Club, one prominent visitor was the deposed King

Tribhuvan of Nepal. He came to Calcutta seeking medical treatment, part of which was relaxation at the 300 Club. He and Boris became fast friends.

"They were very secretive," Inger remembered. "At the time I didn't know what was happening, and Boris never told me, but it wasn't until later that I learned they were planning to put the King back into power."

Ever since 1846 when a shrewd army general named Jung Bahadur Rana took over the powers of government in Nepal and had himself designated prime minister and later maharajah, the Shah kings were kept under strict vigil in their own palace and were not permitted to exercise authority.

Jung Bahadur Rana had made the office of prime minister hereditary, establishing a line of succession that would pass first to his brothers, then to their sons, and in so doing inaugurated the century-long Rana oligarchy. The power structure was reorganized to the sole benefit of Jung Bahadur Rana himself, his immediate circle of relatives and friends, and his successors.

For 104 years, while the Ranas built huge palaces and lived grandiose lives, the people under their reign were neglected and deprived of their rights. Land, for example, was unequally distributed to their friends and relatives.

But major changes began taking place during the years following World War II. India had gained independence from Great Britain, and with the support of the Indian Congress Party, opponents of the Rana rule joined the Nepali Congress Party. They held that King Tribhuvan, still powerless in his palace, was the rightful sovereign of Nepal and the embodiment of the democratic aspirations of his people.

In November 1950, the King fled to India. In Delhi, he was welcomed by Prime Minister Nehru as Nepal's reigning monarch. In Calcutta he went to the 300 Club and there met Boris and Inger.

In the meantime, back in Nepal the Nepali Congress Party called for the overthrow of the Rana tyrants. The "freedom fighters" liberated most of the Nepalese Terai, set up a provisional government in Birganj, and engaged Rana troops in battle. But the action was not decisive, and eventually India presided over a compromise agreement between the rival parties.

On February 18, 1951, King Tribhuvan returned from his self-imposed exile with garlands of flowers around his neck, and began a new rule. The Rana prime minister was forced to step down, thus ending more than a century of extravagant, despotic rule by the Ranas.

Whether or not Boris had much to do with the King's return is uncertain, but King Tribhuvan regained power and in 1951 invited Boris and Inger to come to Nepal to organize his coronation. Boris gladly accepted. He and Inger flew up from Calcutta into Kathmandu Valley aboard a DC-3.

Kathmandu when they arrived in the early 1950s was not the same place it is today. "Kathmandu was like a fairy tale," Inger said lamentingly. "The town was very quiet then, with old brick buildings and carved windows. There was not a drop of cement anywhere, only high mud walls. We had one paved brick road and no more than a hundred vintage cars. Mind you, no buses, no cabs, no pedicabs or rickshaws. We walked. We walked everywhere and thought nothing about it. There were no crowds, of course, and you could always see the mountains, except during the monsoons."

Indeed, Kathmandu then was a privileged place. Life in the valley seemed unperturbed by the outside world; few newspapers ever reached the capital, and no radios disturbed the peace of the streets. No road led into the country, and for the few vehicles the capital did have, they had to be carried into the country on the backs of men and beasts.

They moved into a small bungalow and immediately set to work.

Boris took complete charge and responsibility for the King's coronation. For three continuous days he had three chartered DC-3s flying constantly between Patna, India, and Kathmandu on a bizarre airlift with cargo that included 6,000 live chickens, 1,000 guinea fowl, 2,000 ducks, 500 turkeys and 100 geese. Along with them came a ton of fish, two tons of vegetables and—perhaps strangest of all—a couple tons of ice! Apart from the eternal snows, there was no ice plant in Nepal.

The coronation was a huge success. Guests from around the world attended. Boris had made all their arrangements which, naturally, included accommodations. The biggest and most difficult problem for Boris was finding places to stay for the thousands of people who came. Boris quickly saw the need for a proper hotel in Kathmandu. When the celebration was over and the last guest had departed, Boris confronted the King with a proposition. What Kathmandu needed, he said, was a first-class hotel. The Snow View and the Imperial Hotels, the only ones in town, were inadequate. Not only VIPs needed a place to stay when they came to Kathmandu, but tourists as well.

The King listened to Boris' proposal and finally agreed. Kathmandu would have its proper, first-class hotel. He granted Boris the use of a Rana palace right in town for this purpose, and the famous Hotel Royal of Kathmandu was born. Inger's and Boris' life now became more hectic than ever.

The first formal group of tourists to visit Nepal was a group of wealthy widows from the cruise ship *Coronia*. Since Nepal had never before coped with tourists as such, Boris, with Inger's help, had to arrange everything from scratch. They put on a modest display of handicrafts on the terrace of the Royal. Their friend, Crown Prince Mahendra, met the tourists on the terrace and watched them snap up the handicrafts. Mahendra immediately realized what tourism could do for the country and asked that his father, King Tribhuvan, declare that visas for those who wanted to visit Nepal should be issued without delay upon application. This marked the beginning of tourism in Nepal. Clearly Boris was the father and creator of tourism in Nepal.

King Tribhuvan opened Nepal's doors to the world by welcoming tourists and establishing diplomatic relations with many lands. He died in 1955 and his son, Mahendra, became king. Five years later, in 1960, not wanting himself relegated to a ceremonial role, Mahendra announced that he had taken over direct rule. Political parties and their activities were banned and parliament was dismissed. King Mahendra died in January 1972 and was succeeded by his son, the youthful King Birendra.

With the introduction of tourism and the establishment of international aid agencies after Nepal's admission to the United Nations in 1955, there was an obvious increase in the number of foreigners in the valley. The Hotel Royal soon became the meeting place of Europeans and Nepalese. And Boris, with his buoyant charm and enthusiastic personality, became the leading spirit of the town's social activities. As a correspondent of a large American paper put it, "Boris is the number two attraction in Nepal after Everest."

When Boris opened the Royal, he had a copper chimney with a red brick base built in the very center of the lounge. In a large circle around the fireplace were comfortable reclining chairs where everyone sat with their feet propped up on the bricks. It was here at the fireplace that I first met Boris many years ago. When I asked him about his wife, Inger, whom I had never met, he mentioned she was up in the hills sketching. It wasn't until years later, after Boris' death, that I would finally meet her.

Boris was an exuberant extrovert while it was Inger who protected the privacy of their personal lives. In their flat at the Royal she had the difficult task of bringing up their three sons, Mikhail, Alexander and Nicolas.

There were frustrations, Inger admitted. Life with Boris was not easy. When a journalist wanted to get Boris alone, Inger remarked, "How do you think you can catch him alone? In the first fifteen years we had been married, I had spent only two evenings alone with him."

The truth is that no one, not Inger, not their sons, ever got to know the complete Boris. How can one ever learn about Boris in Russia, Boris the ballet dancer, Boris in World War II, Boris and the Maharajah of Cooch Behar, Boris and his playboy maharajah friends in Hollywood, Boris in Calcutta and Boris in politics? He kept his thoughts very much to himself.

"When you love someone," Inger said, "you want to share their life, their thoughts, their feelings; you want to get to know that person, and you want them to know you as well. I wanted him to talk about himself, but he wouldn't."

Boris had lived a life in fear. He needed to escape, and he did this in this larger-than-life profile.

In Nepal at the Royal, Boris with Inger at his side played host to such celebrities as Presidium Chairman Voroshilov of Russia, Chou En-lai, Jawaharlal Nehru of India, Ayub Khan of Pakistan, and Crown Prince Akihito of Japan, not to mention every ambassador who stayed at the hotel when presenting his credentials to the foreign office. While playing host at the Hotel Royal, Boris and Inger had seen most of the dignitaries of the East, and had added many of them to their already incredibly long list of friends and acquaintances.

Inger often entertained guests in their private flat at the Royal. She would have tea ready for the Tibetan refugee committee in the afternoon and later in the day meet with the King's brother, Prince Basundhara, and his American fianceé, Barbara Adams. Basundhara, the Playboy Prince as everyone called him, was a financial backer for the hotel and came almost every day when he was in town for both business and pleasure. Inger and Barbara became friends.

Inger got to know other foreign women living in Asia and married to Asian men. "You always hear about foreign men marrying Asian women, but you seldom hear the other side, about foreign women marrying Asian men," she said. Two such women, also her friends, were the wives of the Bhutanese and Sikkimese delegations.

The Bhutanese were represented by Lennie Dorji, the sophisticated prime minister and brother-in-law of the King of Bhutan. Lennie was an avid hunter and sportsman. Whenever he arrived on formal visits to Kathmandu, he was always accompanied by his elegant and beautiful wife, Tesla, who, like Boris, was White Russian. To reach Kathmandu in the early days, Lennie and his delegation had to walk and ride eight days to reach India from their capital before embarking on a plane for Nepal.

The Sikkimese delegation was led by the Maharajkumar, Crown Prince Palden Thondup Namgyal, the present Maharajah of Sikkim whose marriage to the American woman Hope Cooke in 1963 became a world sensation. Both women, Tesla and Hope Cooke, confided in Inger when they came to Kathmandu.

Boris' Danish mother-in-law, Mrs. Esther Scott, came to live with the Lissonevitchs at the Royal in 1960 where she spent the last years of her life. "She adored Sir Edmund Hillary," Inger said of her mother. "She would have to get up on a chair to hug him."

Edmund Hillary, the beekeeper who became one of the

most celebrated mountain climbers ever, was a close friend
of Boris and Inger. He had gone to Europe to climb in
the Alps and found his way to the Himalayas in 1951. In
Nepal, he met Eric Shipton, the famed British climber-
explorer and together they charted the most feasible route
up Mount Everest. Hillary returned two years later and
on May 29,1953, he and his Sherpa companion, Tenzin
Norgay, succeeded in becoming the first men to reach
the summit of the world's highest mountain.

Boris and Inger played host to most of the mountain
climbing expeditions. Since Hillary and Tenzin made it
to the summit, more than 200 climbers, including five
women, have attained the summit. They have come from
22 nations on 54 expeditions. More than half that number
whom they also entertained were unsuccessful. "Many were
real characters," Inger admitted. "but we were never sure
we would see them again. It was always tragic when they
didn't return." In 1975, Boris and Inger were witnesses
when Mrs. Junko Tabei, with an all-woman expedition
from Japan, became the first woman to reach the summit.
Aside from Hillary, they were most fascinated with an
Italian climber, Reinhold Messner. He came to climb most
of the peaks in the Himalayas, and in 1980 made the first
solo assent of Everest with no bottled oxygen, no com-
panions, no fixed camps, no ropes and no sophisticated
mountaineering aids. In four days, he climbed from base
camp to summit and back to camp.

Hillary returned to climb in ensuing years and eventually
became involved with the day-to-day problems of the
Sherpa people. The Sherpas had no schools or hospitals
in their remote regions. Hillary founded the Himalayan
Trust Oganization to aid his friends. He supported 20
schools and two hospitals that he himself had taken a hand
in building. He also became New Zealand's ambassador
to Nepal.

"We met them all, from Hillary to Messner," Inger said. "Some of the expeditions had several hundred people, and Boris catered to them all." Until King Tribhuvan opened the country, Nepal's mountains were off limits to foreign climbers. Even today, Inger explained, foreign mountaineers are not free to go and climb any peak they choose.

Unlike Boris who was constantly surrounded by people, Inger felt she needed time to be alone, away from people and especially celebrities. She found her way through art.

When Inger was in school in Britain, she studied commercial art which was to prove beneficial years later when she was in Nepal. With time on her hands while Boris was constantly entertaining, she took up oil painting. She began making long treks into the mountains to paint. In time she became an accomplished artist.

"Actually, my happiest times in Nepal were my trips up to the mountains to paint," she said. "I would go alone, with one Sherpa and some porters to carry paints and canvasses, and spend a month or so in the Everest region or in the area between Pokhara and Jomsom. I would return renewed and able to cope for a while, but then I'd have to run again."

Inger's oils adorn the walls of her son's restaurant in the Thamel district of Kathmandu. The restaurant, aptly called Boris' Restaurant, is where I first met her. "The scenery in Nepal is just begging to be painted by a Monet, a Cézanne or a Van Gogh," she said as she showed me around. "I am fascinated by light as were the French impressionists and I mostly paint outdoors in sun as they did. I'm surprised that most Nepalese artists seem to have jumped from figurative painting, right into abstract, without stopping to absorb the ideas of the impressionists. There is really so much beauty here to be savoured." Inger prefers a pallet knife to a brush for both landscapes and portrait work.

Boris' Restaurant is owned and operated by Inger's son, Mishka. He lived in Nepal until he was 12, and then went off to school in Switzerland.

"I came back to Nepal, always to visit my mother and father, and each time I found it more difficult to leave. I finally realized, Nepal is my home. I can't leave." And by remaining in Nepal, what could Mishka do? He could do what comes naturally. He could get into the same business his father did. He went for a spell to Manila to study the hotel and restaurant business under Axel Goerlach who was manager of the Hilton there. Axel had managed the Annapurna in Kathmandu and was close friends of both his father and mother. Mishka returned to Kathmandu and opened a restaurant.

Upstairs in the restaurant is a shrine to Boris. Here on the walls are framed photographs of Boris and his family from his early days in Odessa in Russia to his last days in Kathmandu. There are pictures of him as a young cadet in uniform, one as a dancer with the Bolshoi, and another family portrait with a very young Boris standing with his brothers and their mother and father. We see him in a poster of the Boris & Kirita dance team at the E&O Hotel in Penang, another in Bali, and there are more of him with heads-of-state, diplomats, famous movie personalities and royalty, including the Queen of England.

"The Queen loved it when he bowed and kissed her hand," Inger remarked when she saw me looking at the photograph.

And there are the early photographs of Inger with Boris, one with them on a royal tiger hunt. Inger and young Mishka both accompanied Boris and members of the royal family and visiting maharajahs on tiger hunts. "I never hunted myself," Inger said, "but I liked the outings." In 1958, Boris shot his sixty-eighth tiger. It was far from a record, as the Maharajah of Sarguja had shot the world record of 1,177 tigers, but it does place Boris among a select few.

"We have a stilted picture of Boris," Inger said. "There was another side to him. Aside from royal tiger hunts and gala parties, he was very industrious. Boris negotiated the first Danish loan for Nepal. Through Baron Thysson's friendship with Boris, the Bhaktapur Project was born. Boris was full of ideas. They didn't always work but they were fun trying out. He had a project to put trout fingerlings into the Trisuli, but then the Nepalese government put carp into the river. Naturally the carp ate all the trout."

Boris also introduced the first domestic pigs into Nepal. "They had to be called English wild boar because importing pigs was not allowed," Inger said. "We started raising pigs for the hotel. Now these pigs are all over Nepal."

When they went to Nepal, Boris' first real business venture, other than the Hotel Royal, was to build a distillery. It landed him in jail. He brewed local style liquor which he labelled Rhinoceros and Tiger Whiskey. He brought his still up overland from Calcutta. But there was a problem. Boris' operation was legal, having had authorization from the King, but there were some 1,400 illegal distillers in his neighborhood. Boris couldn't compete with them so eventually he had to close down. The government then hit him for taxes, including for the time the distillery was closed. They demanded immediate payment. "But Boris never had money," Inger said, "so he went to jail. That was in 1954."

Inger recalls that Prince Basundhara visited Boris every day in jail. One day one of the King's secretaries appeared, and suggested Boris write the King and ask for a pardon. "It worked, and Basundhara came to fetch him. We

Inger Lissonevitch with her son Mishka and a friend in Kathmandu.

celebrated all that night," Inger said. Boris' time of troubles never ceased in Kathmandu, but eventually, after the Hotel Royal closed its doors, he and Inger did find their solitude outside Kathmandu in a modest, Nepali-style brick house on forty *ropanees* of land. Without a bathroom for the first few years, it was a far cry from the glamorous life she and Boris shared at the old Hotel Royal at Bahadur Bhavan in earlier days. But it was home, located on a plateau with a beautiful view near Chapagaon. Boris turned to farming and planted orchards, peaches and plums. Inger indulged in gardening. At last she had Boris to herself, but their happiness was short lived. Boris passed away in 1985.

With tears in her eyes, Inger talked about his death. "He had a tragic ending, which I have a hard time living down," she said. Boris was a great hotelier, raconteur, and generous friend to all who knew him, but he died penniless in a public ward at the Bir Hospital. Only three Nepalese attended his funeral service at the British cemetery. "He died a pauper and yet he did so much for the country," Inger said.

Inger is bitter, and she admits it. "The present generation in Nepal has never been told that it was Boris who put Nepal on the International tourist map."

The fight for Inger is still not over. The taxes are unpaid and the government is trying to take away her land. Then every year, during the four-month fruit season, she fights an unequal battle with scores of unruly villagers who swarm over her wall and strip her fruit trees.

When I finally did met Inger at Boris' Restaurant, I was most surprised how beautiful she still is. She has a silky, little girl voice and her blue eyes flash with excitement. The luster is still there.

"Boris became a public figure," she emphasized as we sat in the garden. "He loved people and was always entertaining the beautiful people from all over the world. Maybe I was a disappointment for Boris, for I couldn't care less about all these people. I hated all that. All I wanted was a family life and to be alone with my husband and children. But that was not my destiny. The only visitors I got close to were Ingrid Bergman and Lars Schmidt. She was wonderful. So kind and unpretentious. The other women, Tesla and Hope, were only in passing. I got to know Barbara Adams rather well. Of course, Basundhara, her prince charming, was very good friends with Boris. And in later years Lisa came to Kathmandu. She is the newer generation, the new blood in Kathmandu."

Before Inger and Boris came to the Himalayan kingdom, there wasn't much there to attract visitors. Not even a restaurant, and certainly not much in hotels. Mountaineers who came to attempt to climb Everest had to sleep in tents on the lawn of the old dilapidated Snow View Hotel or else in open fields. Inger and Boris changed all that. What Inger asks for now is that Boris be remembered for what he did for Nepal. But let us not forget what Inger, too, did for Nepal.

Barbara Adams—An American on top of the world.

Chapter 7

BARBARA ADAMS
Every Woman's Dream

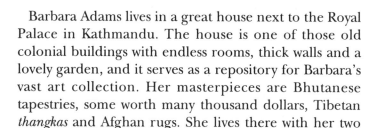

Barbara Adams lives in a great house next to the Royal Palace in Kathmandu. The house is one of those old colonial buildings with endless rooms, thick walls and a lovely garden, and it serves as a repository for Barbara's vast art collection. Her masterpieces are Bhutanese tapestries, some worth many thousand dollars, Tibetan *thangkas* and Afghan rugs. She lives there with her two Labrador Retrievers.

Barbara wears flowing gowns, and her hair, which is now grey, is thick and long. When she speaks you know immediately she is American. She writes a newspaper column called "Barbara's Beat" for a local newspaper. Everyone in Kathmandu knows her, or they at least know about her.

There's a story they tell in Kathmandu about Barbara. They don't tell it when she's around; they whisper it behind her back. I heard it years ago when I first went to Nepal, long before I got to know her.

The story does sound plausible, but even if it weren't true, it wouldn't matter. Everyone believes it. They say that Barbara came to Nepal on her honeymoon, met a real live prince charming and fell in love. When the day for her departure arrived, she and her husband boarded the plane and bid everyone goodbye. But when the plane taxied down the runway and made the turn for take off, Barbara jumped out of the plane. The aircraft took off without her, with her husband still aboard.

Today you could hardly jump out of a 737, but in those days, back in 1961, before they extended the runway, the only aircraft to fly there were the old U.S. Army standbys, the DC-3s. They were noisy, bouncy machines, but very reliable. They could take off and land almost anywhere. It was conceivable that one could jump out of a DC-3 before it took off. It was possible, but no one ever dared ask Barbara if it were true, so the rumor continued. If nothing else, it had a romantic ring about it and made a good story.

In time I got to know Barbara, and finally I dared ask her about the rumor and about her secret life with Prince Basundhara, her prince charming. With the passing of time she was willing to talk about it. We were sitting in her garden drinking tea when she told me her story.

"It's not quite true," she admitted. "Actually I went to the airport three times to leave and I couldn't. I had fallen in love with the prince, that is so, but I also fell in love with Nepal. And I wasn't on my honeymoon. I had been married two years. My husband was Italian." Then she added, "And living with a prince in fairy tale land, that every girl's dream you hear about, well it isn't what you might imagine."

What is even harder to imagine is this young woman, barely twenty-one, from an upper-middle-class Virginia family that was listed in the social register, who ends up living in a distant land, a Himalayan kingdom that few people at the time even knew existed. Barbara became as far removed from Virginia as she could possibly have been. She craved adventure and excitement when she was in college, but this was more than she could have expected.

Barbara was from Virginia but she spent most of her growing up years in Washington. Her father was a stock market analyst who had worked for the Office of Secretary of Defense in Washington during the war. She had a proper high school education, went to George Washington University in Washington and studied languages at the

Georgetown International School of Languages on Massachusetts Avenue. She too was destined to have her name listed in the social register one day, but somewhere along the line she became captivated by the Beat Generation movement. The Beats were a bohemian reaction by young Americans to the so-called "silent generation" of the 1950s. These were the Eisenhower years, the "middle-of-the-road" years that no one questioned. They began with visions of comfort and complacency and ended up with civil rights being the national issue. Barbara found a voice in coffee shops like "Coffee 'n Confusion" on M Street in Washington where she listened to the poems of Ginsberg, Corso and Ferlinghetti. She read with abandonment Jack Kerouac's *On the Road* and traveled with him through the pages across the United States into Mexico. She soon rejected conventional consumer society, everything her family and friends stood for. In other words, she rebelled.

But unlike her contemporaries, Barbara did not flee to New York or San Francisco to embrace an unconventional life-style of Zen Buddhism and drugs. She went far beyond Kerouac's *On the Road.* In 1958, she sold everything she owned, took a boat to Italy and found work writing for Italian magazines in Rome. While on a magazine assignment she met an Italian photographer.

The photographer had been a medical doctor who became disillusioned with the inhumantity he found everywhere he went. He gave up medicine, turned to communism as a solution to the world's problems and became a photojournalist with an axe to grind. He and Barbara found solace in each other's company. A month after they met they were married. They moved into a furnished apartment in Rome and lived there for two years, until they got the assignment that would take them to Kathmandu. Barbara was thrilled. A few years before, she had never heard of Kathmandu; now she was going there. Her life was to turn topsy-turvy. For certain, it would never be the same.

In New Delhi they transferred to a DC-3 that carried them over the Himalayas into the Valley of Kathmandu. They landed on a grass runway.

"Kathmandu then was the most beautiful place on Earth," Barbara said. "The Nepalese were totally innocent, in awe of everything. I was wearing silk stockings and they wanted to touch my legs. We had truly found Shangri-la."

It was Nepal's indigenous art and architecture that captured Barbara's fancy. "I couldn't believe it," she said. "It was like walking through a museum, except virtually all these treasures were still in use." Barbara immediately set out by foot to discover Kathmandu. "You didn't need a taxi, or even a bicycle," she said. "Everything could be discovered on foot. In fact, the streets in most sections were so narrow that even cyclists had to push their bicycles. It's still the same way, I guess."

The old city of Kathmandu fascinated her the most. It was once enclosed by a high wall with narrow openings for gates. The old main gate still stands. To this day the streets within are crowded and flanked with three-story houses with doorways, screens and overhanging balconies carved in wood. The carvings are usually of Nepalese gods and goddesses. All along the ground floor of the houses are open-front shops, where the owners sit cross-legged on pillows and sell their wares.

Barbara found the streets of the old city humming with people. She eyed the Nepalese women wearing saris and men in narrow trousers and shirts hanging down to the knees. She was bewildered by the men and women who came down from the highlands. The women wore bangles about their wrists and heavy jewelry around their necks. Some wore jewels on their noses. Some men wore strips

of cloth wound around their waists from which hung their
khukuris, the Nepalese *scimitar.*

And everywhere sauntered the Hindu cows, and the
never-ending stream of porters jogging along single file,
with heavy, loaded baskets fastened by straps to their
foreheads. How exciting and strange it was for this young
woman with revolutionary thoughts from America.

Barbara recalls trying to get a room at the Hotel Royal
but it was fully booked. They spent their first few days in
the Snow View Hotel. On their third day in the Nepalese
capital they were invited to a reception at the Royal. To
greet them was the hotel's renowned manager, Boris
Lissonevitch, and his attractive Danish wife Inger. Boris
made the introductions and presented Barbara and her
husband to everyone there. "It was like stepping into the
movies," Barbara said. "I had never seen such pomp and
splendor in my life."

Chance brought Barbara and her husband to Kathmandu at the right time. They could not have planned it
better. The palace was preparing for a grand royal function
and had invited dignitaries from around the world. Many
were staying at the Royal. From India came Sikh gentlemen
in bright turbans and their women in saris trimmed in
gold filigree. From Bhutan came emissaries from the King,
and they wore thick robes with wide-open sleeves. There
were Pakistani Muslims and Hindu Parsis, and with them
were their women, in colorful and expensive dress. There
was royalty from Thailand and sultans from Malaysia and
Brunei. And representing King Mahendra of Nepal was
his brother, a suave and debonair man who oozed with
charm. He was slight of build and wore a tailored Bond
Street suit. His accent betrayed his English schooling. Boris
introduced him to Barbara and her husband. "I would
like you to meet His Royal Highness, Prince Basundhara,
brother of King Mahendra," he said.

Prince Basundhara took Barbara's hand, bowing slightly as he did.

"Charmed," he said. Barbara felt she had truly stepped into a story book. This can't be happening, she thought.

Those who knew Prince Basundhara will admit he had an eye for pretty girls, and there's no doubt his eyes were on Barbara when they met. The vibrations were there, and they both felt them.

Basundhara was married to Her Royal Highness, Princess Helen Shah of Nepal. It was an arranged marriage, they say, and Princess Helen was but twelve years old when their vows were made. She was pregnant at thirteen. In the first six years they were married, Basundhara fathered three children with her.

Axel Goerlach, who was the general manager of the Annapurna Hotel at the time, a hotel that Princess Helen owned, knew her well. "It was only natural Helen would be bitter when Basundhara began to show his affection for Barbara," he said, "but there wasn't much she could do. She never showed her feelings. As manager of her hotel, I was often invited to her house. She did not want to engage in any conversation about her personal life, and she never talked badly about Basundhara."

The truth was Basundhara couldn't have cared less what the world thought about him. After Barbara's husband left Nepal, Basundhara arranged for Barbara to meet him in Hong Kong. She then traveled to Japan with him and they toured the country for a month. Barbara returned with Basundhara aboard a royal flight to Kathmandu. They decided that they would not hide nor conceal their relationship. Once back in Nepal, Prince Basundhara and Barbara lived openly together. By Nepalese law they were man and wife.

Barbara's lifestyle changed. While in Nepal and on official royal functions abroad she had to conduct herself accordingly. She played the role magnificently. She gave up Western ways. She dressed in saris and painted her eyes as Hindu women do. She learned to speak Nepalese.

Barbara told me of how she joined Basundhara on tiger hunts in the Terai and went with him on royal visits to India and Pakistan. They were met with motorcades everywhere they went and they were received royally. Barbara was granted the same honors as any lady of standing. When they traveled they traveled in royal splendor.

But Barbara Adams, the American woman from Coffee 'n Confusion and the bohemian world of Washington, was discovering that living the life of royalty wasn't all glamor. "Nothing is ever as glamorous as it appears from the outside," she said. "It was difficult, the social life, the bowing and all the protocol. Suddenly you were being heralded about, squeezed into the back of the plane with all the children. You were not with him. That was the frustrating part, being so close together and yet separated."

As I sat with Barbara in her garden, sipping tea, she revealed her true inner-self and feelings for the first time. "No, it wasn't easy," she admitted. "Basically I am a rather shy person, and now I found myself surrounded by all these strange people. I was listening to a language I never heard before. For Basundhara it came naturally. I began to realize you have to be born into royalty to function as royalty. Basundhara, of course, spoke half a dozen languages. He was patient with me. Instead of me helping him he was helping me."

Barbara and Basundhara spent a great deal of time at the Hotel Royal. When Boris came to Kathmandu and found that the kingdom lacked a proper hotel, he went to the King with the idea of opening one. Basundhara leaped at the idea. The King not only gave his approval, but he gave Boris the use of an old Rana palace.

Basundhara put up the money and the famous Hotel Royal was born. "Friction between the two of them did develop later over business matters," Barbara said, "but it never interfered with their personal relationship. Actually both were poor businessmen. Basundhara never saw a rupee for his investment, but he felt it was money well spent. The Hotel Royal gave Kathmandu the spark it needed, and life with Boris was never dull. "Their friendship was hard on their livers," Axel Goerlach said. "They could party until three in the morning every night, drinking toast after toast, to anyone and everyone. They were fun to be around."

In spite of his heavy drinking, Basundhara was an avid outdoorsman. He and Barbara went horseback riding several times a week, and he played polo every chance he had. "When we traveled he was often invited to play," she said. "He never failed to accept an invitation. He was a fine player and a very good horseback rider."

Basundhara liked to drive and he often took Barbara to Europe where he would rent a car. They motored all over Europe. Sometimes just the two of them; sometimes Boris and Inger would join them. Basundhara enjoyed it most when he was able to travel incognito. "He appeared to be stately but in reality he wasn't," Barbara said. "We once went to Afghanistan, and somehow they found out who Basundhara was. We found ourselves being escorted in a motorcade. Basundhara wasn't too happy. He spent much of his time trying to escape from motorcades."

Barbara revealed that Basundhara was very sensitive. "He was also very lonely. He was frustrated that he wasn't involved in his country's development. He was popular with the people, perhaps because he was extremely democratic. I was with him twice when people proposed a coup, but he would not turn against his brother, and he never did. His only official role was to serve as regent during the King's absence."

Through Basundhara, Barbara did meet many important world leaders. In the stack of photo albums she keeps in her study you can see her with heads of state, like Jimmy Carter and Jawaharial Nehru. There are others of her and Basundhara riding elephants on royal hunts, attending functions, vacationing in the Alps, dining in posh restaurants in Paris and Rome. One photo shows Barbara and Basundhara at Alfrado's Restaurant in Rome, with the Nepali ambassador.

Barbara's life with Basundhara wasn't all protocol and formality. "We often went to visit Boris at his farm," she said. "That was always fun. Boris raised pigs and named them after people in Kathmandu. He named one after me, and another after the French ambassador's wife. I didn't mind but the ambassador's wife didn't take it so lightly. "

The steets of Kathmandu that attracted Barbara Adams to the capital.

Another memorable trip they made together was to Thailand. They were guests of Prince Sandith in Bangkok and journeyed with him and his wife Christina to their weekend retreat in Chiang Mai in the north. "We met Sandith's good friend, Swiss artist Theo Meier, in Chiang Mai," Barbara recalled. "Prince Sandith told us how he would travel to Bali every year to visit Theo. They would have a blast on Bali. Theo had lived on Bali for twenty-five years before he moved to Chiang Mai, at Sandith's invitation." Barbara showed me an oil painting she bought from Theo on that trip. "It's worth a fortune today," she said.

Barbara spent ten exciting years under the same roof with her prince. "I knew it was inevitable, that some day it would end," she said. "The pressures for Basundhara became more than he could endure. He had a severe heart attack and soon after that I was spending more and more time alone. The tragedy was he never stopped drinking.

We finally separated, but still we lived side-by-side one another. I used to see him every day. He'd come with a bottle of vodka at ten in the morning. I was no longer living with him, so I had no rights, and no control over him. I felt that he was killing himself, which eventually he did. He died of cirrhosis of the liver in 1977."

With Prince Basundhara's death, Barbara's time of troubles began. For sixteen years Nepal had been her home. Kathmandu was more a part of her than anywhere she had lived before, Virginia, Washington and Rome included. Her memories were here in Kathmandu. She didn't want to leave, and she was determined she wouldn't. Her fight began.

Over our third cup of tea, Barbara told me how Basundhara's family took everything away from her. That which she did managed to keep, she had to hide, including the sports car Basundhara had given her. But that wasn't enough; the family did everything they could to deport her. "I was fighting for my life. Before Basundhara died he warned me, he advised me to try to cultivate all the powers I could. He said his brother was not well liked and a lot of people were leading him astray."

Barbara demanded to know why she was being deported. Every day she went to the immigration and every day she asked the same question—"Why me?" She insisted she was not going to leave. "I am not leaving," she said. "I have a perfect right to be here. By law I was married to Prince Basundhara. Do you want to truck me down to the Indian border like you are doing to all the hippies?"

A very unfortunate situation had developed in Kathmandu a few years before Basundhara died. The Flower Children from San Francisco's Haight-Ashbury and New York's Greenwich Village discovered Nepal in the mid-1960s. The climate was cool and enchanted, the people friendly and everywhere was the fertility of Shaivist Hinduism and Mahayana Buddhism, the mystic and the sublime. Besides, hashish was growing wild and was sold in licensed shops, and harder stuff was readily available. Along with Goa at the other end of the rainbow in India, Kathmandu became a hippie paradise.

So while the Beatles and Jimi Hendrix sang songs of love, Kathmandu experienced an invasion the likes of which it had never seen before, and will almost certainly never see again. They came from the world over, bearded or shining-shaved, long-haired or skin-headed, in boots or bare feet, heavily robed in ex-G.I. garb or nearly naked, wearing beads or pierced-nose jewels, filthy or scrubbed clean, undernourished or well-fed, with pockets filled with money or with the need to beg and steal or sell themselves to survive. For the most part they were a disreputable lot, and Kathmandu was to suffer for it.

Kathmandu is one of the great attractions for foreign visitors to Nepal.

Something had to be done. The coronation of King Birendra was scheduled for 1975 and Kathmandu had to clean up it's streets before the world could attend the highly-publicized ceremony. Visas were refused and others canceled. And to rid the undesirables from the streets of Kathmandu, free transport out of the country was provided. Those without means of support were trucked down to the Indian border and dumped off.

"Do you want to do with me what you are doing with them?" Barbara asked. Fortunately she did have friends in the right places. She was permitted to stay.

When I first met Barbara a number of years ago she was running the Third Eye Travel agency, one of the few in town in those years. Even though there weren't many tourists in the beginning, Barbara had a good business going.

But still, making a living in the Nepalese capital isn't easy. Aside from her newspaper column and other related articles she writes for magazines, she finds herself involved in projects of many sorts. When I was there a while back, she was renting out her lovely house to movie director Bernardo Bertolucci who was filming what he hoped would be his masterpiece, *The Last Emperor.*

My afternoon tea with Barbara was nearing an end. After knowing her for almost twenty years, she had confided in me the secrets of her private life in Nepal. "I have nothing to hide," she said. The sun was fading when I got up to leave. When I looked at Barbara I pictured her as a student in Washington. She was no less filled with life and ambition today than she was then. She was away from her own heritage, away from her own background, but had she really changed? Tiger hunts don't change people. Ideas do. Barbara Adams had formed her ideas long before she left Washington. She just managed to find a place that could conform to her beliefs. Nepal was that place.

One of these days someone will go to Kathmandu, not to merely talk to Barbara, but to do a film about her. All the ingredients for a great motion picture are there.

Lisa Choegyal—A true lady of the Himalayas.

Chapter 8

LISA CHOEGYAL
At Home in the Himalayas

Whenever I am in Kathmandu, I enjoy nothing better than to go to the home of Lisa Choegyal for a visit. "You must come for a drink," she always says, and then adds, "I'm having a few friends over. I'm sure you'd like to meet them."

Lisa, her husband and their two children live in a sprawling house—she calls it a bungalow—at the edge of town. It's one of those places with rooms attached to rooms, and each room is crammed with eye-catching pieces of art of some sort—*thangkas* from Tibet, carvings from Burma, thick rugs from the Middle East.

It's difficult to get beyond the hallway.

Lisa greets me warmly, and instructs her two young sons to shake hands. They do and run off to hide. "Tenzin will be home later," she says and leads me into the living room.

A dozen or more of her guests are already there. Lisa makes the introductions. Gary McCue, the director of Wilderness Travel, from Berkeley. Khun Bhudhisarn, the Thai International station manager in Kathmandu. Sandy Lieberson, President of MGM International. He wants to talk to Lisa about location shots for movies. There are members of a climbing team preparing to make an assault. They leave before I can meet them and I can't catch all their names. I discover one of them was Reinhold Messner, the noted Italian climber who made it solo to the summit of Everest. Jimmy Roberts comes in. I had met him a couple times before; everyone in Nepal knows him. He made a number of first ascents of Himalayan peaks in Nepal and Pakistan. He founded Nepal's first trekking agency—Mountain Travel—in 1965.

Lisa introduces me to a young bearded man who is writing a trekking guide to Tibet. "How do you research such a book?," I ask him. I feel like a fool when he answers.

"By foot," he says. "I trekked across Tibet, a half dozen times." He then spends the next ten minutes telling me about remote regions of Tibet that no outsider has ever seen. He is called away before I get his name. A day or two later when I see Lisa I ask who he was. She doesn't quite know who I mean.

"Nearly everyone who was there has trekked in Tibet," she says, and then adds, "And nearly everyone is writing a book or a movie script of some sort."

Tenzin, Lisa's husband, comes home from the office. He is Asian, the eldest son of the eastern ruler of Tibet. He speaks English like a New Yorker. He's quite handsome, and he wears a tweed sports coat, gray slacks and brown loafers. He looks more like a college professor than the businessman that he is. "So nice to see you again," he says and we shake hands.

Only at Lisa's house can one meet so many fascinating people. An evening at her place and I can gather enough material to fill my travel column at the *Bangkok Post* for a month. Stories of Nepal make good copy. There's always an amusing tale someone has to tell about a mountain climbing expedition that's about to start, or about one that has failed. There are stories, and opinions, about the Yeti, the abominable snow man, and his probable existence. And one hears talk about such things as a wildlife resort built in a tree top, highways opening up to Mustang, the Japanese bid to build a hotel on top of Mount Everest, a climbing school for people in wheel chairs and so much more.

Then the other reason why I like to visit the Choegyals is for Lisa herself. Now there's someone with a tale to tell.

Who is this woman, Lisa Choegyal? How does she attract all these interesting people? Even more important—why does she? What brings her to Nepal? And her husband, a Tibetan prince? Here, certainly, is a woman who is as fascinating as the country she has adopted.

I first met Lisa back in the early 1970s at Batu Caves north of Kuala Lumpur in Malaysia. She was touring Southeast Asia with a friend, Lady Victoria Yorke, and they had just arrived from Bali. I was at the caves at the time with Hans Hoefer, assisting him with a documentary he was doing on the Hindu Thaipusam festival. I remember little about that meeting with Lisa, except she was English, tall, very attractive and was an admirer of Hoefer's work in Bali. Her meeting with him, however, was to have a pronounced effect on her future.

The years passed, and during this time I often went to Kathmandu, or met travelers who had just come from there, and a name I kept hearing was Lisa Choegyal. I never made the connection. The Lisa Choegyal everyone talked about was the publicity director for Tiger Mountain Group, Nepal's biggest travel conglomeration. Tiger Mountain's operations included the world famous Tiger Tops and the Jungle Lodge in the Royal Chitwan. Then I read that Lisa Choegyal had been appointed Managing Editor South Asia for Apa Productions. Another source said Lisa Choegyal led trekking and rafting expeditions, and that she provided location management for many wildlife films. There was more. Lisa Choegyal was a leading authority on "eco-tourism" and gave talks and lectures to audiences in the US, Europe and Asia. And she was an author and photographer.

The Lisa I knew was Lisa Van Gruisen, a young adventuresome English girl who spoke in rapid, clipped English, and who was probably back in the UK raising a family. Also, the name Choegyal was a Sikkim term that means "protector of the state." It stands for royalty. This could not be the same person.

But Lisa Van Gruisen and Lisa Choegyal were one and the same person. The surprise came when I went to Nepal a few years ago and met her again. It all came back, our meeting at Batu Caves and her connection with Hans Hoefer. She certainly had come a long way since then.

I make a point now, every time I go to Nepal, to visit with the Choegyals. When I sit down and talk to Lisa, and face her across a table over teacups, I see her as a memsahib in the British Raj. She has just played a game of tennis, or whatever the British memsahibs played in the afternoon, and she is sitting down for a cup of tea. But instead of talking about the servants, the dreadful weather and what she plans to do on her next home leave to the UK, she talks about such things as eco-tourism and the government's attempt to keep the mountains clean. She's keen on the environment.

Lisa lives in Nepal, and has done so for twenty years, but there is no doubt, she is the product of her background. When she tells you she went to work for a top antique dealer in London after she left school, it's something that you would expect an English girl with her interests to do. But what you wouldn't expect is for her to break away completely and do some of the outrageous things that she has done. This is where Lisa is different; she made it differently. And it's the Lisas of the world that make life so much more interesting.

Lisa Van Gruisen was born in Northumberland, England and had what she calls "a countryside upbringing." Her father worked for the brewery there and the family moved up to Edinburgh when she was quite young. In her teens she went to Oakfield House School, in Newcastle-upon-Tyne, and later to George Watsons Ladies College in Edinburgh, Scotland. By the time she reached eighteen and had graduated she wanted desperately to travel. "My father insisted I settle down and take a secretarial course," she said, "but instead, in my youthful arrogance, I went to London and worked for a while, but the urge to travel grew strong again."

In 1968, she went to Paris to study. She took a History of Civilization course at the Sorbonne and then studied History of Arts of the Middle Ages at the Ecole du Louvre.

After Paris, Lisa decided to go to America to work for a spell. "I traveled to Houston first, to stay with friends, and then went to Boston to work for the Boston Museum of Art. My next job was with Mallet & Co in New York who had a lease concession in Bergdorf Goodman. The boss was a fabulous character, Sir Humphry Wakefield. I loved my work, and New York, but life there was far too complicated for me, and hectic, so I crossed the Alantic again and went to Dublin and found work in Ireland conserving Georgian architecture and coordinating a book on Irish painting."

In Dublin she met film director Daniel Topolski who was filming a TV series on Marco Polo. The producer was Alexander Macmillan, the son of Harold Macmillan. When Topolski offered her a job as researcher for the production she couldn't turn it down. "The money was lousy," she said, "but the traveling involved was the incentive to make me sign up." Lisa found herself driving around Iran and Turkey in a Land Rover, but, as she regretted, the film never got off the ground. "But it did give me a wonderful experience, and was worth it," she said.

Lisa knew she had to get serious and returned to London and began earnestly working for *Connoisseur* magazine, but the job only lasted two months. Lisa's friend, Lady Victoria Yorke, was going to Bali for Christmas and asked her if she wanted to go along. "Victoria is the daughter of the Earl of Hardwicke," Lisa said. "She was a well-established interior decorator/designer based in London, and she was taking off for a few weeks during the Christmas holidays. She didn't have to ask the second time. I dropped everything, including my job, and went to Bali for Christmas. After Bali we traveled up to Malaysia and that was when we met Hans Hoefer. Hans was the most energetic man I had ever met. He had all kinds of wonderful ideas, and what was great about him was that he was realizing them. He was encouraging, and there was nothing negative about him. Maybe he was the inspiration that I was looking for. He gave traveling a purpose, which was what I needed."

By now Lisa really had the taste of traveling. From Malaysia she ventured with Victoria to Bangkok, toured Thailand, and they then flew to Burma. "I fell in love with everything Burmese," she said. "I wanted to stay longer but you could only get a two-week visa at the time, and Victoria had to get back to England. I decided to take a short trip to Kathmandu before I returned home." That so-called short trip to Kathmandu would change the course of Lisa's life.

Two things of importance happened to Lisa in Nepal. She made her first trek and became enthralled with the beauty of the Himalayas. Second, she met Jim Edwards. Edwards was a name as familiar as Sir Edmund Hillary in Nepal. Not only was he an avid wildlife enthusiast, but he was an innovator and entrepreneur. He had taken over Tiger Tops — the jungle lodge built in the tops of trees.

Lisa became completely captivated by Tiger Tops. She liked it so much she convinced the manager to give her a job for the rest of the season. "Jim Edwards said if I could talk my way into a job at Tiger Tops I could talk my way into anything," Lisa said. "Once I began I didn't want to leave. I stayed and I stayed, right up to the monsoons. I guess I thought if I left I may not be able to get back.

Finally, with the rains, I had to leave. I returned to Singapore overland, saw Hans again and then went back to England."

Lisa spent that winter in London, cold and miserable. Her thoughts were on Asia, especially Kathmandu. She wrote to Jim Edwards and asked if she could have another job at Tiger Tops. His reply was positive. In October 1975, she returned to Kathmandu, and she has been there ever since.

Lisa put all her energies and efforts into her work in Nepal. She made up her mind she wasn't going to limit herself to one job. At Tiger Mountain she became a jack-of-all-trades. She became their public relations director which included overseeing the wildlife lodges and running operations for both trekking and river rafting. She was soon preparing marketing plans, distributing sales promotional materials around the world and developing media and press relations. She was called upon to arrange conferences and special events, such as the annual World Elephant Polo Association championships, and giving filming support and film location management. She has become Kathmandu's unofficial host for celebrities and dignitaries coming to the country. Her work brings her in close touch with anyone of importance who comes to Nepal.

Lisa kept in close contact with Hans Hoefer in Singapore, who by now had his own printing company for his guidebooks. In the early 1980s she produced *Insight Guide to Nepal* for him, followed soon after by *Cityguide Kathmandu Valley*. Hans then appointed Lisa his Managing Editor South Asia for Apa Productions and she has since supervised the updating of insight guides for India, South Asia, Pakistan and Sri Lanka. She has written *Insight Pocket Guides* for Tibet, Sikkim, Bhutan and Sri Lanka and *Kathmandu Valley Bikes & Hikes*.

"I'm making it sound like all work," Lisa said, "but Nepal has always been a fun place. When I first arrived Kathmandu was overrun by hippies, but all that was soon to change. Almost every day I would go to the Om Restaurant to eat."

The restaurant was owned and run by two brothers from Tibet, Lobsang and Yeshi. One day when Lisa was there a third brother came to the restaurant, and they introduced him to Lisa. "His name was Tenzin," she said. "He had been educated in America, and I found him very fascinating and interesting. I often thought about him and wondered what happened to him. Then in 1985, I met him again, at the Marine Bar in Kathmandu." The bar is run by the U.S. Marine detachment at the American Embassy. "I never go to bars," Lisa continued, "but this night I did for some strange reason, and Tenzin was there. He too said he never goes to bars. This was his first time. He was still the interesting man I met ten years before. We began dating. Eventually we got married."

And Lisa Van Gruisen became Lisa Choegyal.

Lisa's husband, Tenzin, was born in Kham, a region of eastern Tibet, near the town of Kanze. His mother, as was often the custom, was married to two brothers. His father was the ruler of the region and Tenzin was his eldest son. The Choegyals were an established family of farmers and traders. Tenzin had passed his early years in the relative grandeur and comfort of a three-story mud-brick house. He recalls growing up in a male-dominated society in which boys were taught to break wild horses and carry a rifle as soon as they reached their teens. The climate was harsh, and in winter snow drifts blocked them in for months on end. "Sides of meat hung from the rafters would remain fresh all winter," Tenzin said. The hot, dry summers were no less severe.

But the tranquility of far-off Tibet was not to last forever.

The turmoil was about to begin. As the world stood by and watched, the communist Chinese army marched into Kham in 1950 and Tibet entered into its time of trouble. Tenzin's father and uncle led the resistance and his brothers became guerilla fighters in the struggle against Chinese domination. In 1956, when Tenzin was fourteen, his parents decided to send him to Lhasa. They packed him off in the company of relatives to the Tibetan capital in the back of a Chinese truck.

Two years passed, and as Tibet descended steadily into utter chaos, Tenzin received the rudiments of a monastic education. By then, the resistance had been defeated in Kham and its leaders attempted to regroup their forces in the mountains of Lhoka, immediately to the south of Lhasa. The war had reached a decisive phase and as the Chinese clearly could not be defeated, Tenzin's father decided that he should be sent to safety and freedom in India.

Tenzin's objective was the UN sponsored Tibetan Refuge Center in Kalimpong, a hill town near Darjeeling in northern India. He left Lhasa on the main road south to the town of Phari and made the difficult crossing over the Himalayas through treacherous mountain passes to Gangkok, the capital of Sikkim. From there he made his way to nearby Darjeeling where he resumed his education. He no longer studied Tibetan Buddhist classics. Under the instruction of American missionaries, he learned the Roman alphabet and conversational English.

A few months after Tenzin made good his escape, the Dalai Lama crossed the Indian border and a general exodus from the mayhem of southern and central Tibet began to gather momentum.

In 1963, after a year of compulsory service in the Indian army, Tenzin returned to Darjeeling and began working for the Tibetan language newspaper, *Tibetan Freedom.* Then on one auspicious day in 1965, he was told he had been awarded a special one-year course for selected elite Tibetans to study civil and business administration at Cornell University in New York. Tenzin Choegyal, a young man who twenty-three years earlier had been born in one of the wildest and most inaccessible places on Earth, was going to America. He now found himself on board a Boeing 707 bound for New York.

His studies completed, he returned to India to work for the Home Affairs Department of the Dalai Lama's exiled administration in Dharmsala. By 1968, however, he was back in Darjeeling: the new editor of *Tibetan Freedom*. Unfortunately, this journalistic career was brought to an abrupt end only two years later by a severe attack of pleurisy. To recuperate, he went to stay with a cousin in Kathmandu. There in 1975, at his brothers' restaurant, he met Lisa Van Gruisen, a wide-eyed English girl looking for romance and adventure. He couldn't forget her.

In Kathmandu, his health restored, Tenzin found work in the carpet business, eventually founding, with his brother Lobsang, a company manufacturing handwoven rugs for export to Britain and Germany. One evening, several years later, Tenzin went to the Marine Bar for a drink, and there he met Lisa again. Their romance began, and in 1985 they got married. They have two sons, Sangjay and Rinchen.

Lisa has seen great changes since she first arrived in Nepal, and we can credit her with being one of the prime movers of these changes. She unwittingly got herself involved with eco-tourism, a name she dislikes very much. "You see the name everywhere these days in the travel business," she said. "It sounds impressive, but what actually does it mean?"

We were sitting in Lisa's garden when she began expounding on tourism. She can be very vocal at times.

"The problem," she said, "is that no one, even those in the travel trade, are quite sure what it means, yet it's a word that has become widely used and even one that throws around a lot of weight. You want to go trekking, white water rafting, elephant riding in the hills, biking, hiking, name it and the chances are the outfitters who sponsor such trips tell you they adhere to eco-tourism. Ask them what it means and each one will tell you something different."

I asked Lisa for her own interpretation of the word. "It's travel without doing harm to the environment," she said without hesitation. She explained at Tiger Tops they have been involved in eco-tourism for nearly thirty years, but they called it by another name—environmental tourism."

As the director of Tiger Mountain, Lisa has done wonders. Tiger Tops is an example of environmental tourism that does work. Ten years ago Nepal was getting bad publicity from the damage climbers were doing in the country's mountains. Climbing expeditions were leaving behind literally tons of discarded supplies. "It was reflecting on Tiger Tops which was unfair," Lisa said. "We had working proof that you don't have to have electricity and central air-conditioning, nor wall-to-wall carpeting to get five hundred dollars a day for a room. We have been getting that for the last ten years."

Lisa admits that without abundant wildlife there wouldn't be a Tiger Tops. "You have to help the wildlife, by protecting the wildlife, and in return the wildlife helps you. It's mutually beneficial. It's also necessary to involve local people which helps the local economy."

Lisa poured me another tea. As she continued: "Tiger Tops appeals to all sorts of people and all sorts of nationalities, and people of all ages. It's comfortable enough to appeal to the eighty-year-old, round-the-world tourist and it's specialized enough to appeal to the ultimate bird-watcher. Everyone from Mick Jagger to the Prince of Wales has enjoyed it."

Lisa credits the government support for the country's success. "They call us into meetings and ask our opinions about things. The next day we read in the newspaper that the things we discussed are now the new law."

She gave Mount Everest as an example. "Everest was getting very overcrowded and Nepal was getting negative publicity that reached around the world," she said. "Overnight the new government changed the law, and by a simple stroke of the pen Everest was cleaned up. Expeditions now pay extra surcharges, and they use kerosene instead of wood. They now have to carry out everything they take in, even if it requires helicoptering it out."

Lisa believes that through environmental tourism Nepal was able to clean up its act. "The mountains have never been so clean as they are now," she said. "Nepal is very poor and it depends upon tourism revenue. Through proper control, the government has increased the revenue and at the same time limited the number of expeditions. It does work and Nepal can now set an example for other countries in Southeast Asia. The problem is countries are interested only in tourist numbers. Let people pay and limit their numbers. Not everyone will agree, but I do believe we have no alternative."

.Aside from her position as public relations director at Tiger Mountain, Lisa has done all sorts of tourism consulting in the region, including Southeast Asia. She wants to see environmental tourism expand, and not only to wilderness areas. She contends that certainly Asia's resort areas, and in some cases many cities themselves, should adhere to some type of environment policy. Can the infrastructure of a country take unlimited tourists? She says no. Caution must be exercised.

As a result of Lisa's perseverance, the government has

opened up some of the government's remote areas. One area is Mustang. "Fortunately," she said, "they now limit visitors to six hundred a year."

Lisa has also become the Director of the Kathmandu Valley Preservation Trust. She's very involved in fund raising for that project. She is also an advisor to the World Wildlife Fund Nepal Program, working on areas of conservation awareness, and government and media liaison. She was the Marketing Specialist on the Tourism Resource Consultants' team for the Sarawak Tourism Masterplan project that was completed in 1993.

In 1992, the government put Lisa in charge as production liaison in Nepal and Bhutan for the feature film *Little Buddha*, directed by Bernardo Bertolucci and produced by Jeremy Thomas. She was responsible for government liaisons, locations finding and local coordination. It was her most exciting achievement. "I got to know the Italian director Bernardo Bertolucci and so many other interesting people," she said. Bertolucci made a name for himself when he directed Marlon Brando in *The Last Tango in Paris* and the epic film *The Last Emperor.*

"Bertolucci is not like most directors I've worked with," Lisa said. "There's something beautiful, crazy, and very special about him. He's funny too. He operates like a writer. No one knows what he's going to do. Millions of dollars are riding on him alone. He has the power and he exercises it. He goes ahead as he sees it, and often upsets those who plan schedules. He takes his own time, and follows his own genius."

In choosing the sites, Lisa picked Patan for the setting. Three miles southwest of Kathmandu, Patan is the oldest metropolis in the valley. It was a flourishing city when Asoka visited it three centuries before the birth of Christ.It is a majestic place that attracted Lisa when she first came to the valley. The town is surrounded by many-roofed temples and decorated with carvings and lattice work. The square is dominated by the several beautiful temples, with its gateways guarded by a huge figure of Hanuman, the monkey god. The air in the square is heavy with the odor of burning incense and the sound of clanging cymbals. Monks sit within the temples, chanting and spinning prayer wheels. "The sights and sounds in Patan are never dull," she said. "Early dawn and late evening are the most dramatic times, when mood is at its best."

Lisa contends that *Little Buddha* is a brilliant film. "We put so much into it," she said. "Nothing like it has ever been done in Nepal before, and most likely never will be again. We had the full cooperation of the Prime Minister's offices, and we got cabinet permission. The film company arrived in March 1992, and it took ten months to complete. Bertolucci uses thousands of regulars, and very few actors. He does everything in scenes, and insists on shooting 360 degrees. We had to build whole sets, even if he used only a small portion. He is extravagant." Then Lisa added, with subdued pride, "Bertolucci named his leading lady after me."

During the long months of filming *Little Buddha,* the Choegyal house was filled with film producers, script writers, actors and extras. "The problem is film people can be very demanding," Lisa said. "They take up all your time."

Many people Lisa met in Nepal have become close friends. Sir Edmund Hillary, who was High Commissioner to India and Ambassador to Nepal from 1985 to 1989, is a frequent visitor to her home. Reinhold Messner calls upon Lisa when he is in town, which is often. "Reinhold is a remarkable person," Lisa said. "He has total focus and complete concentration. He also has a fantastic collection of Tibetan art which he houses in his very own castle in northern Italy. He's the world's greatest mountain climber, and he's very, very articulate, and charming."

Lisa and Tenzin are building a new home, a place with a view overlooking Kathmandu. It is being designed and built by local craftsmen. We can be certain, with Lisa's background in the arts and Tenzin's knowledge of all things Tibetan, that it will be a beautiful place. And we can also be sure, it will be filled with interesting people.

The General Manager, Kurt Wachtveitl with Elizabeth Taylor, above, and
James Michener, below.

Chapter 9

WACHTVEITL, GOERLACH & OTHERS
The General Managers

Rudyard Kipling brought Asia to the Western world through his vast collection of writing—essays, novels, ballads, poems, plays and short stories—and had there been TV in his day, we most likely would have included that too. Much of Kipling's writing has become classic, and is still popular. What child isn't moved by *Kim* and *The Jungle Book*? And who hasn't enjoyed his short stories, and his novels like *The Man Who Would Become King* and *Captains Courageous* that have reached the motion picture screen. And how many times have we heard the lines, "Though I've belted you an' flayed you, By the livin' Gawd that made you, You're a better man than I am Gunga Din?" Or the other immortal lines, "Oh, East is East, and West is West, and never the twain shall meet."

Kipling painted some very graphic portraits of the fascinating people he met in the East at the turn of the century. He tells readers about adventurers and wayward wanderers, loyal military officers and missionaries, remittance people and opportunists and scores of other interesting characters. He refers to some as "a special breed of men."

Yet for some reason there was one special breed of men that Kipling didn't chronicle: the expatriate hotel managers who lorded over the many grand, Victorian hotels that existed throughout Asia during his time. He couldn't have missed meeting the Sarkies brothers, the three Armenians—Martin, Tigran and Arshak. They founded the famous Raffles Hotel in Singapore, and later the E&O in Penang and the Strand in Rangoon. The

205

parties they gave were so grand they made the newspapers in Paris and London. Kipling surely must have met Captain H. N. Anderson, the general manager of The Oriental Hotel in Bangkok. When Kipling was at The Oriental, Anderson's accountant had been tampering with the books. To escape the wrath of the authorities who were coming for him, the accused man dove into the Chao Phraya River and drowned after attempting to swim to the other side.

For some unknown reason, Kipling never wrote about these people, although he is certain to have met them.

Hotel managers have become legends in Asia as elsewhere around the world, some within their own lifetime. Libraries are filled with their biographies. Magazines contain countless articles about them. Hotel managers create images that are often hard to live down. We picture them as suave and composed, and tailored in Bond Street suits. They stand in the lobbies of their fine hotels, ready to thrust out firm hands to visiting VIPs. They converse in at least four languages, remember names, even complicated hyphenated ones, and have disarming smiles that make unhappy guests happy.

And we hear that good managers can find rooms for guests with reservations even when no rooms are available; how they manage seats on flights that are over-booked; produce tickets for operas or cultural performances that are sold out. They are travel adviser and tour guide, valet, medical practitioner and father confessor. And if they cannot do something themselves, they know someone who can.

There is more. They never perspire, become angry or have harsh words even for their enemies—publicly that is. They consider no request impossible. Indeed, they have been schooled in every grace and are *par exemple* of savoir faire. And most important, especially for someone in their trade, they have the gift of gab that keeps people entertained with their easy flow of words. They are all skilled raconteurs.

But are these impressions of hotel managers outdated? Does this nostalgic image we have of them reflect a distant time when travel was solely for the rich and leisure class, and when writers who came after Kipling, like Somerset Maugham, Noel Coward and Graham Greene, roamed the world and wrote about what they saw and whom they met.

Those days are gone forever; but travel is not gone. We might live in an age of computers when travelers are often reduced to blurred numbers on a hotel printout and group travel means being herded cattle-style in and out of hotels–but we continue to look for some vestige of that glamorous past. In Asia we can still find it.

Asia has replaced Europe as the place to find quality hotels; Asia has become the bastion of hotel excellence. Several Asian hotels are today considered the best in the world. The reason is that Asia can provide first-class service whereas Europe no longer can, and in Asia the art of hotel managing in the old tradition is still very much alive. Graham Greene was delighted when he sat in the museum-like office of General Manager Frans Schutzman of the Manila Hotel, listening to the tales Frans had to tell of history and intrigue, stories that most likely inspired novelist Greene to pen another great mystery about Asia. Noel Coward found a character he could recreate into another play when he sipped mint juleps with Boris Lissonevitch at the Hotel Royal in Kathmandu. And were Somerset Maugham to come back today he would be pleased to step into the lobby of The Oriental Hotel and find Manager Kurt Wachtveitl there to greet him. Maugham may not like it when guests call him "Kurt" instead of "Mr. Wachtveitl," but he would be impressed with the master hotelier's chatter about having lunch with the Sultan of Brunei or about the reception he is giving for the Prince of Monaco. And what writer, or anyone for that matter, wouldn't be intrigued to check into the Royal Garden Riverside on the Chao Phraya and meet manager Axel Goerlach, and listen to his anecdotes about kings and queens, and befriending people like boxing champ Mohammed Ali?

The general managers of Asia's great hotels become, in time, quite knowledgeable of the affairs of the country they are in. They have the unique opportunity of meeting the right people in the right places. In a sense they are father confessors. At lunches and dinners they become sounding boards for their guests. They listen with an assumed air of interest to whatever their guests have to tell them. They hobnob with actors and actresses, entertainers of all sorts, renegade playboys, royalty, and wealthy dowagers. They are the envy of writers, for they have secrets they dare not tell locked up inside them. And this becomes the problem, for general managers develop two faces, one for the public and one for their private selves. They develop a public facade in which they present the world as a most pleasant and enjoyable place. They seem to like everyone and have no bad words even for their enemies. Breaking down this facade is most difficult, but once you do, you find some incredible people with some incredible stories to tell. We are often misled to think that a manger is merely a handshaker who sits at the head of the table entertaining special guests. What we don't know is that they often get to know these people intimately. Frans Schutzman met actor William Holden at the Raffles when he was manager there, and they became good friends. When Frans had the time, he often went to visit Holden at his ranch in Africa. Kurt Wachtveitl at The Oriental was very close to Elizabeth Taylor and her friend millionaire publisher Malcolm Forbes. When the couple came to Bangkok aboard Forbes' yacht and anchored down river on the Chao Phraya, they often invited Kurt aboard for dinner. When Malcolm Forbes suddenly and unexpectedly died, Kurt held a private ceremony marking the one hundredth day of his death, a period according to the Buddhist tradition when friends gather to pay their last respects. Neither the press, the media, nor any outsiders were invited. And Axel Goerlach down river at the Royal Garden Riverside knows more about the private lives of Nepalese royalty and Mohammed Ali than he dared tell.

No, we cannot underestimate hotel managers. They are, Mr. Kipling, a special breed.

Frans Schutzman is in a class by himself. He never trained to be a manager, nor even for the hotel business. It was by chance alone that he became a manager. But, he boasts, he grew up dining in the best hotels of Vienna and that is training enough. "You don't have to go to Lausanne Hotel School to learn what good service is," he said. "Nor do you have to peel potatoes to enjoy eating them. You learn from dining on them."

Born in 1915 under a Dutch colonial regime in Surabaja in what then was the Dutch East Indies, and is now Indonesia, Frans served with British intelligence as an undercover agent in Italy during the war. After the hostilities ended in Europe he became a successful music publisher, but he squandered away all his profits on good living. Then, for excitement, he decided to turn to journalism. The year was 1951. He managed to get an assignment with a Dutch newspaper to cover the action taking place in Malaysia and Indonesia. It was the time of troubles in Southeast Asia, the Emergency, when communist guerillas refused to give up their arms after the war. Being Dutch, Frans discovered after arriving in

Singapore that he had little chance of entering Indonesia as a reporter. The Indonesians had just spent half a dozen years ridding the country of the Dutch and they weren't about to grant a press pass to a Dutchman even if he had been born there.

Disappointed but not disheartened, Frans found himself in Singapore without a job and little money. He turned his misadventure into a new career. He accepted a job at Raffles Hotel as head waiter; six months later, through some shrewd maneuvering, he became the general manager. But he did more than manage the place. He moved the hotel from the red into the black. He found that the major hotel expense went for food, partly because the staff was stealing food from the kitchen. They had quarters but were not given meals, and consequently were dining on expensive roasts, lobster and Swiss cheese. He called in the hotel carpenter and had him build tables and benches, and had the cook prepare meals for the staff without cost to them. He reduced operating costs to one-third of what it had been.

Frans liked his position at Raffles and would have stayed but when the Chinese owners became annoyed with him— he had let Somerset Maugham stay at the hotel without paying—he resigned. "No money could pay for the publicity we were getting," he said.

After Raffles, Frans managed six of the world's top hotels. The last one he managed was the grand old dame, the Manila Hotel in Manila. He was there ten years. He retired at the age of seventy-eight a few years ago and now lives in Spain. The last I heard he was looking for a small hotel to manage. "I'm too young to retire," he quipped.

Unlike Frans Schutzman, Kurt Wachtveitl, general manager of The Oriental Hotel in Bangkok, did go to school to learn the hotel business. But that was only after attending the University of Madrid to study philosophy and the Dante Alighieri School in Rome to study the history of art and literature. While he was in Rome, the hotel business captured his interest. He had a choice. He could peel potatoes and work in the kitchen to learn to become a hotelier, or he could go to school. He chose school. He went to Switzerland to study.

Four years later, Kurt graduated from the world-famous Lausanne Hotel School in Switzerland and soon after found positions with some of that country's most prestigious hotels, including the Beau Rivage in Lausanne, the Three Crowns in Vevey and the Suvretta Haus in St. Moritz. Kurt then went to work for the elegant Hilton in London. His future looked bright. He was destined for the top. Then suddenly, Kurt did a complete about face. He resigned from the Hilton. He was quitting.

Why the sudden change of heart?

Kurt had fallen in love. A young woman whom he had met in Switzerland had totally captured his heart. He had met her when he was studying at the Lausanne school and she was attending a finishing school in an Alpine village. She too was interested in the hotel business. Her father owned a hotel back home.

The romance faired well as long as Kurt was in Switzerland, but once he accepted the position at the Hilton in London, his world was turned topsy-turvy. The young woman with whom he had fallen in love was from a kingdom in the East. She was from Thailand. Her name was Sukhuma Bunnag.

Sukhuma, or Penny as everyone called her, was from a noble Thai family. She wasn't actually a princess, like story books say, but she was as close to it as one can get. The Bunnags are an important family in Thailand, and this didn't make it any easier for Kurt..

Prince Chula Chakrabongse in his book *Lords of Life, A History of the Kings of Thailand,* traces the lineage of the

Bunnag family back to the seventeenth century. Queen Amarindra, the first wife of King Rama I, the founder of the present Chakri Dynasty, had a sister who married Nai Bunnag, an important nobleman and high official with the title of Chao Phraya Akara Mahesena. He was the sixth generation descendant of a Persian, Sheik Ahmed, who had settled in Ayutthaya in the 1600s, served in the royal service, and was made Phraya by King Songtam.

Peter Bunnag, Penny's brother, claims that his great ancestor, Sheik Ahmed, brought Islam to early Siam.

As was the custom, Penny was sent abroad to study. Her father, who owned the Trocadero Hotel in Bangkok, placed her in a finishing school in Switzerland and there at Beau Rivage she met a young and handsome student named Kurt Wachtveitl. Penny too fell in love, but she realized their situation was hopeless. She was from the other side of the world, from an eastern kingdom where customs and habits differed greatly from Kurt's. He was from old Europe, from a world staid and set in its ways. Penny and Kurt dated, and they were in love, but they both knew one day it must end. Penny finished her courses and returned to her homeland. Kurt started work at the Hilton in London. They resigned themselves to the fact that their romance was over.

But theirs was a love that distance couldn't kill. Kurt was unable to drive Penny from his mind. When he heard about an opening for a hotel manager at a beach resort called Pattaya located a few hours southeast of Bangkok, he applied for the position and was accepted.

Kurt gave up Europe for another life, for a life of uncertainty. "I realized that as long as someone is around, as Penny was when we were in Switzerland, it's easy to take them for granted," Kurt said. "But when there are certain things in life that you treasure, then you realize you have to make an effort." Kurt's move to Thailand was that effort

The year was 1965 when Kurt took over as general manager at the Nipa Lodge at the beach resort in Pattaya. The resort then was an outpost, but Kurt could see it had a promising future. He immediately set to work to put Pattaya on the tourist map. First on his agenda was to hire Penny as his secretary, and his second was to ask her family for her hand in marriage. The following year the couple married. A short twelve months later, Kurt gained the top position at The Oriental Hotel in Bangkok.

The Oriental that Kurt stepped into wasn't anything like it is today. Although it was widely known around the world, as every author from Joseph Conrad to Noel Coward had written about it, it wasn't by any means a world-class hotel. But things were about to change. The war in Vietnam had started and tourists by the score began to arrive in Thailand. Kurt was soon to find himself faced with one of the greatest challenges a young hotel manager could ever have, to transform a sleepy hotel on the Chao Phraya River to the world's best hotel. He was to perform miracles. "We only had 110 rooms then," he recalled. "But that was only the beginning."

The Oriental Hotel had been purchased by the Italthai Company in 1967, the same year Kurt took over as general manager. The Normandie Grill was the first to undergo a complete transformation and didn't reopen until January 1969. Then came the Tower Wing.

In 1972, after refurbishing the Tower Wing, the management turned their attention to what was to become the main section of the hotel, the River Wing. The old Chartered Bank, which had been The Oriental's next-door neighbor for some eighty years, agreed to sell a piece of riverside property that enabled The Oriental to expand. Drawings for the extension were worked out in due course, capital was raised, the first piles were driven and the new Oriental Hotel was in the making. The 350-room River

Wing was completed in 1976. A few years later a group of
bankers were polled and they voted The Oriental the best
hotel in the world. The record was held for ten straight
years. And Kurt Wachtveitl was the man at the helm all
the while.

Kurt had the foresight to surround himself with good,
reliable staff. One was his public relations manager,
Pornsri Luphaiboon. A few years before Kurt took over,
Pornsri walked into the office to apply for the position of
secretary to the manager. "I never thought I would get
the job," a smiling Pornsri said as we sat in the Sala Rim
Nam Restaurant across the river from the hotel and she
told me her story. From time to time I looked up from
our table and glanced over at The Oriental. I tried to
imagine the young and inexperienced, nineteen-year-old
Pornsri, fresh out of commercial school, nervously seeking
employment.

"I went home and told my mother I would never get the
job," she said. "Two other women also applied. They were
older and had experience. I felt so bad."

Her two older brothers worked as receptionists for the
hotel, and Pornsri often went there to visit them. She
looked around the hotel and dreamed. How wonderful it
would be to work here, she thought. She got the job, and
when Kurt took over, he promoted her to be his public
relations manager.

Another talented staffer was Ankana Kalantananda
Gilwee. Ankana, the longest-serving employee at The
Oriental, joined the hotel when Madame Germaine Krull
was the manageress after World War II. Ankana was the
first Thai woman to enter the hotel business in those days
and went to Paris to train. She has worked for six managers
and has seen many changes at The Oriental. She recalls
with great humor the days of mosquito nets and no
running hot water. A deluxe room depended on the

thickness of the kapok mattresses and the quality of the mosquito nets.

Serving as special guest relations consultant today, Ankana's friends include James Michener, Gore Vidal, Morris West, Barbara Cartland and hundreds more. They are actors and actresses, authors and journalists, photographers and painters, dancers, singers, composers, and musicians. In fact, anyone who is somebody, or who has been, stops to pay a visit to Ankana in her office next to the Author's Wing.

Kurt left Pornsri much to herself. She concentrated on helping journalists, attending to their needs. Pornsri's creed was that you must let international writers promote the hotel. "If journalists find they are happy with the hotel, then they will say nice things about you," Pornsri said. It paid off.

Pornsri is convinced the success of The Oriental is largely due to Kurt's management. "He is familiar with every operation at the hotel," she explained.

Every morning at exactly 8:30, Kurt holds a staff meeting. Present are his secretary and the resident manager, the food and beverage manager, housekeeping, the sales department manager, the public relations director and maintenance—eight people including himself who make policy and who are kept abreast of things with up-to-date information. They discuss the activities for the day, they go through the arrival list and discuss what has to be done with VIPs, they decide about functions and parties and air any trouble each department might be encountering.

One of the topics at the morning briefings concerns arriving guests. Who is coming? What do they require? Sylvester Stallone is arriving. Alert security he will be accompanied by half a dozen bodyguards. Barbara Cartland tomorrow. Tell housekeeping to fill her suite with pink pillows and cushions. Detail for Barbara is important.

Kurt's other meetings are with section heads that include head waiters and butlers. Kurt keeps atop everything, including budgeting and advertising. "He has an amazing memory," Pornsri disclosed. "He forgets nothing. He's firm but also understanding."

Every day at noon, Kurt does stand in his Bond Street suit in the lobby of The Oriental, shaking hands with important guests, and he doesn't sweat and he remembers even hyphenated names. He doesn't actually find rooms for guests with reservations when no rooms are available, but he does have a trained staff who can. And I don't know about his managing seats on flights that are overbooked or producing tickets for cultural performances that are sold out, nor would I imagine that he's much of a medical practitioner or father confessor, but he is schooled in every grace and is himself *par exemple* of savoir faire. And he does have the gift of gab that keeps people entertained with his easy flow of words. In many ways he's much like Frans Schutzman. He too is outspoken. He speaks his mind and guests like him for it.

Kurt admits his biggest concern is keeping an eye on the rich and famous guests. When John Steinbeck was staying there, writing a book, he didn't want to be disturbed, which meant screening all his calls. But which ones? Burt Lancaster's daughter Susan wanted to go on a *klong* trip to the Floating Market but what about security? Kurt had to provide it without alarming her. Gore Vidal spends four to six weeks at the hotel during Christmas, in the Noel Coward suite, and likes to work out with barbells. How do you sound proof a room with two-hundred pound weights bouncing on the floor?

Every day from noon to one you can see Kurt standing in the hotel lobby, greeting some guests, saying goodbye to others. And every afternoon he does a tour of the kitchen, the laundry, and even the parking lots. "It's not easy to pull things over on him," one of the staff remarked.

Kurt has some fixed ideas about expatriates in Asia. He says his moving to Thailand was like coming home. "Never, in all my years here, have I felt like I was living in a foreign country. I enjoy the whole mentality—the joy of life, the food, everything. It's much easier to live in an environment where you're happy; it's complimentary to your whole being. Living in the Thai society where people believe in other lives I've almost wondered if maybe I've had another life here too. I feel so at home."

One of the great plus points of an international marriage, he explained, is the benefits a couple can witness in the development of their children. The Wachveitl's three children, daughters Inka and Carla, and son Kim, are, according to their father, true citizens of the world. "They attended boarding schools in Germany and they speak fluent German, plus Thai, English and French— they're very cosmopolitan."

Kim went to Cornell to study hotel management, and Inka is married and living in Normandy, France. She and her husband own a chateau that they have converted into a hotel with 25 rooms, restaurant, bar, tennis courts and swimming pool. The youngest daughter is studying fashion management in Paris.

Life at the family home, The Oriental, is nonstop. "We haven't had an argument in thirty years of marriage. There are always other people around and you don't want to wash your dirty linen in public," explained Kurt with a smile and a wink.

The couple share a great many things together, and their business lives, although professionally very different, are both stimulating. They have a house in Germany and go back for a visit once a year.

Kurt is convinced mixed marriages can only be good

for mankind. He explained, "All borders and nationalistic boundaries have softened. Obviously twenty-five years ago it was not very common. But now people do not blink an eye and that's certainly healthier."

"If we are going to survive on this planet it will only be by understanding each other," he added. "I know some people are very conscious of not watering down cultural characteristics by marrying out of your own society, but I truly believe more harm is done because people don't understand the person who lives across the fence than the other way around."

Kurt has in his office three "Golden Books" as he calls them. It would take days to go through them all. They are filled with photographs of guests, many with Kurt standing at their sides, and with their autographs and inscriptions. The photographs and names are those of everyone of importance who has stayed at The Oriental since Kurt took over. The list is impressive: Takeo Fukeom, Prime Minister of Japan; Lee Kuan Yew of Singapore; HRH Prince Albert of Belgium; General Moshe Dyan of Israel; Beth and Chamos Romula, Foreign Minister of Philippines, with the note his first time at The Oriental was 1941, hers in 1968; HRH Crown Princess Sonja of Norway; King Carl Gustaf of Sweden; Madam Deng Ying Chao, wife of Chinese PM Chou En-lai; King Birendra of Nepal; HRH Prince Rainer and Princess Grace of Monaco; Prince Nordam Sinhaniuk and Princes Moneque of Cambodia; King Hussein of Jordan; Richard Nixon, dated September 9, 1985; Henry Kissinger; Pierre Trudeau, Prime Minister of Canada; Her Majesty Queen Sirikit of Thailand. And that's only a few.

Just a glance at the Golden Books tells us all we need to know about Kurt Wachtveitl, General Manager of The Oriental in Bangkok.

Axel Goerlach sits at the top, but for him it didn't come easy. He had a tough time right from the start. He had to

The General Manager, Alex Goerlach, as a movie actor in Hong Kong, above,
and with Mohammed Ali, below.

escape from East Germany before he could start a life for himself. It has been dramatic ever since. He is proof that managers can lead adventuresome lives. He at least has had more than his share of adventure.

Axel Goerlach was born in Germany, on the eastern side, in 1940. His father served aboard a minesweeper in the German navy during the war. As a very young boy Axel remembers seeing dogfights in the sky between German and Allied planes. He recalls going to visit his grandparents by train in the west. They had to jump down from the compartments and run for cover when the planes came overhead.

The war ended and Germany was divided. "Our home became headquarters of the U.S. Army when they took over," he said. "We had to move in with the neighbors for about six weeks. This was the first time I saw grown-up people crying, when the war ended. I couldn't understand why. They were the elder Germans. They knew things we didn't. Everyone was in the war, my father, my uncles, everyone, and the only ones left in the villages were old people, wives and the very young. When the tanks rolled up that was the first time I saw a Negro; they threw chocolates and chewing gum to us."

After six weeks the Americans pulled out and the Russians moved in. "The difference is that they stayed," Axel said. "Germany had been divided and we knew that was the end. My father was held as a prisoner-of-war by the British in West Germany. He wanted to be with his family again and managed to flee from the British zone into the Russian zone where we now lived."

In 1948, East Germany became the German Democratic Republic, a communist state; and the Goerlachs decided it was time to leave. Axel's father, who had his own bakery, devised a plan. In May 1950, when Axel was ten years old, they made the attempt.

Axel's mother and children got a permit to visit their grandparents in West Germany. However, one person had to stay behind, and that was his father. The children were informed they could tell no one their plans, not even their best friends. "It wasn't a happy moment for us kids," Axel admitted. "We were frightened, and somewhat saddened. We were frightened when we saw the Russian soldiers at the station. When they looked in our direction we thought they were after us. We had been in trouble with them before, and I had spent three days in a Russian jail with my mother and sister." It was the first time they had tried to cross border.

The toughest guards they had to face were East German women. "They were mean, far meaner than the men," Axel said. "We had to hide all our money which my mother taped to the body of my sister who was only three. She thought it was a game that we were playing, and we feared she would talk. Fortunately she didn't."

Axel had a faraway look in his eyes as he told me his story. We were sitting in the Garden Restaurant at the lovely Royal Garden Riverside, the hotel he now manages. Through the floor-to-ceiling glass windows I could look out over the swimming pool where hotel guests lounged on deck chairs and waiters in trim Thai costumes brought them tall drinks. I thought of the world I was viewing then and there, and I tried to visualize the world that the young, ten-year-old Axel Goerlach was attempting to flee. I had met Axel twenty-five years before, when he took over as manager of the Rama Hotel in Bangkok, and I met him again when he was GM of the Hilton in Kuala Lumpur, and I traveled with him and three others into remote Bhutan, but I never knew much about his early years and the privations he had suffered–until now.

Axel continued his story, with a voice out of the past.

"Once we were on the train, we had only five or six hours

to travel," he said, "but it seemed like an eternity. We kids were terrified. We had one stop after another, and each time there were guards to check us. Russians and East Germans. Finally we crossed the border. Everything was over, the pain, the anguish, the fear. We found our new home, and a new life."

I was afraid to ask Axel about his father, for fear of what might have happened to him. Axel smiled. "One week after we made good our escape," he said, "my father made his attempt. He had it all planned. He knew when, where and what time to cross. He planned to leave one morning. The police came to visit him at the house. "We know you plan to escape," they said to him. "You had better do it tonight because tomorrow we have to come and arrest you." He quietly closed the bakery, locked the door, got on his motorbike and made a daring suicide drive across the border that very night. He made it! "The next day we were back together as a family," he exclaimed.

Axel grew up in West Germany, going to school, doing what boys his age do, but times were not easy. His family was together but it was hard for his father to find work. "He longed to get back to sea," Axel said, "but deep inside he knew the good old days were over. He claimed that working on ships had lost all its romance."

Axel envied his father's free lifestyle, but he didn't long for a seaman's life. He thought about becoming a chef. "It was one way to travel and see the world," he said. "A chef is always in need. I made up my mind. I decided this was what I wanted to do, to be a chef."

Axel left school when he was fourteen to begin his apprenticeship. He had to labor for three years, five days a week on the job and one day a week at school. He earned hardly enough money to pay for his tram fare to and from work. His parents had to help support him. "I had to buy my own uniform, and even my own working knives," he explained. "My father had no other choice but to go back to sea, aboard a tramp oil tanker. It meant he never knew where he would go, and sometimes he might be away for two years. He was at sea from 1951 to 1973. My brother also went to sea. I was living with an aunt in Hamburg."

Altogether Axel's father was at sea forty years. After he retired, he sat on the front porch at home, looking at the sunsets, watching the ships coming and going. "He died when I was the general manager of the Hilton in Manila," Axel said.

When Axel was seventeen he graduated as a young chef, and then went off to work in Sweden. "Sweden was exciting," he said. "I liked it because I was in a part of the country that was close to the Arctic Circle. The town was Arvidsjaur, in Swedish Lapland. For three months of the year it was night, completely dark, and the weather averaged 30 to 36 degrees below zero. We dressed in furs. I had to smoke a pipe to keep my hands warm."

As we talked, I looked out the window at the Royal Garden and watched a shapely, well-tanned European woman dive into the swimming pool.

"I enjoyed it because the people were nice," Axel continued. "We didn't do much when it was dark. We took it easy. Then we had three months of daylight, and the skiers came to town."

After spending two and a half years in Sweden, Axel went to the Jersey Channel Islands "basically to learn English." He worked for a hotel during the day and attended school in the evenings.

"I was happy with what I was doing, and that's all I wanted out of life. I guess because life had been so hard when I was young, without food. As a chef I was always well fed. I probably would have stayed, but when I was in my third season in Jersey I saw an ad in the paper for young chefs who wanted to work in Bermuda. My God, I thought, away from Europe, into the tropics. So I wrote, and within ten days I had an offer. They said to come ahead. I had to pay my way, which meant I had to borrow money again. But this was a new start. I reported to the Carlton Beach Hotel."

Axel explained that once someone has served their apprenticeship in Europe, they are more or less guaranteed a job. Management is aware they not only know how to cook but also have a basic knowledge of hotel operation.

"The more you move around, the better it is," he said. "You learn all types of operations, in hotels, clubs and restaurants. I was at the Carlton when an offer came that I couldn't turn down–chef at the Officers Club at the American Naval base." This was an exciting period, during the Cuban crisis. Axel got to know submarine commanders and officers who planned the Bay of Pigs operation. It was also there at the base that Axel listened to the tales sailors had to tell about good duty in Asia.

"Little did I realize that Asia was going to be a reality to me," Axel said. "The manager at the club, Paul Wirthlin, was accepting a job in Hong Kong and asked if I would like to join him. He went ahead and cabled back. He had found an opening for me as a chef at the Mandarin."

Axel remained at the Mandarin for one and a half years and then joined the staff at the Hong Kong Hilton. He did well at the Hong Kong Hilton. The chef in him blossomed. He added a personal touch to his style of serving the guests. He came out of the kitchen and indulged in tableside cooking, even recommending menus.

From the very start Axel liked Asia, and he liked the work. He also liked the time he had to himself. He almost became a professional actor. Director Shelton Leonard from the U.S. was filming a pilot TV film called "I Spy." Comedian Bill Cosby, who had a serious role, was a leading actor, and Axel was hired as a heavy, a Mafia gangster.

But Axel didn't become actor; the Hilton needed him more than Hollywood. The chef at the Hilton in Bangkok had been fired and Axel was asked if he would take over for a few months until a new chef was brought in and trained. He accepted. That was 1965. Bangkok then was in its heyday. G.I.s by the thousands were arriving in the Thai capital for much needed R&R and the tourist industry was booming. Axel liked the excitement, and he liked Bangkok. The new chef arrived, received his training, and Axel was free to return to Hong Kong.

Before leaving Bangkok Axel told the Rama Hilton general manager that he would like to come back. Two months later, his prayers were answered. Rama Hilton recruited him as restaurant and banquet manager. "I knew nothing about banqueting," he admitted candidly. "But they gave me a crash course in banquet management under the guidance of Peter Daetwiler. I discovered to my surprise, that I could handle it very well." Two years later Axel was promoted to food and beverage manager.

Just a year and a half after that, Axel was promoted to sales manager, yet another job in which he had no experience. After spending six weeks at Hilton Corporation's Career Development Institute in Montreal, Axel fitted well into the new mold.

When a new general manager took over the Rama, he made Axel executive assistant manager. This was when I first met Axel.

Just six weeks after he became assistant manager, Axel received another SOS, this time from the Vice President of Hilton.

The Annapurna Hotel in Kathmandu, which was operated by Hilton, was having problems. Over a three-month period the hotel had two managers. Neither of them were liked by the owners and were dismissed. Hilton thinking the cause might be that they were married — it was said their wives were not happy — insisted the next manager be a bachelor. Axel was unmarried and the right candidate.

Kathmandu in those days was considered a hardship post. The town folded at sundown and there was virtually no nightlife. When the position as general manager was offered to Axel, he was at first reluctant to accept it. "What happens to me if they don't like me too?" he asked. He was promised that he would be made general manger no matter where he went after that, even if he only lasted twenty-four hours. Management also agreed that every three months he would be given a long weekend of R&R in Bangkok.

Axel accepted, and he did well in Kathmandu. He not only did well but he loved it. He remained twenty months, until the Hilton gave up management of the hotel.

"The owner of the Annapurna was Princess Helen Shah, the wife of Prince Basundhara, brother of the King," he said. "The first year I got along fine with everyone, but then I became aware that Princess Helen had a private secretary, Sahdev Rana, who had different interests from mine. I wrote a confidential report and sent it back to our main office in New York. What I didn't know was that the secretary was opening my mail. Overnight things changed. Suddenly I was a *persona non grata*. From one day to another I became an enemy of the royal family owners of the hotel. Before that I was at every function, the King's birthday, the Queen's birthday, sometimes I was the only foreigner. 'You are part of our family,' they would always tell me. My driver was fired and a new one installed. I was under observation twenty-four hours a day. But you know, none of this mattered to me. I had a job to do and I did it. And I still liked Kathmandu, and I must admit, I liked the excitement. I felt I was playing a bit part in a cheap

Hollywood movie. In Hong Kong I was acting. In Kathmandu it was real."

After a time, Axel knew everyone who was anybody in Kathmandu. He got to know Barbara Adams and became close friends with Boris of the Hotel Royal and his Danish wife Inger. He spent a great deal of time with Boris. "After I left Kathmandu, Boris came to visit me when I was at the Hilton in Kuala Lumpur. He was always traveling, buying hardware and supplies for the Hotel Royal. He gave me a copy of his book that had just been publsihed, *Tiger for Breakfast*. He had autographed it, with the inscription— "Since you've left my liver improved." He was probably telling the truth. We used to sit up drinking and talking until three or four in the morning."

Axel found Inger always charming, and they would sit and talk for hours, about Sweden and Norway and the cold winters they endured. "But there were periods when she would disappear, for weeks on end," Axel said. "I found out she would run off to paint. She was a very private person. Boris always treated her with respect, and there was no doubt, he loved her very much. But sometimes his work stood in the way."

Prince Basundhara became Axel's close friend. "He was living with his American girlfriend, Barbara, when I first arrived. They lived openly together, and he could care less what people thought about it. He used to come to the hotel and I'd give him steaks and he would take them home for Barbara to cook for him. She was a great sport about it, and it was obvious she was deeply in love with him. But it could get awkward at times. His wife, Princess Helen, was the owner of the Annapurna. Basundhara continued to come to the hotel, even when he was living with Barbara. He was a good customer, and as the brother of the King, we had to treat him well. But that wasn't the point. I liked him and we got along splendidly."

Axel remained good friends with Princess Helen even after he left Kathmandu. He was the manager of the Hilton in Kuala Lumpur and she often came and stayed at the hotel. But I am getting ahead of my story.

Axel was unable to take his R&R in Bangkok during his last year at the Annapurna. The Indian-Pakistan war had broken out and Nepal was isolated for six months. Only a half dozen of the hotel's one hundred and twenty rooms were occupied at any one time. "We had enough wine and enough beer to have a party every night," Axel said.

With the difficulties Hilton was having with the owners of the hotel, the management decided to pull out. "It was a sad moment," Axel recalled. "We gave three months' notice. On December 31, 1971, the contract expired. We walked out at midnight. Many of the royal family were there to see us off. We took the next Thai International flight to Bangkok."

As a reward for his service in Kathmandu, the Hilton sent Axel to Kuala Lumpur to open their new hotel that had just been built. That same year, in 1972, the Malaysian government hosted the Pacific Area Travel Association conference and delegates from around the world were making the Hilton their home base. Major functions and receptions for PATA were also held at the hotel. At the conference was the second time I met Axel. I had completed a book on Malaysia for Hans Hoefer's new *Insight Guides* series and was there with Hans to promote the first books in the series. Axel was the perfect host. Everyone knew him.

The early 1970s was an interesting time in Malaysia. The country decided to open its doors to tourism. Great changes came. To let the world know more about Malaysia, Dato Shahrum, the curator of the National Museum in Kuala Lumpur, put on an exhibition on the history and development of boxing, with a few actual boxing matches.

It was set up to coincide with the Mohammed Ali-Joe Bugner title fight that was held in Malaysia on January 1, 1975. Ali won a fifteen-round decision over Bugner in the title fight. Joe Frazier was also invited to present a gift to that year's millionth visitor to the musem.

Weeks before the match, Mohammed Ali arrived with his legion of supporters–sparring partners, trainers, family members, friends. He made the Hilton Hotel his headquarters. He and Axel became the best of friends. "He rented seventy-two rooms," Axel said, "and he stayed six weeks. We were together almost every day." Mohammed Ali and Axel were to see each other again a few months later, in Manila.

After the Ali-Bugner fight, Axel was vacationing on Bali in 1975 when word reached him that he had to take over as general manager of the Manila Hilton. Off he went to the Philippines on his new assignment, and no sooner was he settled at the hotel when Ali came to town, with his camp and hundreds of followers. He was there in Manila to defend his title against Joe Frazier in what he called the "Thrilla in Manila." When Ali learned that Axel was the general manager of the Hilton there, he moved his whole camp to the hotel. Axel had a ringside seat at what some called the "battle of the century." Ali survived fourteen rounds of punishment and won by a TKO.

What Axel thought would be a short stay turned out to be the opposite. He ended up spending two and a half years in the Philippine capital, and what an unexpected and exciting two years it turned out to be. "It was one continuous celebration after another," Axel said. "The Filipinos had a cause for a party every night." He dined with President and Imelda Marcos; he knew all the cabinet ministers and chief justices; and he stood judge of more beauty contests than he can remember. He was close friends with Filipino artist Frederico Alcuaz who occupied a suite of rooms on the eighteenth floor at the Hilton. "He was flamboyant and added color to the hotel," Axel said. "Every day for lunch you could see him dining in the Hilton Rotisserie. He had his private table there, and you can be sure, someone at that table would be the subject of his painting later that afternoon."

It was while Axel was still at the Manila that he got a tempting offer from All Nippon Airways. ANA wanted him to set up a new five-star hotel in Singapore. "The salary they offered me was double what I was drawing and I couldn't say no," he said.

The hotel that Axel launched in Singapore was the elegant Century Park Sheraton off fashionable upper Orchard Road. The opening was grand and the future looked good. At the Century Park another event took place that would change his life. Axel fell in love with a lovely Singapore Chinese woman who worked in public relations at the hotel. A whirlwind romance followed and soon after they married. Axel's bachelor days were over.

Few economists at the time foresaw the coming fuel crisis. High fuel costs in the early eighties had ANA tightening its budget. Axel's three year contract was nearing its end. He negotiated a contract with the New World Hotel in Hong Kong. But within a year he realized the futility of working for just a single family. "I was missing the thrill of working in a chain hotel," he explained. Nevertheless, he helped the owners of New World set up The China Hotel in Guangzhou.

Later he switched over to the Meridien chain. He helped set up two properties simultaneously in Singapore before getting transferred to Hong Kong to manage Hong Kong Regal Meridien.

This was his third return trip to Hong Kong. It was then in 1987 that Axel and his wife decided to migrate to Australia. They had by now two daughters.

No sooner were they settled when Axel was invited by Thai International Airlines to travel with a research group to the remote kingdom of Bhutan in the Himalayas. Niels Lumholdt, vice president of the airlines, had been asked by the Bhutanese government if he would assist with their plans to open up the country to tourism. Unplanned tourism to a fragile destination like Bhutan, with a population less than two million, could be devastating. Bhutan had been independent for all its recorded history, more than two thousand years, and only in 1974, did the monarchy open its doors to the outside world. Less than a hundred tourists arrived that year. The figure has risen to a thousand a year. Axel couldn't resist the offer and flew to Bangkok to meet the group.

Lumholdt took two assistants, Vivat Boonyavanich, the area manager for India and Nepal, and Tom Hackett from the airline's office in Seattle. He invited two writers, Robin Dannhorn, who had been on the staff of the airline, and me, reporting for the *Bangkok Post.* Axel would survey the hotel situation and make recommendations to the government. We had no idea what to expect.

From Bangkok we flew to Calcutta. We left Dum-Dum Airport in a 16-seat Dornier aircraft and flew over the towering Himalayas to reach Bhutan. Some 16,000 feet above Paro, the nearest village to the capital and with the only airfield in Bhutan, the pilot had to search for an opening in the clouds, and after finding one, we dropped suddenly in narrow spins through the skies to make our landing. We had reached James Hilton's Shangri-La that he portrayed so well in *Lost Horizon.*

Everything caught our attention, the high mountains that sealed us in, a monastery with white walls perched on a cliff, the Bhutanese in their native dress, and the silence that seemed to press down like a weight. A van waited to carry us the short distance to Thimpu, the capital, where a young king and his four wives, all sisters, resided.

For the next ten days we were awed. "I thought I was remote when I was in northern Sweden," Axel said, "but nothing compares to this."

Bhutan is cut off from the world. There isn't a television set in all the country. There is a weekly newspaper, but it can't be found readily outside the capital. Radio broadcasts are limited to a few hours daily. There's no crime, no beggars, no prostitution, no suicides, and no threat of bombs, hijacking or terrorism. In fact, you don't even see policemen, except traffic cops in Thimpu. Nor are there jukeboxes, pool halls or neon lights. There are but two thousand kilometers of road and less than five thousand vehicles. The country's biggest expenditure is maintaining roads throughout the kingdom.

We stayed at the Motithan Hotel which overlooks Thimpu. Axel approached it as though he were the new general manager taking over. He missed nothing.

Like the town, the hotel came as a surprise. It sprawls, with wings and corridors and spacious bedrooms. Everything is neat and clean. The style of decor, characteristically Bhutanese, includes splashes of color with hand-painted ceilings, eaves and beams all decorated with minuscule designs. There is an abundance of hanging banners and drapes of all sorts, fashioned from brightly-colored cloth. Framed black-and-white photographs from a past era hang on the walls.

In the next ten days we traveled over much of the country's five thousand kilometers of road, to as far as the Chinese border, to places like Punakha, Tongsa and Bumthang. It is quite impossible to find a hundred yards of straight road in Bhutan; there is only one curve after another; and they are treacherous, with sheer drops of hundreds, sometimes thousands, of feet into deep canyons below. Roads are only one-way without guardrails.

We crossed high passes, where great Mongol hordes once marched through this east-west passage on the first silk route. Sheep, cows and even yaks fed along the roads. Their herders made no effort to shoo them away. At times we drove through the clouds. Villages were scattered, where old folk gazed and kids waved as we passed. The mountainsides were gardens of flowers; some trees in blossom looked like exploding fireworks. Magnolias and rhododendrons were predominant.

At Tongsa we had special permission to visit the monastery, an honor granted to very few. The Tongsa monastery dates back to 1543, and here, cloistered behind its thick walls, seven hundred monks live out their lives. Their robes are thick dark-red, handwoven cloth. They are as baffled by us as we are by them. They offered us rancid salted yak butter tea. It was inhospitable to refuse them.

The monastery had wide plank floors polished smooth by hundreds of years of bare feet marching over them. Embroidered drapes hung from lofty ceilings, altars with heavy silver trays and bowls flanked by ivory tusks cracked and yellowed with age. Pillars were square timbers painted red. Huge wooden doors swung not on hinges but on pins. Chambers were dark and ladders that connect the levels were steep and menacing to climb. Everywhere were large brass bells and gongs. In small hidden side rooms, monks chanted, doing their *pujas*, and in the stone courtyards blackbirds and crows disrupted the silence with the heavy flapping of wings and mocking cries.

The road to Bumthang was even more thrilling and nerve shattering than the others. Just as we passed one narrow section, the road collapsed into the canyon. We knew we had to return the way we came, and that night it worried us as we sat around a log fire at the bar in our inn. We tried to decide what drinks to have from the bottles behind the bar, all locally made—Pure Malt Whiskey, Bhutan Mist, Magpie Apple Brandy, Khambu Spirits, Dragon XXX Rhum, Jachung Brandy. Axel served as our host and suggested we try the Dragon XXX Rhum. We did and soon forgot about the road.

The next day, as we returned, with hangovers, we found an Indian work force had the road patched. Eventually, after a week and visits to a dozen monasteries and an estimated 12,000 curves, we arrive back in Thimpu.

The town that first appeared so comically small now loomed as big as Paris does to the farmboy seeing it for the first time. It was a welcoming sight.

We spent a memorable evening as guests of Lennie Dorji, uncle of the king and ex-prime minister. We sat in his elaborately decorated house, with skins and tusks on the walls and elephant feet with red stain covers for stools to sit upon. Lennie told us about hunting wild boar and leopards and mountain thar and game we never heard of before. And he had fishing stories to tell, about trout bigger than New Zealand trout, giant carp, and mashseer which grow up to five feet in length. Then he laughed. "In the rivers in the lowlands you might snag a crocodile." He also talked about traveling overland across the Himalayas to attend a royal wedding in Kathmandu. He and Axel exchanged anecdotes about the people they both knew–Boris Lissonevitch and his Danish wife Inger and Prince Basundhara and his American fiancée Barbara Adams.

We all left Bhutan, by plane the way we came, and said our goodbyes in Calcutta. Each went his own way. Axel returned to Australia.

Australia did not prove to be lucky for Axel. In Melbourne he met a Singaporean Indian friend who wanted to open a waterfront resort. He convinced Axel to join him. Together they set the project into motion when suddenly the banks financing the project dropped out. Axel and his friend had not yet recovered from their loss when the president of SAS hotels called him to Hamburg, Germany, to manage a newly acquired property there.

So after thirty-one years, Axel was on his home soil. But Europe was no longer to his liking. He and his family— he had two daughters now—returned to Australia where he joined a new Japanese hotel management company as director of operations.

Australia for the second time proved unlucky for Axel. In barely nine months the management company went broke. The Japanese owners had lost a fortune on the Tokyo stock market.

For a rest and a change of pace Axel took his family on a long holiday in Europe. While he was in Switzerland, a Bangkok-based entrepreneur approached him to set up an all-suite hotel in Bangkok .

After his holiday trip he returned to Bangkok but things really did not work out according to his scheme. He dropped out of the project.

Axel then answered an SOS from entrepreneur William Heinecke who had opened the posh Royal Garden Riverside resort downriver from The Oriental. He is the hotel's general manager.

"The hotel industry has changed over the past two decades," Axel said. "I feel that the human touch is rapidly disappearing. But I try to keep it alive. I personally attend to all our important guests. That, I think, is important."

Rudyard Kipling would agree to that.

Bill Heinecke, as a race car driver, one among his many sports.

Chapter 10

BILL HEINECKE
Call to Adventure

No one thought Bill Heinecke could do it. To some it was a mystery why the Ford Company in Bangkok ever gave him a car in the first place–to make an impossible drive from Singapore to Bangkok in record breaking time. I don't mean that the drive itself was impossible, but to do it in less than thirty hours was something else, maybe even bordering on lunacy. I had made the same trip in a four-wheel drive the year before Bill's attempt, and it took me five days. Now Bill was betting he could do it in one third that time. He was so sure of himself he was able to convince the Ford Company to give him not only a car but a bundle of money to boot.

Today, more than a quarter of a century later, it's an easy drive. The roads are paved all the way, and some have become superhighways. But back in 1967, the odds were stacked against anyone going the distance without a mishap. The route covered a gruelling 897 miles, much of it over potted, unpaved roads, across unbridged rivers and through rough jungle terrain. Bill would have to drive from one end of Malaysia to the other, from the south to the north, and through mountainous southern Thailand where there were few gasoline stations and fewer garages. He had to contend with monsoon rains, floods and cattle on the road, and if the driving conditions didn't get him, the bandits might. Muslim rebels in the south in those days were always holding up cars and buses and from time to time even the Bangkok-Singapore Express train. And there was always the unexpected. I was delayed along one stretch of road in southern Thailand when a herd of elephants blocked my way.

To succeed, Bill would have to average better than thirty miles an hour. On some sections he could only do five or six miles an hour.

Also working against Bill was his age. He was only eighteen years old and had just graduated from high school in Bangkok. Not too many people took him seriously. But for as young as he was, one thing he did have in his favor was experience, racing experience. When he first went to Thailand with his father and mother four years before, in 1963, he was interested in go-carts, a sport that was very popular in America. But there were no go-carts in Thailand. This didn't stop him. From America, he imported Thailand's first go-cart. "My parents weren't about to give me money for some crazy sport," he said, "so I had to earn the money myself." He took a part-time job selling classified ads for the *Bangkok World,* an English-language daily where operators used to say: "I'm sorry the ad man is in school now. Please call after 3:30."

"With money I was in business. My first go-cart wasn't very powerful, with a lawnmower engine, but it was a start. I convinced a couple of other people to import go-carts and soon Bangkok had an active group of go-cart racers. Before long go-carting became the craze."

Bill's fetish for go-cart racing eventually put him at odds with his father, which was one reason he had to break the Singapore to Bangkok driving record. He needed the prize money. Bill's father had felt as long as go-cart racing was merely his son's pastime, something that kept him out of trouble, it was fine. But when Bill graduated from Bangkok's International School, his father had other thoughts. He had high hopes for his son. He had arranged for him to enter Georgetown University in Washington. He knew that a solid education in a prestigious university would guarantee his son a good job, perhaps an appointment in the Foreign Service. He emphasized to his son that college was essential.

Roy Heinecke had spent a lifetime in Asia, and if anyone knew the score, he did. He saw the vast opportunities a young person with an education would have, for Southeast Asia was on the move.

But Roy Heinecke's skinny teenage son did not want to go to college like most of his classmates were doing. He wanted to remain in Bangkok and race go-carts. Roy gave his son the ultimatum: Go to Georgetown, with all expenses paid, or get a job and move out of the house. He thought the prospect of booting his son out might make him change his mind. It didn't.

"I wasn't rebellious, a dropout, nor was I on drugs," Bill said. "I had a car and a motorcycle and was doing something exciting. I felt there was adventure here in Thailand; I could pursue my driving here. I knew I couldn't do that at Georgetown."

Bill did have all the things most teenage boys desire–a go-cart, a motorbike, his own car. And he felt proud that he had earned the money to buy these things himself. He got his start selling newspaper ads, and he started his own advertising agency working out of the living room of his parents' house. Later when go-cart racing became popular in Thailand, he convinced the editor of the *Bangkok World* to let him write a weekly go-cart column. But Bill didn't stop here. He asked if he could sell ads that would support the column, and he wanted the newspaper to split with him whatever advertising fees he generated. The editor was amused at this brash kid with so much self-confidence. A half of nothing is nothing, he thought. He agreed to the arrangement, but he underestimated Bill Heinecke. "He had such enthusiasm you couldn't say no to him," says Barrie Cross who was then the general manager of The Oriental Hotel. "I ended up buying ad space for The

Oriental and I didn't even know what go-carts were." In a very short time, at the age of fifteen, Bill was earning 20,000 baht a month, about a thousand US dollars, more than most reporters and sub-editors were getting.

To further add to his income, he began cleaning offices at night. He had noted that businessmen around town would complain about erratic office cleaning crews. So he started a professional janitorial service. He hired a couple workers, printed a few dozen calling cards and set up a company. "I used to go to school during the day, sell ads and work at my advertising company after I got out of school and in the evening I would go around and help my workers clean offices," he recalls. "Friends would often see me washing a window or something. I was a regular laugh-in."

But now that he had to move out of the house, Bill knew he had to make some changes. He was making money but not enough to support both himself and his expensive racing hobby. He turned to the *Bangkok World* once more, but the newspaper now had a new owner and the editor he had known was no longer there. Bill approached the owner with a bold idea. He announced that he wanted to become the paper's advertising manager. "I have the experience, and I have brought a lot of advertising money to the *World.*"

"You're only a kid, barely eighteen," the new owner barked, puffing on a cigar, "and I just bought the newspaper. Do like your old man said; go to college. Then come back and see me."

"Look, I want this job," Bill insisted. The man behind the desk sat there looking at him. "If you don't give it to me," Bill continued, "I'll resign. You hear! I'll resign."

Bill not only didn't get the job as advertising manager but he also lost the only sure income he had. No more go-cart column, no more selling ads.

Bill was now in a dilemma. If he intended to make it on his own, he had to expand his business operations, his advertising agency and his janitorial service. To do that would take an increase of capital, but how? He had difficulties convincing customers that the minor standing before them was really in the Big League. The local American Chamber of Commerce wouldn't even let him in at first (he later took revenge by becoming chamber president).

"When I first started I couldn't open my own checking account," he quips.

Bill knew he was on the right track, and success was within easy reach, but still, what could he do to raise more money? He couldn't go to his father. But he could race. If he could win a couple races he could pump his winnings into his business ventures. The quickest and most simple way would be to get sponsors to back him on a Singapore to Bangkok drive. He boasted that he could do the drive in less than thirty hours, and he let the sponsors he approached take up the challenge. Furthermore, he told them, if he didn't win, they didn't have to pay. It worked.

Also, as they say in the public relations business, he needed "an additional peg" to hang his campaign on. He did this by announcing that his co-driver would be the famous race car driver from Hong Kong, Albert Poon. Albert was an old friend who had given him some pointers on how to race go-carts. To entice Albert to join him, Bill offered him half the purse, and when Albert accepted, Bill emptied his bank account and paid him in advance. Bill also agreed to foot his expenses and sent him an air ticket to Singapore.

Now all Bill had to do was set the record. If he lost he would be in serious financial trouble. He might even have to go to college. But he didn't think about that. "I didn't intend to lose," he said. He set the date–Friday, October 13, 1967.

Aside from Ford Motor Company, Bill's other two major sponsors were Singha Beer and Movado watch company. He placed their names and logos on the side of his Ford Cortina, jumped behind the wheel and headed south to Singapore. The drive gave him the chance to study the route. He didn't like what he found. The road in southern Thailand, if it could be called a road, would be the most difficult. It was mostly dirt, with fallen trees blocking the way every few miles. He had to ford rivers and streams. There were often wide detours, and heavy logging trucks commanded what little driving space there was. It didn't look good, but it was too late now for him to change his mind.

In Singapore Albert Poon was waiting. Representatives from the three sponsors, Bill's mother and father and the press were there to see them off. In 1967, Malaysia didn't have the superhighways it does today, but the roads were hard surfaced and in spite of heavy traffic they made good time. After crossing the Causeway from Singapore to Malaysia they followed the main trunk road to Kuala Lumpur, then turned north through Ipoh to Butterworth—across from Penang Island—and thundered on to Alor Star before reaching the boarder at Ban Klonh Pra-Vawn. Taking turns at the wheel, they reached the Malaysian-Thai border in good spirits. They were on schedule, but still ahead was the most difficult section to drive, through southern Thailand. The Ford agents were there to greet them with words of encouragement, and the press eagerly fired questions at them. Strobes flashed. Everyone was thrilled. "It looked like we could do it," Bill said. "Then the bubble burst." Albert didn't have a visa for Thailand.

"No amount of pleading could make Thai immigration change their mind," Bill recalled. "The Thai authorities wouldn't budge. I could see my purse suddenly vanishing.

I would have to return what advances they had already given me, and I had already given Albert his take. I had no choice but to do it alone. The pressure was even greater than before. Albert headed to Penang and I headed north. I had lost almost two valuable hours at the border."

There could be no rest stops and no slowing down even for potholes and river crossings. Bill had to put faith in his horn, hoping the blast would drive sleeping cattle off the highway. Logging lorries moved when they saw his dust. Kids in villages stood by the roadside and waved as he shot past. His face and body were dust covered and his Cortina splattered with mud and he kept his foot pressed hard on the accelerator pedal. Nightfall came and through the black of night his headlights picked his way across streams and over bumpy detours. Dawn came and with it thick fog. Still he could not slow down. The fog cleared, the sun came out burning hot and by late afternoon he saw the outskirts of Bangkok. He had driven nonstop all the way from the border. Twenty-eight hours and forty minutes after leaving Singapore he arrived at his destination. He received a hero's welcome. His sponsors were pleased with the results. He set a record that has yet to be broken.

Bill collected the rest of his prize money and put every baht into his businesses. There would be no stopping him now.

Bill foresaw the money to be made in advertising, and now with capital to invest, he was able to expand his advertising agency. He had experience with newspapers, but what about radio? He gambled. He bought radio time and became the pioneer of radio advertising in Thailand. Then came a chain of art galleries which sold original paintings by Thai artists who at the time had few commercial outlets. Help came from his high school sweetheart, an attractive American girl named Kathy. He began investing in restaurants and food outlets. By the time he was twenty-one-years-old, when his classmates were graduating from college, Bill Heinecke had 400 people working for him. He was grossing US$2.5 million a year, and made the pages of *Life* magazine. The mere high school graduate with a slick, duck-tail haircut and a beard to make himself look older was rolling in money.

But racing was in his blood and he couldn't quit. He admits it began with go-carts. He can be defensive about the subject and is quick to point out that go-carting is more than a kid's sport. The first go-cart was devised in 1956 by a Los Angeles mechanic. Interest developed rapidly throughout the U.S. and quickly spread to Europe. Bill brought go-carts to Asia. At first the vehicles were powered by lawnmower engines, but after numerous refinements the cart became a sophisticated racing machine. The engine was capable of reaching speeds greater than one hundred miles per hour. Suspension was minimal, with the driver's seat, a bench, just inches above ground. Steering was responsive to the slightest touch of the wheel, and because carts cornered quickly, they could be dangerous. Three of Bill's friends were killed in go-cart racing. "One year we went to Indy," Bill said. "I was representing Thailand. We were turning the circuit faster than Parnelli Jones. His machine was twelve to fourteen inches above the ground. We were barely inches and doing 110 mph. If you consider we were on a five- inch wheel, that's equivalent to 220 miles per hour on a regular wheel."

Go-carts, Bill explained, were the training ground for later champions. He was the youngest driver on the track in those days.

After setting the record from Singapore to Bangkok, Bill's next motor event was a race from Vientiane in Laos to Bangkok. "We drove a Honda S600, starting from the Monument in Vientiane and made it to Bangkok in six hours," he said. "Roads were unpaved in those days, and it was rough. I got back to Bangkok and the entire suspension was gone and engine was barely hanging on."

The next race he entered was billed as the "First Asian Highway Rally." It was from Laos all the way to Singapore. "I was with another friend from my go-cart days, Grant Wolfgill," Bill explained. "There were three of us taking turns driving. The third driver was a Thai, Vorakul Punyashthiti, one of the best in the country. I had just turned over the wheel to him and had curled up in the back seat to get some sleep. We were in the lead, nearing the Malaysian border. As I later learned, they had just paved a section of the road but had covered it with sand to keep the tar down. Vorakul hit the section doing a hundred miles an hour. He skidded, hit a stone kilometer marker and we went rolling over the side of a steep hill. We came to a halt right side up. The roll bar had saved us. I didn't know what happened except that Grant was shouting to some villagers to help push the car back up hill on to the road. It did us no good. We found the rear axle was broken."

In Singapore Bills' girl, his mother and father and all the news media were waiting. The first reports were that Bill was in the lead. The next reports said he had suddenly disappeared. There was no more news about him or his two fellow drivers. A gloom fell over the gathering. Everyone expected the worst.

Bill, with his forehead bruised and jumpsuit torn, began hitchhiking. He made it to Penang and from there caught a plane to Kuala Lumpur and another to Singapore. All cars had arrived and their drivers were gathering at the Goodwood Park Hotel on Scotts Road. Just then Bill walked into the hotel. "It was like attending my own funeral," he said.

A year after graduating from high school, Bill and Kathy

married. They went to Pattaya Beach for part of their honeymoon. Kurt Wachtveitl, general manager of the Nipa Lodge, gave them accommodations as a wedding present. The date was September 1968. This was Kurt's last act at Nippa Lodge before taking over as general manager of The Oriental hotel in Bangkok.

They spent the rest of their honeymoon in Hong Kong at the posh the Mandarin Hotel. Now it was Bill's turn for surprises. He bought Kathy a beautiful gold watch and pearl earrings at Lane Crawford, and for a present for himself he bought a Jaguar. "I had been in business a year now and had a little money," he said. "It was an E-type Jaguar. I bought it for racing, from my old friend, Grant Wolfgill, the guy who raced go-carts with me. Grant worked for NBC as a cameraman. He was captured by the Pathet Lao and held for about eighteen months. After his release, he lived in Hong Kong where he continued to race."

With his new Jaguar, Bill graduated to the big time. He shipped the car from Hong Kong to Macau and qualified for the Macau Grand Prix. His early boyhood ambition, to drive the Macau Grand Prix, was fulfilled. "The Macau Grand Prix is one of Asia's greatest motor races," Bill said. "You do thirty laps around the circuit, and each lap is three miles." His was the first non-formula car to finish.

From Macau he shipped the Jaguar to Bangkok and then drove it to Kuala Lumpur in Malaysia. He put on new racing tires and qualified to drive in the Malaysian Grand Prix. "I did okay in Macau," he said, "but now my brakes kept failing. Everyone but me knew that Jags didn't have good brakes. Jags look great. They are powerful and are good on a straightaway, but when you get on a hairpin turn the brakes always fail. I learned this from Grant who had sold me the car. He was there in the pits." I was sitting with Bill and a couple of his associates in the coffee shop at the Royal Riverside when he told me the story. He had everyone at the table spellbound, hanging on his every word.

"I'll never forget," he continued. "I came into the pits after my first trial. I've been married for three months now; I'm seated in the first racing car I ever owned, and I've been around the Grand Prix circle. I worked up my courage, three laps, building up speed all the time, and on the forth lap I was going as fast as I could, got to the hairpin turn, and went for the brakes, and there were no brakes. My foot went to the floorboard." The sound of other customers in the coffee shop, and even our waiter's voice, faded into the background. Bill Heinecke was leading us around a hairpin turn. "I went through the gears from fourth, to third, to second and finally to first, and somehow I got around that corner. It scared the living daylights out of me. I managed to make it safely into the pits and went over to Grant Wolfgill and said, "Grant, the goddam brakes failed. How could you sell me a car whose brakes fail?" He said, "Don't worry. They come back after thirty or forty seconds. It's just a temporary failure when they get warm." He was right. They did come back but that didn't help on the track.

"We tried many modifications to get the brakes to work," Bill said. "They failed again in my second Malaysian Grand Prix and I swore I would never drive it in another race, and I didn't." We all laughed and Bill went on to another yarn about racing.

Failing brakes didn't stop Bill from racing. He sold his Jag and bought a BMW Elva. "A great racing machine," he said. "I bought it from Walter Haskemp. The Elva is an open racer, faster than my Jag, and I could compete in all the Grand Prix races now."

Bill then went on to tell about an accident he had in Macau, the worst in his racing career. "I remember I had two big gas tanks, one on each side. They were made of alloy, and all you needed was one spark and you were finished. New safety belts had just been fitted and I strapped myself in. I set off in the race, did a couple laps and was picking up speed, going around a turn when the steering rod broke. It broke as I reached the corner and I went into the wall." He stopped for a moment, leaned back in his chair and then continued. "I'll never forget it. I was temporarily knocked out and when I came to all I could hear was the fuel pump—which doesn't turn off unless you switch the ignition off—I could hear it pumping gas. But now the engine wasn't running. That pump was the first thing I heard when I came to. And then I smelled the fumes because both gas tanks had burst. I was covered with high octane fuel. I realized I wasn't badly hurt but I also realized that at any moment I could become a big ball of flames. I grabbed the side of the car and heaved with all my strength to get out, but for some reason I couldn't get free. I had attached my safety belt for the first time ever." Then Bill smiled. "I damaged two ribs, which I like to say I did in the accident, but I didn't."

Bill enjoys doing the Far East circuit to this day. "I love it," he said, "but I also realize my limitations. My abilities were not to be a world-class racer. I enjoyed it for what it was. What has happened, just like yacht racing in Asia, is that they have started to bring in professional drivers, from Europe, New Zealand. I was into racing as a hobby, and making enough to pay my bills. I was always sponsored because my background was advertising and public relations. Also there was no one representing Thailand in any of these events."

Bill took racing seriously for ten straight years, until 1979. "I did a couple of races for Teddy Yip; he raced the Formula One. I raced a Porsche 906 for him, the GT Class. Now all I do is a Grand Prix every now and then."

In the meantime, business for Bill Heinecke was booming.

By 1974, his Inter-Asian Publicity Co. Ltd. had become a major advertising and marketing outfit, operating not only in Thailand but in other Southeast Asian cities. Looking for an international partner, he teamed up with one of the world's largest ad agenices, and he became managing director of Ogilvy and Mather Thailand Ltd.

Clients flocked in, billings soared but after four years he stepped down as director, tired of the "politicking of international companies." Bill is not a corporation man. "Work for yourself. No wealthy entrepreneur got that way by being on someone else's payroll."

Today, William E. Heinecke has more than thirty companies variously tied into his empire and they gross more than $60 million a year. He's no longer a will-he-or-won't-he-make-it phenomenon but an EEE—Entrenched Expatriate Entrepreneur, one of the most successful in Asia. And when Bill marches into a bank, bank managers don't suggest to him how to invest his money. If anything, they might ask him for tips on investment and the market.

One would imagine with fame and fortune, and his name appearing in *Times* and *Newsweek* and in the pages of the *Los Angeles Times'* financial section, he would have changed his ways and settled for a more sedate life. On the contrary. Bill now has more money to pursue the adventure trail. He does it by mixing business with pleasure. He took up flying.

The idea came to him when he bought a hotel in Pattaya. He never intended to get into the hotel business but it was a deal he couldn't turn down. Then came another property in Hua Hin. "My plan was to resell the properties, but there were no buyers. We had no choice but to make a go of it, which in a sense was what Italthai did when they bought the Nipa Lodge. They couldn't sell it so they had to take it over, and once in the hotel business they expanded and bought The Oriental."

Bill Heinecke was now in the hotel business. "So we started building this hotel, and it required that I go to Hua Hin twice a week. The road was dangerous to say the least. And then I had the other business in Pattaya. I thought maybe I should learn to fly. I could be in Pattaya in thirty minutes after leaving my office in Bangkok, and the next day I could be at work in Hua Hin."

Bill began his flying lessons at the Thai Flying Club at Bang Phra near Bangkok, and then went to the U.S. and did a crash course in two weeks. He got his license and returned to Bangkok. Now he needed a plane.

"You could fly in Thailand then but it was a rather complicated way you had to go about it," he said. "What you did was buy an airplane, and you donated it to the Thai Flying Club. You gave away the rights to it—which takes a bit of courage—and then the Flying Club says since you are so nice we are going to grant you the privilege of being the only one allowed to fly that plane. In those days it was the only way. So I bought my own plane, a two-seater Grumman Lynx. Later I bought a Mooney M20, until I got my present aircraft, a Beechcraft."

On a drive to the Flying Club early one Monday morning, Bill told me how he flew his Beechcraft from London to Bangkok. His story was reminiscent of the great London to Sydney air races that took place in a 1920s and 1930s. In a sense nothing had changed. "You might have all the sophisticated navigation gear money can buy," he said, "but you still must fly your aircraft by the seat of your pants, over the same terrain those early aviators had to fly–across Europe and the Middle East to Southeast Asia."

Now Bill was making the attempt.

"I hired a pilot to deliver the plane from Kansas, where it was built, to Bangkok, but I wanted to accompany him from London to Bangkok." I felt like I was one of the famous Smith brothers.

The Smith brothers, Keith and Ross, set the first record in a Vickers Vimy when they left England on November 12, 1919, and arrived in Darwin on December 10, a total of twenty-eight days. In October 1933, Charles Kingsford Smith, no relation to the brothers, flew the first solo flight from England to Australia in seven days and five hours. He was knighted in 1932 but disappeared in 1935 after passing over Calcutta in a flight from London to Australia.

Bill continued with his story: "In London I discovered my pilot was a woman, Margrit Waltz, a German lady. She was thirty-eight years old, married to a school teacher in Pennsylvania." Margrit had flown the Beechcraft from Wichita across the Atlantic, refueling in Newfoundland and Greenland, and arrived in London only a few hours before Bill arrived. She handed Bill her card—TNA Aviation. She saw him studying the card and laughed.

"Tits 'n Ass Aviation," she said. "All women pilots. I employ a number of women, all housewives. I can keep the costs down."

The Beechcraft, Bill explained, cruises at about 170 miles per hour. It had four fuel tanks and carried two fifty-gallon drums in place of four passengers. They had a range of fifteen hours. Since it was neither equipped with oxygen nor pressurized, they would fly at 10,000 feet, except for the Alps where they had to climb to 16,000 feet. Bill had arrived on a Friday morning. "We had a couple of meetings," he said, "and then flew to Biggin Hill where we fueled and immediately took off for Frankfurt in Germany. This lady pilot wasn't wasting any time." While crossing the English Channel, Bill had his first fright.

"We left Biggin Hill and were flying a few thousand feet above the channel. It was dark, pitch black outside, when suddenly the engine failed. The prop stopped, without warning. It just stopped. You could hear the wind whistling past the plane and we started descending, going into a glide. I didn't know what in the hell was happening. I then realized I didn't know anything about the pilot. I met her only a few hours before. She was calm, like nothing was wrong. She reaches down and switches tanks, and then restarts the engine. She now tells me, after scaring the hell out of me, what the procedure is. I didn't know it but she drains every last drop in a tank before switching to the next tank. In the meantime I'm ready to start swimming."

Bill admits he is a "super-conservative individual," and by spending thirty to forty hours with an experienced pilot flying from Europe to Asia, he could learn a lot. It was his chance to learn more about his aircraft, and about some of the idiosyncrasies of his pilot.

They landed in Frankfurt, and at eight the next morning they were back in the aircraft. By noon they were flying at 16,000 feet above the Alps. "It's a bit dicey," Bill said. "You need oxygen at that height so you can't dally. In an hour of crawling over the top of the Alps we descended to 10,000 feet. We stayed at the altitude for the rest of the trip."

They arrived exhausted in Alexandria, Egypt. "We were flying twelve-hour legs, so by the time we refueled and checked into our hotel every night, there was little time to sleep. And this woman didn't want to stop." They were up before dawn every morning and racing down the runway just as it was getting light. "I have to admit, it was beautiful," he said.

"Twelve hours driving on dry land is not like flying twelve hours in the air," Bill said. "No rest stops. No toilet facilities, and it's all non-stop." From Alexandria they flew across the desert wasteland of the Middle East to Oman. It was midnight when they reached their hotel room. "We were flying into the night and our days were getting shorter and shorter. We were losing about four hours of daylight and had to do more night flying, which makes it much more difficult."

Their most difficult sector was flying across the Indian subcontinent. "We had to fly into Dum-Dum Airport in Calcutta under instruments," Bill explained. "The weather was bad and we were surrounded by hills. The sky was alight with continuous flashes of lightning. We were jolted around so violently we could hardly read the instruments. I couldn't stop thinking about Charles Kingsford Smith, and that didn't help matters. It was here somewhere above Calcutta, after flying the first solo flight from England to Australia, that he disappeared."

Their shortest run was from Calcutta over the jungles of Burma to Bangkok. They arrived just as the sun was setting over Don Muang Airport. From London to Bangkok, with four stops, in four days. "I was ready to sleep for three days," Bill said, "but not Margrit. She was back on a commercial plane that afternoon on her way to Paris. She was making another delivery the next day."

Since he has had his Beechcraft, Bill has flown to every landing strip in Thailand, and he was the first private pilot to fly into Burma since before World War II. "Flying in Southeast Asia has opened up for the first time," he said. "Once a person is licensed he can file a flight plan and leave the next day. He can even fly abroad if he wishes. And he can own his own plane." For his next plane, Bill would like a pressurized turbo jet.

Bill became close friends with the chairman of his Hua Hin hotel. The chairman was keen on scuba diving and introduced Bill to the sport. That was in 1977, and since then Bill, often accompanied by his wife Kathy and their two sons, dove in every dive spot in Thailand and then started going abroad. He makes two adventure dive trips every year, and these include the Grand Caymans, the Maldives, the Red Sea, Papua New Guinea, the Solomons, Truck in the American Trust Territories and the Australian Great

Barrier Reef. He charters a private yacht in the Red Sea and dives in a cage along Australia's Great Barrier Reef looking for the great white shark. He has dove on World War II wrecks at Truk Island and located Japanese zeros in the shallow waters around Rabaul in Papua New Guinea.

Bill becomes enthusiastic when he talks about the great white shark. "I know this character, Rodney Fox," Bill begins, slowly at first. "Remember the film '*Blue Water, White Death*'? That's him. He was carried away by a great white and survived, and he is now a protector of the great white. We go with him." Bill talks now in rapid rhythm. "We leave out of Adelaide, aboard an old 1926 schooner, one hundred and twenty feet long. We sail to Port Lincoln and load with two tons of blood and a ton and a half of horse meat. Another ton or two of fish on deck, for chum. That movie is true. I have never been scared of a shark in my life until now. You could never get me out of the cage. They are real man-eaters, and ferocious, afraid of nothing. They would come at us and would try to take bites out of the hull of the steel boat. They would actually leave their teeth embedded in the hull."

You have to ask Bill to slow down. You can see the sharks attacking the cage. He continues: "Eight days. We get the sharks to follow our chum for two days. We get them to hang around and they become committed to the boat. Then we put the cage down. Four people to a cage. You can go into the cage anytime, or come out anytime. You drop straight in from the surface. It's an unbelievable experience."

From viewing great white sharks in a cage, Bill goes to diving on wrecks on Truk Island.

Anyone who knows Bill will acknowledge he enjoys his life. He is making money from his many businesses; he is happily married with two fine sons; he goes on two diving expeditions every year; he flies his own plane; he lives in a great Thai house filled with priceless antiques; and he still races. He mixes business with pleasure and takes along Kathy (she's out of the art gallery business now) and his two sons, John Scott and David William, as often as he can. Bearded but still boyish looking, he pads around in jeans and T-shirt.

In an article in *Asia Magazine*, writer Dennis Gray noted: "Most entrepreneurs' principal night-time and weekend hobby is catching up on work... they often engage in other activities, like sports, but they are not most likely combining it with a business call." Bill Heinecke does.

But Bill is not your typical die-hard expatriate, the so-called Old Asian Hand. One might even wonder if he is an expat at all. And he's not old. Asia, actually, is the only life he knows. While other kids back home in America were interested in the Beetles, Woodstock and protesting the war in Vietnam, Bill was growing up in Asia. He came to the Far East when he was three years old.

Bill's father, Roy Heinecke, had served with the U.S. Marines in Shanghai long before the Second World War began. During the war he had seen some of the toughest fighting in the Pacific. After the war he became Far East Bureau chief for *Leatherneck* magazine, a Marine Corps publication. He was stationed in Japan, with his wife and two sons. His eldest son, Skip, was nine, and Bill had just turned three. "We could speak Japanese better than we could English," Skip said. "I guess we were what you called U.S. government brats."

After the Korean Peace Talks in 1952, Roy and his family returned to California. Roy took his discharge and for two years wrote for the *Santa Anna Register* and the *Garden Grove News*. In 1956, he joined the State Department and that summer went to Hong Kong on his first assignment. Bill was seven. He went to elementary school in Hong Kong while Skip, now thirteen, went to the Naval Academy prep school in the U.S.

In 1962, Roy took his family to Kuala Lumpur where they remained for a year. They then went to Bangkok where Roy became a founding member of the Foreign Correspondents Club—they met in Mezu's Kitchen in Patpong Road before moving to The Oriental Hotel—and Bill enrolled in the International School. No sooner was he settled in school than Bill imported his first go-cart and began selling adds for the *Bangkok World*. When Bill was graduating, his brother Skip was on a U.S. destroyer in Vietnam.

When I think of the colossal success that Bill Heinecke has enjoyed, another man comes to mind—Albert Foreman. Novelist Somerset Maugham wrote about him in a short story called "The Verger." Albert was a verger, a kind of caretaker, at St. Peter's in Neville Square in London. A new vicar had been appointed, a red-faced energetic man in his early forties, and he called Albert into the vestry one morning after service.

Albert wondered what the matter could be. His deportment, he knew, was irreproachable and his character unimpeachable. He had been with St. Peter's sixteen years.

"We've got something rather unpleasant to say to you," the vicar said. "I discovered to my astonishment that you could neither read nor write."

Albert didn't deny the charge.

The vicar then said, for the sake of the church, he had no alternative but to let Albert to go.

Albert walked slowly home. His heart was heavy. He did not know what he should do with himself. He was a non-smoker but now felt he would like to have a cigarette. He looked about him for a shop where he could buy a pack. He couldn't be the only man who walked along the street and wanted a smoke, he thought. A month after he left St. Peter's, he set up a tobacco and news shop.

He did very well and opened a second shop, and in ten years he had a dozen such shops. He was making money hand over fist. One morning he was depositing a bundle of money when the bank manager called him to his office.

He explained that Albert had a considerable amount of money on deposit and would do well to invest it. All Albert had to do was sign the transfers. Albert had to tell the manager he couldn't read or write.

"You mean to say that you've built up this important business and amassed a fortune of thirty thousand pounds without being able to read or write? Good God, man, what would you be now if you had been able to?"

"I can tell you that, sir," said Albert Foreman. "I'd be verger of St. Peter's in Neville Square."

Had William E. Heinecke not won his first race from Singapore to Bangkok, he might well still be selling ads for a Bangkok newspaper.

"In spite of what I have done in business," Bill told me, "I have made enough time for a lot of adventures, diving, racing, flying. The secret for survival is getting the best instructor you can find, and then get the best equipment. Everything I have been done has been stacked in my favor." Then he thought about it for a moment. "A little money helps too."

Bill Heinecke with the King of Thailand at the boat races in Hua Hin.

Bill Mathers at Yale.

At the press conference after release from prison.

Chapter 11

BILL MATHERS
Treasures Beneath the Sea

When Bill Mathers was released from prison in Vietnam in 1984, after spending nearly ten months in solitary, waiting to be executed, no one ever thought he would go back to sea again, at least not to hunt for sunken ships. But he did. Only now he was more secretive, more circumvent than ever. It was obvious he had something in mind, something big, but only those working with him knew what it was, and they weren't about to tell. In time, when the news broke, we would all learn Bill Mathers' secret. It was just a matter of waiting.

Salvage divers are this way. They are a peculiar breed of people. They are all secretive, worried that someone might steal their ideas. Maybe their treasure maps. They trust few people, and certainly not writers and reporters. Bill made no pretences about that. We are great friends, and I have known him since he came to Singapore in the late 1960s, but every time he was on to something, he excluded me. "I'll let you know about it later," he always said. But I do have to admit, I did make some exciting dives with him. We dove beneath a lake in Malay jungle looking for a lost city, and I was with him when he located and dove on the *HMS Repulse*, the British battleship sunk in the opening days of World War II.

It would be wrong to call Bill a treasure diver. He's not like some of the characters we have both known in Singapore. Some are outright thieves. They find wrecks, take what they can salvage as quickly as they can, and then blow up the remains to keep other divers from moving in. "It keeps the prices up," one noted treasure diver said. It's a pity, for sunken vessels are time capsules.

I would have to classify Bill Mathers more as a marine archaeologist than a treasure diver. He did study Asian history at Yale, and he admits being fascinated with Asia's rich exchange of goods and cultures, but this wasn't the reason he came to Asia in the first place. The U. S. Navy sent him to Vietnam, but not for his knowledge of Asian history. He was sent as a salvage officer, to clear harbors and rivers of the vast Mekong delta of wrecks and sunken vessels. He spent his time and did his hitch in Nam, but after the war, rather than return home, he went to Singapore. Initially he worked for commercial diving and salvage companies and then spent nine years participating in the development of his own marine construction company.

Underwater construction became his pipeline to an underwater world few people even realize exists. Trading had been going on in Southeast Asian waters when Rome was still an outpost of the Greeks. The South China Seas are littered with wrecks, from ancient thousand-year-old Chinese junks to World War II wrecks. Their locations had remained unknown until Bill and a handful of other divers began their searches.

It was during this period when Bill was a salvage diver in Singapore that I first got to know him. I was building my own sailing schooner on the Pandan River and every now and then he would appear to see how I was progressing. He too had plans of owning his own boat, but for different reasons. I wanted to go sailing off to the South Seas looking for romance. Bill wanted to go diving for lost wrecks.

Eventually we both achieved our ends; I completed my schooner and sailed the South Seas; and Bill found the vessel he wanted, an 80-foot schooner called *So Fong*. She was a beautiful wooden vessel built in Hong Kong in 1937. Bill equipped her for pleasure cruising and scuba diving. She lacked nothing.

Even long before Bill bought *So Fong*, he began systematically looking for archaeological wrecks in Asian waters. And as I said, I was fortunate to have dived with him on several expeditions. We made the trip into the Malay jungles and dove into the inky depths of a hidden lake in search of a lost city, a thriving Khmer-type walled city that was reported in early Chinese chronicles dating back to the 11th century. The aborigines who lived on the shores of the lake also claimed a Loch Ness-type monster lived in the lake. It doesn't make for comfortable diving when you think a monster might be lurking in the dark waters. We found no monster but we did uncover some artifacts that could indicate a ruin of some sort. Without the right equipment to further explore the lake bottom that was silted with layers of glutinous mud there was little we could do. We put the lake on hold.

Another time, after Bill had acquired *So Fong*, I was with him when he began the search for the British battleship *HMS Repulse* that was sunk off the Malay coast, along with the *HMS Prince of Wales*, by Japanese dive bombers during the opening days of World War II. The two mighty warships, the pride of the British Navy, and their destroyer escorts had left Singapore the evening before and headed up the coast in a last-minute effort to intercept and stop the Japanese invasion of southern Thailand and Malaya. Ninety minutes after Midshipman Masame Hoashi had spotted the British ships in his scout plane and radioed his sighting to Admiral Sadaichi Matsunaga in Saigon, the indestructible *Prince of Wales* and *Repulse* were lying on the bottom of the South China Sea.

Now, after lying untouched in her watery grave for more than four decades, Bill had located the *Repulse* in 180 feet of water. We spent three memorable days diving on her. Bill didn't only look for wrecks. Once a U.S. film-maker chartered *So Fong* and produced a one-hour documentary film about whales in the Indian Ocean. The film was narrated by actor Gregory Peck.

All seemed to be going well for Bill, with one diving success after another, but then in July, 1984, his luck ran out.

Bill and a crew of five were sailing *So Fong* from Bangkok to Hong Kong. Winds carried them precariously close to the Vietnamese coast and consequently they were apprehended by a heavily armed Vietnamese patrol boat.

Armed men brandishing automatic weapons stormed aboard *So Fong* and dragged Bill aboard their vessel, tied him to the ship's mast and then with *So Fong* in tow took him to Can Tho, a small town fifty miles southwest of Saigon. There the authorities informed him he was charged with espionage and violating territorial waters.

The situation did not look good for Bill. The authorities could not understand why a pleasure yacht had to have a depth sounder, radios, satellite navigation and other such sophisticated equipment aboard. To make matters worse, the year before Bill had chartered *So Fong* to a Dutch television crew in the search for a World War II Dutch submarine that was sunk, with all hands aboard, by the Japanese off Malaysia in late 1941. Aboard *So Fong* was the son of the deceased Dutch submarine captain. The submarine was located and Bill recovered the wheel from the wreck which the captain's son donated to the Dutch Maritime Museum in memory of his late father.

Bill was given a blueprint of the submarine for his help during the expedition. He had the blueprint aboard *So Fong* when the vessel was seized.

Bill's scuba diving equipment further puzzled the Vietnamese. When they found the blueprint of the Dutch submarine, they suspected that there must have been a foreign submarine operating in their waters.

The suspicions of the Vietnamese were further heightened when they found Bill's much worn naval uniform jacket. Bill had kept the jacket as a memento of his Naval service, wearing it to serve cocktails for the amusement of his guests. The jacket had once fitted him snugly, and he had now put on a few pounds over a period of fourteen years. The Vietnamese mistakenly concluded that the old jacket belonged to another naval officer who had been secretly put ashore somewhere in Vietnam.

Bill never saw *So Fong* again. During his prolonged detention no foreigner was permitted to visit him nor was he allowed to send or receive mail. He was constantly interrogated and brought before mock trials in which he would be informed that he was to be executed. On two occasions the Vietnamese dragged him from his cell and threatened to shoot him.

Between interrogations he spent his time in solitary confinement, awaiting his execution.

Bill had no idea that his crew—four Frenchmen and an Australian—having paid heavy fines, had been released after spending two months in jail. Bill was left behind and held incommunicado.

To retain his sanity, Bill knew he had to keep his mind occupied, and he did this by exercising. He worked out a routine. His room was exactly twelve feet square. It had a bed and two tables, which once a day he shoved into the center of the room. He then began walking around the perimeter, one and a half miles each day, 385 circuits around the bed and tables.

During the last three weeks of his incarceration, the threats became more frequent. He was constantly reminded that those before him who had been tried for espionage had been sentenced to death, and their executions were carried out. On one occasion his guards bound him to a post in the courtyard and there he remained until nightfall.

The next day the Vietnamese gave him two alternatives: to go to prison and stand a humiliating public trial or become a spy for Vietnam by using his contacts as a businessman.

"They wanted me to enter a confidential relationship with the government of Vietnam," Bill later said. "They wanted me to basically provide them with information about the military manoeuvres of the US and ASEAN...to give them as much information as I could about the refugee camps, about any kind of disabling efforts that might be directed against Vietnam, and information about the offshore exploration program for oil that was conducted during the war years by the US Government and US companies."

He said that he refused both alternatives.

When Bill's interrogators refused to listen to his defence, he went on a twelve-day hunger strike but stopped when it made no impression on them. "It may work in the West," Bill said, "but these people couldn't have cared less if I died of hunger."

Bill endured a total of fifty-four interrogation sessions and was made to sign more than fifty pages of documents on charges made against him. A four-man counter-espionage team from Hanoi was especially rough in questioning and accusations.

Bill was told that no one was trying to secure his release, not his government, his family nor his friends. No one. What he didn't know was that along with the United Nations, the governments of Australia, France, Indonesia, the Netherlands and a number of US congressmen had interceded on his behalf. Efforts to obtain his release were made and publicized on a worldwide network and hundreds of people at all levels of authority were involved.

On March 31, nine months after his capture, Bill was

taken from his cell and marched into a room where three Vietnamese officers were seated behind a table covered with a white cloth. To one side stood a bust of Ho Chi Minh flanked by Vietnamese flags.

Bill was ordered to stand at attention. An officer read the results of their investigation: Bill Mathers was guilty of intelligence gathering activities and was found guilty of violating the territorial waters of the Republic of Vietnam. They sent him back to his cell to await his execution.

Four days later, on the morning of April 4th, he was awakened at 5 am and told to quickly dress. His hands were tied behind his back and he was herded into a van waiting in the street. Although it was still dark, he could recognize the streets—he was being driven to Saigon, to Ho Chi Minh City. He presumed it was here, in the center of town, that he would be publicly executed. The van seemed to travel forever, and soon he had no idea where he might be. He passed through a gate, which he didn't recognize, and the van stopped. An armed soldier opened the door. Standing next to him in a Western suit was a foreign man, the first Caucasian he had seen since his captivity. He gave his name, stating that he was the Australian consul, and shook Bill's hand. "Come this way," he said.

Bill was now shocked beyond belief. He was dreaming. Soon he would awake and find himself in his tiny cell. This had to be happening in a dream! But it was no dream. It was real. He was at Tan Son Nhat Airport, and directly ahead of him, catching the morning light, was an Air France commercial jetliner. His legs became almost too weak to support him as they walked toward the aircraft. Eyes were staring directly at him but he didn't know who they were. His mind was foggy. He would awake and find it wasn't so! The consul helped him up the portable stairway.

A pretty hostess showed him to his seat. She spoke to him in French and then English. She could have spoken to him in Swahili and it wouldn't have registered. Later, Bill couldn't remember what he ate or drank aboard the flight, or if he ate or drank at all. He was that muddled. All he remembers is that he was landing in Bangkok and there was a multitude of people waiting to greet him.

He still couldn't comprehend—he was free. Faces greeted him, men in uniform, in tailored suits and ties. Strobes flashed. He was standing in front of a cluster of microphones and bright lights. He was asked to give a speech.

On March 25th, ten days before Bill's release, and four days before his mock trial, the Vietnamese Government had formally notified the U.S. Government in Washington, the Australian and French Governments in Hanoi, and the Secretary General of the United Nations in New York City that Bill would be released sometime after March 30th and before April 10th. In accordance with the agreement, on Monday, April 1st, $10,000 in U.S. currency was paid in advance to the Vietnamese authorities in Bangkok. In addition, based on the accusation that Bill Mathers was a spy, his schooner *So Fong* was confiscated.

I was in Singapore when a consul at the U.S. Embassy informed me that Bill would be released in two days. Along with a number of Bill's friends and diving buddies, I had been cooperating with the embassies and writing personal letters to the Vietnamese government hoping to secure his release. When I heard the news, I caught the next flight to Bangkok. I was at Don Muang International Airport when the Air France flight arrived.

Members of the press, photographers, television cameramen, reporters, official embassy representatives, all crowded the arrival hall at the airport. This was big news and everyone from the wire services to local newspapers was there to report it. Bill appeared, gaunt, heavily bearded, a bewildered expression on his face. His sunken, searching eyes revealed the ordeal he had gone through. I rushed up to grab his hand but he withdrew and looked at me as if I were from another planet. He was led to a podium lined with microphones. For the longest time he stood there. Then he spoke. His voice surprised everyone. It was clear and concise. "I am very, very happy to be released and able to talk to people who can understand me and are willing to return my conversation," he said. It was almost as if he were reading a written speech.

"My emotions are somewhat confused right now," he continued. "I haven't seen anybody—any Westerners— except my friendly interrogators for nine months now." He then went on to thank those who arranged his release. Embassy officials then whisked him off in a government car to take him to an unknown hotel where he would be debriefed. Two days later Bill phoned me. He apologized for his behavior at the airport. He explained he was returning to America, and he didn't know his next move. I think he knew, and for nine months in prison he had been thinking about it, but he wasn't about to tell me.

Bill disappeared from the Asian scene for the next few years, and there were those who believed he would not come back. They didn't know Bill Mathers. He was not idle during this time. As we all learned later, he was busy in archives and libraries from Mexico City to Madrid. In Asia, however, people soon forgot about him. Occasionally someone would ask, "What ever happened to what's his name, you know—Bill Mathers." Then in the fall of 1987, the name Bill Mathers surfaced. The wire services flashed the news around the world—a Manila Galleon with a cargo worth millions had been discovered off the coast of Saipan in the Marianas, less than a hundred miles north of Guam. The expedition leader's name was given—William

Mathers. Soon everyone remembered him. And no longer was the secret his to keep. In September, 1990, *National Geographic* published two full-color articles on Manila Galleons–"Track of the Manila Galleons" and *"Nuestra Señora de la Concepción ."* The latter was authored by William M. Mathers.

After the *National Geographic* article appeared, Hans Hoefer's APA Press in Singapore published the *Treasure of the Conception, The Archaeological Recovery of a Spanish Galleon,* co-authored by William Mathers. It tells in detail the story of the recovery of the Galleon *Nuestra Señora de la Concepción .* Bill was in the news everywhere. How did it all happen?

After the loss of the *So Fong* and his release from prison, Bill formed another company, an underwater recovery group called Pacific Sea Resources which was to become the first archaeological team to excavate the remnants of a Manila Galleon.

For his exploration, Bill outfitted a salvage vessel, *Tengar,* and equipped her with some of the most modern diving equipment he could muster. For depths far beyond safe scuba range, *Tengar* carried a two-man diving bell. They had an ROV (Remotely Operated Vehicle), a mobile video camera guided from the surface. In addition, she carried a submersible that held two observers and a pilot to be used for even deeper searches.

Bill handpicked his crew, thirty men and women from seven nationalities—Thai, Malaysian, Singaporean, Filipino, Australian, English and American. He had archaeologists, conservationists, computer programmers, artifact illustrators, photographers, writers, engineers, cooks, riggers, welders, marine biologists and a secretary. Everyone was a qualified diver as well, and had to swear secrecy to the project.

Bill was determined that if he found a galleon, the

excavation would be conducted under rigorous archaeological standards, with the cooperation of academicians throughout the world.

As Bill explained in the *Geographic*, the Manila galleon trade was one of the most hazardous, and yet most profitable commercial enterprises in European colonial history. Between 1565 and 1815 these top-heavy sailing vessels carried the treasures of the Orient via Mexico to the West in exchange for New World silver and the manufactured goods of Europe. Perhaps as many as a hundred galleons were lost in treacherous seas over the centuries, but the search for their remains has traditionally focused on the Atlantic and Caribbean legs of the trip.

Bill would focus on Asia and the Pacific leg.

The trade at its best was haphazard. In his research Bill found that Manila Galleons under sail from Mexico and elsewhere from the New World's Pacific coast en route to the Islas del Poniente, better known as the Philippine Islands, made an important stop at Guahan (Guam) to take on fresh water and other provisions necessary to complete the final 1,400 miles of their 8,400-mile journey across the Earth's largest body of water.

Ferdinand Magellan discovered Guam on March 21, 1521 after a voyage of three months and twenty days from the southern tip of South America. Magellan Monument at Umatac Bay on the eastern side of the island marks his landing site. Magellan's men were met by a number of triangular-sailed canoes filled with friendly, smiling people with long black flowing hair. They boarded the vessel and when ordered off by the Spaniards several were shot and killed. This was Guam's first contact with the West. It is interesting to observe that these islands which are relatively close to both Japan and China were not discovered by either, rather it was a European sailing from the other side of the Earth who first discovered the islands.

Under the best conditions galleons were difficult to navigate due to their poor design, their large size and overloading. During a typhoon they were a navigator's nightmare and many were blown off their intended route and ripped apart on treacherous reefs and shoals. Westbound vessels carried cargos of silver coinage necessary to operate the island governments and other items necessary to support Spain's Pacific outposts. Eastbound galleons were bound for the Western Hemisphere–Acapulco or the Isthmus of Darien in Central America, where a landfall could be made within the most narrow strip of land separating the Pacific from the Atlantic Ocean.

Sea charts of the period were practically nonexistent and navigation instruments rudimentary. A captain had to keep the bow of his ship pointed toward the day's rising sun and hope wind and currents did not deflect the ship too far from its intended track.

In the late 17th century, the galleons which sailed eastward from Manila carried cargos of silk, porcelain, spices and gold for the Spanish treasury of King Carlos II. Their cargoes were priceless.

While some vessels were bound for Acapulco, others carried cargo which would be transferred to an Atlantic fleet of Spanish galleons for shipment to Cadiz, Spain. At the Isthmus of America (what is now Panama) the precious cargo was carried on the backs of burros through the jungles to the Atlantic Ocean for reloading on ships bound first for Havana, thence to Spain.

Many of the Pacific galleons never completed their journey to or from the Philippines as they were blown off course during storms and wrecked, some in the vicinity of Guam. Locating them is the problem. Shipwreck sites are rapidly camouflaged by nature and by the sea's natural surroundings. Wrecks of ships over one hundred years of age are marked only by sand and coral. All exposed timber would have been destroyed by shipworms. Gun barrels are the most prominent remains. Boarding axes, swords, flintlock muskets and cannon balls have a good chance of survival. Usually, however, ballast rock are all that remain of an ancient ship.

For the adventurous, Manila galleons spell romance. Their remains have been sought after for centuries. The most prized of these vessels, it is believed, is the *Nuestra Senora del Pilar,* Our Lady of the Pillar, under sail from Manila to the New World in 1690, with a cargo of one and one half million pesos in coin and bullion. She ran aground on a reef and sank in the vicinity of Cocos Island off Guam's southern shore. Another vessel, *Senora del Buen Viaje,* Our Lady of Good Voyage, sank off Pago Bay in Guam.

Bill's basic research on the galleon *Nuestra Señora de la Concepción* took two years. He pored through archives in Seville, Rome, Guam, Mexico City, Washington and Manila. He believed that *Concepción* was wrecked through mishandling after leaving Guam on September 20, 1638, en route east from Manila with a cargo of Oriental silks, porcelain, ivory, and precious jewels.

Concepción was the largest Spanish ship built up to her time, 160 feet long and displacing some 2,000 tons, with a loaded draft of between eighteen and twenty-two feet. By today's standards she would be a small freighter. She was also one of the richest galleons of her day, with cargo valued at four million pesos, worth tens of millions of dollars on today's market.

Bills' research ship *Tengar* arrived in Saipan on March 14, 1987, and anchored a hundred yards off the southwest coast. Bill had negotiated an agreement with the Commonwealth of the Northern Mariana Islands, and agreed to work closely under the U. S. Army Corps of

Engineers. The search began. It was to last two years.

The first three weeks of diving yielded ceramic shards and scattered concentrations of ballast stones, but little else. Then while Bill and another diver were moving from seaward toward shore, they made their discovery.

"And then I catch a glimpse of metal—a small luminous object poking from the sand," he wrote. "Probing carefully, I uncover a three-inch wide fragment of hand-tooled gold plate. I am captivated by the image on the fragment: A woman in a swirling gown cradles a vase of flowers. Her left hand holds a cluster of roses. A small dog springs up at her feet. Floral designs embellish the fragment's border."

Other discoveries were soon made and brought to the surface: a small gold shoe with forty-one inlaid diamonds; a mass of thirty-two gold chains, each about five-feet long, all held together with a twisted gold wire; beads of Chinese origin; ornate brass tacks that bore remnants of gold leaf; ceramic shards; gold and brass buttons; two silver sword pommels; and much more.

Altogether the excavation yielded more than 1,300 pieces of 22.5-karat gold jewelry—chains, crucifixes, beads, buckles, filigree buttons, rings and brooches set with precious stones.

Some of the less valuable finds from the *Concepción* were just as fascinating. For example, they discovered 156 intact storage jars at depths between 140 and 250 feet. Full of waterlogged sediment, the jars weighed more than a hundred pounds each and had to be winched aboard. Later study revealed that they had come from kilns in South China, Vietnam and Thailand. Most of them were used for carrying water, a precious item on long trans-Pacific voyages that lasted months.

But it is the excitement of the find that Bill so dramatically writes about: "The seas along this reef off

Saipan can be extremely rough, and it is frightening to imagine the ordeal of the *Concepción*. The galleon trying desperately to clear Saipan's southwest shores, being hurled into the reef by towering waves and pulverized against the coral, spilling ballast and cargo from gaping holes below the waterline, passengers and crew leaping into the churning seas and facing the spears and slingstones of waiting Chamorro islanders. I can almost hear, above the gale, the terrible screams of helpless men and women. Of some four hundred aboard, only a few dozen survived."

Other than what Bill and his crew were able to salvage from the cargo, there was little archaeological study to be made. Nearly 350 years of typhoons had played havoc with the ship's remains. Nevertheless, all items were measured, photographed, and drawn on paper, and their images recorded on disks in the ship's computers. The findings were plotted on archaeological site maps, and all details, including precise locations, were entered into their computerized data base for the final archaeological report.

The *Concepción* is only one of the many Manila galleons lost in a trade that lasted for some 250 years. Perhaps another of these gallant vessels might be lying peacefully on the bottom, exactly as it went down, waiting to be discovered. I'm sure the world will be hearing about William M. Mathers again.

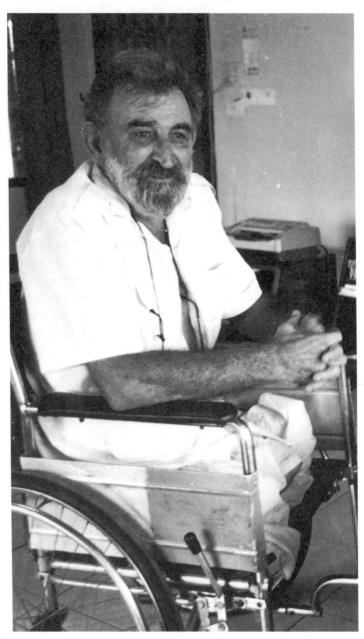

Tristan Jones—Author, sailor, explorer beyond dreams.

Chapter 12

TRISTAN JONES
Sailor Extraordinaire

When a man has written fourteen books about the sea, most of which are autobiographical—and you have read them all—there's very little you can ask when you meet him. It's all there in print. I felt this way when the chance came for me to meet Tristan Jones, one of the finest sailing adventure writers of our time. I knew, for example, all about Tristan's records, that he holds most of the single-handed sailing records in modern sailing history. That he has traveled to the Arctic Circle, and that he has sailed the world's lowest stretch of navigable water, the Dead Sea, and that he had sailed an ocean-going vessel on the world's highest waters, Lake Titicaca in Peru. To be precise, Tristan Jones has sailed 345,000 miles (more than the distance to the moon) in boats under forty feet long, 180,000 miles of this distance single-handed. He has sailed the Atlantic eighteen times, nine times alone. And he stayed alive on an iceberg for fifteen months by living off seal blubber. His adventure-filled articles and books had been translated into seven languages.

I knew these things about Tristan Jones, from his articles and books, but I still wanted to meet him, not to ask him about himself, or his accomplishments; I wanted to tell him something.

Tristan had been a great inspiration for me, and ever since I began reading him, I hoped that one day I would meet him, so that I could thank him. I had my reasons. For as long as I can remember, I wanted to own my own boat and sail the South Seas. I didn't have a bankroll to go out and buy a yacht, so I decided to build one. Everyone

I met told me it was hopeless to even attempt such a thing. Tristan told me, through his written word, that I could do it. And there were still others who said, even if I did get my boat built, it was an impossible dream, to sail the oceans without a bundle of money, and most important, without experience. Tristan taught me dreams are what living is all about. And so I built my own boat, a 71-foot schooner, and sailed the oceans, and all the time I was at sea I hoped that one day I would meet Tristan Jones. He had been the inspiration I needed. He had provided me with hope.

The years passed, and still our paths hadn't crossed, but Tristan always seemed close at hand. He was forever making the news, either something new and exciting he was doing or else he had a new book that was being released. Then in 1982, I suddenly had doubts that I'd ever meet Tristan Jones. He might never even go to sea again in a small boat. I was in Singapore, aboard my schooner, when news reached me that doctors in New York had amputated his left leg above the knee, the result of a wound sustained while serving with the Royal Navy in Yemen.

But I was wrong. Tristan didn't give up the sea. The next news I heard he had been thrown out of a hospital in New York for organizing a wheelchair race among the other amputees —"They were too much younger, but so miserable." He then raised the money, mostly through writing, to buy and outfit a trimaran and take it from California on an eastward voyage halfway around the world to Thailand. He sailed his thirty-eight-foot trimaran, *Outward Leg*, down the west coast of Mexico and Central America to Panama and through the canal to England. He then crossed Europe via the Rhine and Danube rivers, through the Iron Curtain, the first-ever crossing of its kind, to his destination—Phuket in southern Thailand. He had a reason for choosing Thailand.

When he was in New York, before he had his leg amputated, he had formed a society to investigate the legend of the sunken continent of Atlantis. After the operation, he says, he realized who the people of the sunken continent were, the disabled, and he redirected his efforts for them. He registered the Atlantis Society as a non-profit organization dedicated to helping raise funds for the poor and the disabled. He started the voyage to inspire other handicapped people, especially youngsters, to reach for their own star and achieve their own ambitions despite the obstacles, natural and man-made, placed before them. "I concluded that the only way this dream could be realized was if I could discover and provide some way for the handicapped themselves to participate in achievement," he said. "In a small sailing craft, on a world voyage east-about, this was impossible. The only solution was to find some time and place where all the intricate, disparate skeins that would realize the dream might be brought together."

Why western Thailand? "It was in the moderate, cyclone-free tropical climate of the west coast of Southeast Asia," he said. "It was stable, evidently; and it was reputedly cheap." Once Tristan reached Phuket, he began his work with handicapped youngsters.

Tristan hoped to spread his word about the Atlantis Society by taking *Henry Wagner*, a 40-foot Thai longtail boat, rigged with sails and designed for the ocean waters, across Thailand's Isthmus of Kra, which he described as "the thinnest part of the long peninsula that dangles down from Indo-China like the tentacle of a dead octopus."

There is no known record of a sea-going vessel ever having done it before. To help him cross the isthmus, he had gathered a crew of Thai youngsters: the orphan Nok, a scruff of a lad with a hideous cleft palate; Som with one arm; and Anant, like Jones, a leg amputee. To make up the complement he had Thomas Ettenhuber, a 23-year old German who was nearly blind, and a Thai dog named Rambo. Tristan had signed Thomas as mate aboard *Outward Leg* in Europe. He had been with him for three years.

Tristan and his handicapped crew sailed the boat part way, via the Ta-Pee River, and for two days had an elephant named Plai Thongchai haul the two-ton vessel six miles through the jungle. The entire crossing took six weeks of incredible effort by the disabled captain and crew. After making the crossing, unaided by any others, Tristan and his crew voyaged northward, a further 1,500 miles by sea and river, to Chieng Rai on the border of Laos.

Tristan showed the world that disabled people could not only do the same as their able-bodied brothers, they could do it better if they tried hard enough.

I learned that Tristan was living ashore in Phuket, writing another book. I got his address and wrote to him, asking if I could come visit, and then awaited his reply.

What I hadn't known when I wrote to Tristan was that he had suffered another tragedy. After several operations to remove blood clots, the doctors found it necessary to amputated his right leg. He was now a double amputee. Soon after I head the sad news, his reply to my letter arrived. I couldn't believe what he wrote. His letter was filled with deep sympathy. He had heard about the loss of my schooner in a typhoon in the Pacific, and now he expressed his regrets in hearing the news. He said for me to come ahead. I was welcome any time. ·

Phuket is a beautiful island connected to the Thai mainland in the north by a causeway, and bordered in the west by the Andaman Sea. It's beaches are superb and the clear shallow waters around the island and neighboring islands offer some of the finest scuba diving in Southeast Asia. It was no wonder that Tristan chose such a beautiful spot to set up his headquarters.

Tristan's house wasn't difficult to find. Everyone on the southern end of the island knew him and knew where he lived. At Rawai Beach, across from his house, was a sign: ATLANTIS LAND-SEA ENABLEMENT. Beneath the name, a message in small print tells a unique and tragic story. "The Henry Wagner," it reads, "was captained by Tristan Jones from Liverpool, with his disabled crew, to attain the first-ever recorded crossing of the Isthmus of Kra by a sea vessel from the Andaman Sea to the Gulf of Thailand." It tells about the difficult crossing and then relates the memorable voyage to northern Thailand. Henry Wagner voyaged north, a further 2,600 kilometers by sea and river, to Chieng Rai, reached July 4, 1988. Then comes a note of sadness. "There on 26 December 1988, Thomas Ettenhuber, mate, died of an enlarged heart. Henry Wagner was returned to Rawai by Tristan Jones and the surviving crew to rest here as a memorial to the gallant mate, a triumph of faith, and as an inspiration to all." It concludes with an inscription that appears on the grave of Robert Louis Stevenson in Samoa: "Home is the sailor, home from the sea, and the hunter from the hill."

Tristan's house is a two-story building set among tall coconut trees. A collection of men and women, including those from the Kra expedition, live downstairs, helping care for Tristan and business for the Atlantis Society. A rampway leads from the lower level to his quarters above, providing him easy access for his wheelchair. He was at his desk when I entered his quarters, a bedroom cum office. "You're late," he barked. "I expected you days before this." I made some excuse for my delay, which he seemed not to hear, and then he said, "Sorry about your schooner."

I tried to picture Tristan Jones, the intrepid yachtsman whom I knew from his books, but what I saw before me was Tristan the writer. I remembered seeing photographs of him. In one book he is sitting at a table in the main saloon of his boat, pounding on a typewriter. He has the machine gimbaled, so it would rock with the motion of rolling sea. Now I found him sitting in front of a computer with a wide screen. To his left was a second computer and a fax to one side, and from a CD player came the Schubert C Major Symphony, or I think that's what he said it was later.

He swung his wheelchair around to face me. He asked me to pull up a chair, and as I was doing so, he saw me glance out the window toward the beach. He then asked if I could hear the leaves. "I listen to them day and night," he said. "They are like a Beethoven symphony, like the waves that were my only companion for so many years."

Instantly I liked Tristan Jones. It was easy to see this was no ordinary man. He continued the conversation by telling me he watches birds settle on a tree near one window every day. "They come at different intervals and sing. I know them now, they are so regular. These birds are not an accident," he said. "They are part of something. I know there is a God, everything fits in so wonderfully. There is some idea there."

His voice is deep and commanding. He speaks more like a college professor than the sailor he is. He laces his conversation with a combination of metaphors and axioms. He is witty; his mind quick and incredibly sharp. We begin talking about writing, the books he wrote and those he is writing. "I'm much better known in Australia and America than I am in my own country. In America I'm accepted. I have entry to clubs, even universities there."

He could see the puzzled look on my face.

He continued: "I wanted to raise this sailing interest for handicaps in England, after all this is where yachting originated, but it's very difficult for me. It's difficult because first of all I'm a Welshman; secondly, I'm working class; and thirdly, I've been in exile since 1938. I'm an outsider, and a bit of a bounder. If I had been born richer it would have made it easier for me, but not different."

He offered me a cigarette. "It's my only vice these days," he said. "I no longer drink, and I take no drugs whatsoever, not even for pain." He adjusted the sarong that covered the stubs of his legs. "I have to keep my faculties," he explained. I asked him about the pain.

"Pain, it's like a friend from many years back," he said. "It's a friend, not an enemy. It's like loving someone with a wart on her nose. You just have to deal with it." Still, he admitted, he is waiting, and hoping, for the pain to subside and the wounds to heal. And until then, he fills his hours with work. He is writing one book and has another two or three dancing around in his head.

Even though his ocean journeys have made him famous, what came as a surprise was to hear that he adamantly respects but doesn't love the sea. "No self-respecting sailor over fifty-five or sixty is going to dream about spending the rest his life at sea. We sailors know from hard experience that the amount of physical and mental stress endured when ocean weather really lets loose is almost enough to tempt us to drop to our knees and weep and plead and beg God, and the devil if need be, before we are beaten into a black void of an unknown death. That we don't do it, that we resist the temptation to do it, even when hope is but one last ragged thread stretched to breaking point, is our badge of sanity."

In spite of his suffering and constant pain, Tristan hasn't given up sailing nor the sea, not completely. He showed me his latest invention—a motorized wheelchair. He fitted a steel chair frame on his motorcycle sidecar to produce a novel high-speed wheelchair. At the beach he studied ways to get himself into and out of boats. "After all, once in a boat the world is your oyster," he said gleefully.

He also designed a ten-foot dinghy, which he named *Little Legend,* and succeeded in making the tricky solo transfer from chair to boat. Soon after we met he went on an offshore inter-island trip with his dog Rambo and a disabled boy aged eleven.

Tristan is the old mariner from storybooks, and the spinner of countless yarns. He has faced the odds so many times in his forays against ignorance, bigotry and doubt that adversity has become his friend, and despair his ally and inspiration.

Tristan is a fighter, from a long line of Welsh sailing people—even his grandmother was first mate on a wool-trading ship. He was born fighting, feet first after a difficult labor on board a Commonwealth vessel traveling from Australia. The first landfall two days after the ordeal was the island of Tristan da Cunha in the South Atlantic, one of the most remote islands in the world, and hence his name, Tristan. The ship was bound for Halifax, Nova Scotia, when the skipper received a message redirecting her to Liverpool, England. So young Tristan became British, for the law was that a child born aboard a Commonwealth vessel took the nationality of the first Commonwealth port at which it docked.

Tristan was orphaned at the age of six, received a rudimentary education and at thirteen took off as a barge hand through the rivers and canals of Europe—exporting scrap iron to Germany for wages of five cents a week. He's been at sea ever since. World War II broke out and in 1940 he joined the Royal Navy, served on Arctic convoys, and was sunk three times before he was eighteen. After the war he transferred to the Royal Hydrographic Service. His service ended in 1952 in Aden when an inshore survey vessel he was on was blown up by guerrillas. He suffered a severe spinal injury that left him paralyzed. Told he would never walk again, he was given a physical discharge.

But he did walk again, and now he took to the sea in small boats.

Tristan spent fifty-two of his years at sea, many of these alone, sailing solitary, not because he particularly liked it, but because of budgetary restraints. Alone he was driven into himself. "Good for writing. And I always felt so free. Five minutes at sea is worth a day at shore. You can feel the shackles dropping off."

"I remember once, I was crossing the Atlantic alone, in 1969, and I heard on my small radio that men had landed on the moon. I thought about it, but I was much happier where I was on my boat and the ocean. I felt I had a freedom they did not."

Freedom is a word that Jones uses frequently, freedom of spirit, of mind, and of body. He is a fiercely independent man who has shaped his own philosophy and moral code over the years of chasing his dreams and doing exactly the opposite of what people said he should do.

Tristan wrote a host of books, using the proceeds each time to pay for the next adventure, the endless quest. He loved a thousand women, but never stayed long enough for anything permanent. In all the years of wandering he has retained his faith in human nature, even though he's met the worst, from drug runners to pirates, from drunkards to politicians.

"There are more good people than bad," he says. "People fascinate me. I can forget a million places, but I can't forget the people I met. They keep coming back to me. I like simple people; I can accept the things they do much easier. People are what counts. I spent so much time at sea, I feel like Rip Van Winkle waking up after a hundred years, like a child. Every time I look at people, especially a baby, I think, this person may live to the next century. It takes all my wishes and dreams with me."

Tristan had more difficulties on land than he did at sea.

He was arrested and worked over in Buenos Aires, then clapped in a torture cell in Montevideo. When he finally did make it home to Britain, his vessel—the tiny, nearly indestructible *Sea Dart*, which he had shipped back home—was impounded by customs officials because he couldn't pay the "import" tax.

In his quest for the means to liberate *Sea Dart*, he took any work he could get: stoking the boilers of Harrod's Department Store in London, regaling TV talk-show viewers with wild stories, and skippering one-day "around the lighthouse" cruises for jaded New Yorkers.

Tristan Jones made his American debut at the Explorers Club in New York City in 1976. Every year on April 15th, at the Waldorf Astoria Hotel, the famous Explorers' Club of New York holds its annual Club dinner and meeting.

But this is no ordinary club meeting. On this special evening, explorers, scientists and adventurers from all over the world are honored by fifteen hundred of the most prominent people in America when they gather in the Waldorf Astoria's ballroom to trade stories, to nibble on exotic dishes and to catch up on the state of travel and exploration. Here the prime goal is to keep the business of adventure very much alive, and the members and their guests do it quite well indeed.

Guests of honor are not necessarily men of letters and astronauts. A little old man in a tuxedo thrills the audience when he talks about just returning from two months in an uncharted Chocho jungle in the wilds of South America. Later he tells the small group gathered around him that he saw animals and plants nobody had ever seen before—even the scientists that were in the party.

Another speaker gives graphic details of his encounters with Bengal tigers in the Sunderbans and his voyage down the crocodile-filled Ganges tributaries and the way it felt to be in tropical rain forests where some flora, as best as could be determined, never had been described in any scientific book.

Tristan was asked to speak, but his was not simply a task of getting up in front of an audience. He was asked to bring his 21-foot ocean-going cutter *Sea Dart* into the world's most famous hotel and appear with it on stage in the Grand Ballroom on the fourth floor.

The feat required that the cutter be brought up through the goods elevator, through the kitchen and through the very posh anterooms and dance halls to reach the fourth-floor ballroom. Tristan nevertheless agreed, only to discover the ship which was bringing the cutter from England was delayed. It was due to arrive the day before the ceremony. Tristan did get *Sea Dart* to the Astoria on time, but only after a mad drive through the streets of New York. Once there, he had more obstacles to overcome.

The boat had to pass through the doorways from the kitchen with hardly a paint-coat's thickness to spare after they removed the doors from their hinges. By heaving, shoving and pushing they got her into the Grand Ballroom and then only after cutting away *Sea Dart's* dog house.

Tristan described in his book *Adrift* how *Sea Dart* was concealed behind a curtain, standing proudly on a ten-feet-high stage while the ballroom filled with guests.

While Tristan dined on fish soup, the guests munched on "lion loin from Uganda, nibbles of hippopotamus, buffalo sausage, wild boar paté, elk deer, wild goose, the hump of a Lake Titicaca ilams, musk ox, bear meatballs, moose, caribou, walrus, kangaroo, red deer, ibex, and Alaskan salmon."

Not one of the guests knew *Sea Dart* was behind the curtain.

The speeches began. James Lovell, the astronaut, claimed that "The vast unexplored continents have been traveled. Space travel is now a reality and man has now set foot on the moon." He concluded by stating: "We also look to the future and hope that the inspiration of past accomplishments will stimulate the youth of today to continue on the trail that has been so brilliantly blazed by these eminent men."

Lowell Thomas, who was in his eighties and the author of fifty-three books, gave his talk and showed a film on his travels to Tibet.

Now it was Tristan's turn. He stood on the raised platform behind the curtain, a microphone cord around his tuxedo collar, nervously waiting. The curtain silently opened, with blazing lights aimed at the stage, and then came the dead hush followed by a gasp of fifteen hundred souls. He talked about his gallant little vessel *Sea Dart.*

That tiny boat upon which Tristan now stood, he had managed to haul—smuggle he called it—through Peru from the Pacific coast and across the Andes Mountains to Lake Titicaca four and a half kilometers up, and back down to the headwaters of jungle rivers that lead to the Atlantic. He had sailed *Sea Dart* upon the Dead Sea, the lowest body of water in the world and now on the highest, Lake Titicaca.

It is men and women like Tristan Jones that give the Explorers' Club of New York the meaning of adventure.

One of Tristan's most memorable trips was not across forbidden seas but to the slums of New York City. He was having drinks with friends at the Explorers Club when the club's president immediately began telling him about his forthcoming trip. "I'm going to Pantagonia," he said. "What about you, Tristan. Where are you planning on going next?"

"I want to go to the Bowery," Tristan said.

"You want what?"

"I want to go to the Bowery," Tristan replied, and he was serious. "It's just right down the street, and for most of us, it's unexplored."

"You're mad," the president said.

"Look," Tristan said, "what I want to do is leave you all my money. All I will keep is enough for a subway token."

Tristan gave the president his money and went down to the Bowery. He remained three months.

Some of Tristan's most powerful writing comes from his living in the Bowery. He discovered that the two most powerful groups of people in New York are those who have everything and those who have nothing at all. He left the former behind, at the Explorers' Club, and found the latter when he went into the lower East Side. Tristan explains his reasoning: The power of the rich is derived from fear, while the have-nots derive their power from the pure strength of having nothing to lose. "The most powerful people in the second group are those who wish to gain nothing," he said. He was privileged to know some of them, on the Bowery and in Lower Manhattan, and among them were some of the most remarkable people he had ever met in a lifetime of wandering the Earth. "They taught me not to apologize, that circumstances will apologize for themselves. They also confirmed what I had already guessed—that the only true riches are to be found between your ears. That the only thing you should regret is what you did not do, not what you did."

Tristan was the first, as far as he knows, to sing the song of the homeless when he was living among them in 1979. As we sat in his room in Phuket, he explained that the homeless in America and Europe differ greatly. "In Britain, for example, a hobo exists under the form of socialism; in New York it's capitalism. These people, from opposite sides of the Alantic, with absolutely nothing, develop under different systems. Under capitalism, everything is organized; money, as little as there is, goes through the channels."

Aside from his sea tales, Tristan gives us some powerful insights on life in cities. "Some of the great cities of the world are sailors' cities, built by people of the sea for the sea people," he wrote in *Outward Leg*. He names these cities—Bristol, Liverpool, Copenhagen, Amsterdam, Lisbon, Venice, Hong Kong, Singapore, Sydney, San Francisco and New York.

The most obvious sailors' city of these, he claims, is Amsterdam; the least, New York. New York does her best to ignore the sea—to treat it as though it does not exist. In describing New York he tells a side of the city even New Yorkers don't know. He writes: "The finest sea trip, and the cheapest, in all the Americas, aboard public transport, is from Battery Park to Staten Island. Battery Park itself, off which the Dutch ships lay to their moorings in the days of Peter Stuyvesant, lies like an anchor to the high towers of Wall Street, to the bows of the huge ship of Manhattan Island. Farther along the shore on the port side of Manhattan, the old three-master *Peking* lies disdainfully off South Street. On the starboard side of Manhattan, in the West Village, warehouses where Melville labored as a Custom's inspector still show their red-brick faces to the sometimes sweating, sometimes freezing streets. Farther amidships the incredible, man-built cliffs of Midtown are piled up—but always, under them, lies the sailors' town. Below them are Broadway and the Bowery—celebrated in a hundred shanties even now sung from the English Channel to the South China Sea."

Tristan's fondness for New York stems from his living in Manhattan for six years on and off. "When sailors have asked me how I could live there, so far from the sea and things of the sea, I did not tell them that I thought New York was the world capital of the oceans and that every time I walked down any street anywhere in that sprawling hubbub I was continually reminded of the sea and of things of the sea and of peoples of the sea, for how would they have believed me? But how else could it be for a city whose main river is named after one of the greatest and bravest sea navigators of all time, Henry Hudson?"

Tristan felt he was closer to the sea in West Greenwich Village than even when he lived by the sea. "There, in my scruffy room in the Village, I did my best to do what I had promised myself I would do—tell the world that sail and sailing and sailors are not dead and long gone, and that the spirit that peopled a continent, that overcame unimaginable difficulties, is still alive and well."

In Manhattan Tristan learned the true meaning of solitude, even though, as he claims, he had probably been more truly alone than anyone else on Earth—for fifteen months during his Arctic voyage.

It was in New York that he encountered the very real solitude of the writer. "In New York I learned to care about what I should care about—and nothing else," he said. "I learned that I care about people and the world in which they live."

Tristan is preoccupied with loneliness. He delineates between loneliness and solitude. "Solitude not loneliness is a wonderful thing, the mainstay of freedom," he said. "There is no freedom within a group. Each one is chained to the others. It is only in solitude that we can go into a dream and stay there as long as we like. The only harm that solitude might do is to isolate us from those who might understand us."

In New York, and not at sea, he learned that it is easier to be courageous when you are alone than when you are with a group. "It is easier," he said, "because you never apologize to yourself for your own courage and not to have to apologize is the hallmark of achievement. This is quite a discovery, and it is important to anyone who is afraid of being alone for any length of time."

After nearly seven years ashore and after having his left leg amputated, Tristan decided to return to the sea. Hoping to inspire other handicapped people, he began to piece together Operation Star. He devoted months of writing and lecturing to raise money for his very special project. In mid-1983, when in San Diego to do a single lecture, he spotted the perfect sailing vessel for his physical needs. He found a 36-foot trimaran that would eventually become *Outward Leg*—the missing and most important piece of Operation Star. Four months of manic outfitting and preparation followed, including the invention of "cool-tubes" designed to prevent the trimaran from capsizing in heavy seas. On October 17, 1983, Tristan and his only crew member, Wally Rediske, set out in *Outward Leg* from San Diego to Europe and eventually to Asia. They crossed the Atlantic—the twentieth time for Tristan—and at St. Katharine's Dock in London Tristan made a poignant return to where he began his seagoing life thirty years before.

Tristan's emotional range of his sea sagas covers a great geographical sweep from the Arctic islands to the steaming jungle coasts of the Guianas. He writes superbly of the sea. It is forever in his heart, even when he is landlocked, surrounded by "landsmen." When he sailed for San Juan through the Devil's Triangle with a United Nations of a crew, he wrote with flair about the joy of one's return to his element. And the glory of success is so well capped when, after being down-and-out on three continents, *Sea Dart* arrived from England for an eye-popping "sail" through the streets of New York where it ends so triumphantly at the Explorers' Club.

Probably what was among the most futile of his expeditions was to the frozen Arctic. "It was made for the wrong reasons, with the wrong boat, meager finances and unsuitable equipment," he wrote in the introduction to his book *Ice.* "The first leg of this voyage took me into the Baltic, on a futile detour of two thousand miles or so, to find a Finnish girlfriend. I eventually found her, well married. I have not dwelt on this. Some parts of a man's life are his and his alone. To complain is not my function."

Tristan's attempt to sail up the Amazon, the world's largest river, ended in defeat, but to him it opened up other avenues of adventure.

Tristan Jones has the unique ability of turning hardships into victories. He writes about his failures as well as his victories, and in either case, he writes from the soul. He might tell his readers about the hazards of sailing, but he also tells the truth of the sea. He makes us feel life to the very tips of our fingers, and in turn he makes us become aware of life to its fullest. "The sea shows no sign that she knows anything about mankind," he wrote in *Adrift,* which I consider one of his best books. "We can not carve wide swaths out of her, nor huge monuments. A thousand of us can ride over one square mile of her in a day, yet when we have passed she shows no sign that we even exist. Out of sight of any vessel, the sea appears today exactly as she did ten billion years ago. It is as if mankind had never been."

In another passage in the same book he writes: "Out there you are on your own, confined to your own resources. There is no doctor, no chemist, no dentist, no lawyer, no mechanic, no grocer, no policeman just down the road."

To many the thought of no doctor and no grocer might turn them off, but Tristan asks: "Isn't adventure the thought of the unknown? Is this not what separates the adventurer from the traveler?"

No, as Tristan Jones so often expresses it, our world is still a magnificent place to live, and the unknown is out there waiting for us. Today there are few places the

National Geographic hasn't gone that we can't read about and see in pictures, but experiencing them ourselves is the true meaning of living.

In spite of his handicap, Tristan still dreams, and one such dream is a voyage to the Andaman Islands that lie some five hundred miles west of Phuket.

"Here we have a group of islands that have been locked away in the annals of history while modern man has gone to the moon and dropped Smart bombs in an oil war," said Tristan. "It's likely that the last time some of these indigenous people sighted a white man was when he stepped ashore clutching a cutlass."

The Andaman Islands, there are more than a hundred, were discarded by the early British, Spanish, and Portuguese explorers. The islands were of little resource or strategic importance when the British set out to colonize India, Burma, Malaysia, Australia and New Zealand. And, during World War II, the Japanese ignored the Andamans as they sought to establish their Pacific empire.

After the war had ended, the Soviet Union set up secret nuclear missile sites on the islands as part of a "forward defense" policy and banned all shipping in the region, including private yachting. Now that the Cold War is over, all missiles (nuclear and others) have been removed and the Indian Government is planning to open the Andaman Islands to the world.

Tristan sees his journey to the Andamans as a link between modern man and the peoples of a bygone era.

"The communities living on the Andamans don't know anything about modern man, what we've done and what we think. I intend to make contact with these people and they are likely to be suspicious and protective. But the time seems now right for a worthwhile encounter."

Tristan and I talked at length about the Andamans. He acknowledges that some of the islands are populated by cannibals, but he is not concerned. He has never carried any weapons while under sail—even in waters where pirates are known to exist.

"Writing is in my blood, but getting there and back keeps my spirit going and my human condition satisfied," he said. "For me writing is the creative aftermath of doing."

With a wink, Tristan Jones admits the Andamans may be his next "doing." He may never do it, but the dream is important. It was the dream that he passed on to me.

Karel van Wolferen—An expert on Japan and the Japanese.

Chapter 13

KAREL VAN WOLFEREN
Mightier Than the Sword

Pens are most dangerous tools, more sharp by odds
Than swords, and cut more keen than whips or rods.
—JOHN TAYLOR, *News from Hell, Hull and Halif*

When I first met Karel van Wolferen in Bangkok in the summer of 1966, I never expected that one day he would brief members of the U.S. Senate in Washington, give talks to the faculty and student body at Stanford and Harvard Universities and have lunch in Los Angeles with noted writers like Michael Crichton of *Jurasic Park* fame. In fact, in Crichton's best-selling novel *Rising Sun*, the author lists Karel in the bibliography as one of his sources of information.

And none of us who had met Karel in Bangkok then would have ever suspected that one day he would be elected president of the Foreign Correspondents Club of Japan and receive the highest Dutch award given for journalism.

The truth is, when I first met Karel, I wondered if he would ever make it in Asia. He didn't have much working for him. But back then, I guess, it really didn't matter. None of us had much working for us. We had little money, but we were happy doing what we were doing, and it didn't take a great deal of money to live. I was writing newspaper and magazine articles for a pittance, and in Karel's case, he was teaching English to Japanese students in Japan.

An old friend, Al Podell, a magazine editor from New York, had introduced me to Karel. They had both arrived

295

in Bangkok from Yokohama aboard a Messageries Maritime passenger ship. I had been anxiously waiting to see Podell, for I wanted him to join me on a Jeep trip to northern Thailand, up to the Burmese border. I had gone down to Klong Toey, Bangkok's waterfront, to meet the ship when it arrived. I knew I would have to do some fast talking with Podell, for it wouldn't be an easy trip. The roads then were poor, and in some cases, nonexistent. There was also reported Communist activity along the Thai-Burmese border.

The ship docked and Podell came down the gangplank, all smiles, followed by Karel who was wearing a straw hat, shorts and sandals. His straw hat was fastened with a cord under the chin, and he carried a heavy rucksack. Podell made the introductions. "Meet Karel," he said.

"Karel van Wolferen," the young man said. He had a slight accent. I surmised he was Dutch, which later proved to be correct. It was terribly hot that afternoon, and Karel removed his hat to wipe the perspiration from his face. He had blond, kinky hair.

I didn't give much thought to Karel. He was just someone Podell had met on the ship. But later that day, after revealing my plans, Podell got me aside and asked if Karel could make the trip north with us. I was rather hesitant. I explained we would be crowded in the Jeep. "Hey, listen," Podell assured me, "he's worth it. He'll keep you entertained the whole trip."

Podell was right. Karel did keep us entertained. For five days he told us stories about life in Japan. He spoke with authority about the Japanese, their culture and their habits, their history, their philosophy and their determination to succeed. He made the hours slip by on what would normally have been a monotonous bumpy motor trip. For endless miles we rumbled over potholed roads, forded rivers and had to wait while fallen trees were chopped away. And all the while Karel kept talking. Most of the time we weren't even aware of rutted roads and detours and the torrents of monsoon rain that flooded the countryside. Karel kept us entertained with his endless tales.

Karel's analysis of the Japanese came from experience, not from something he had heard in school or read from a textbook; he learned it by being there, by keeping his eyes and ears open, and by closely studying the Japanese. His keen perception eventually paid off. Today Karel van Wolferen is the most sought after speaker on Japanese affairs from Europe to America. His books are read in a dozen languages. He has changed the way the world thinks about Japan.

Karel is a self-made foreign correspondent. His name ranks with such other noted Far East journalists as John Reed, Lowell Thomas, Dennis Bloodworth, Richard Hughes, Marguerite Higgins and Martha Gellhorn.

Foreign correspondent is a loosely defined term. We have to agree, it has a certain ring of romance about it. We picture foreign correspondents in trench coats, with battered typewriters at their sides, winging off to the troubled spots around the world, covering the news as it is happening. We see them belonging to a privileged group, the hallmark of international intrigue.

We can't deny their importance, and their influence. With determination and persistence, and an unrelenting will to get the story, foreign correspondents have reported all the great and catastrophic events of the past century. They have covered wars, riots and revolutions, poverty and famines, humanity's struggle to survive, and the dream of peace. They have traveled around the globe as staff correspondents for newspapers, magazines, radio, and more recently, television. Thousands more have reported from abroad as stringers, free-lancers, and reporters on special assignments. Some have played a part in the history they recorded. Foreign correspondents have had grandstand seats at every major event that has shaped the world we live in today. Through their voices we have been able to learn firsthand what they saw, heard, and felt during those tumultuous events.

Karel van Wolferen is one of these people. He reminds me of John Reed, a thirty-year-old correspondent who went to Russia with notebook in hand and no experience, and ended up covering one of the most significant events of modern times—the birth of the world's first Communist state. Reed knew no Russian. He knew little of the struggles that had led to the March Revolution and even less of its leaders and the political parties vying for power, but he had superb reporting tools: a quick and inquisitive mind, sharp eyes, good ears, boundless energy, and strong legs.

As an eyewitness, Reed gave an account of not only what occurred, but he also vividly portrayed the sights and sounds of revolution: the tramp of boots as the Red Army marched to battle, the sound of rifles echoing across the vast squares of the former imperial capital, the endless meetings and the voices of angry debates. He was able to tie human beings to the events so that a coherent picture emerged.

Out of Reed's encounter with revolution came a masterpiece of reporting, *Ten Days That Shook the World*, the most vivid description we have of the events that led to the Bolshevik seizure of power and the men who shaped them. Reed brought the foreign correspondent to the foreground.

Karel van Wolferen was witness to a similar situation taking place in Japan, the emergence of the country as an economic world power, and he reported what he saw, as John Reed had done in Russia.

Some foreign correspondents turn to writing books as a

medium of expressing their thoughts and beliefs. Lowell Thomas who began as a foreign correspondent became a noted newscaster, lecturer and author in later years. He is best known for befriending Lawrence of Arabia and riding with him across the African deserts. He wrote fifty-three books in his lifetime.

Richard Hughes, a name that rings a bell in Hong Kong, reported the news for more than thirty years. Anyone who visited the Hong Kong Foreign Correspondents' Club could see him sitting at his table near the window holding court. A heavy set, roly-poly man with a red face, Hughes played host to younger journalists, and to those who came to have him autograph his books. Richard Hughes authored *Hong Kong: Borrowed Place, Borrowed Time and Foreign Devil, Thirty Years of Reporting in the Far East.*

Another correspondent to make his mark in Southeast Asia was Dennis Bloodworth, the Far East correspondent for *The Observer* of London. He came to Asia in 1954, and in 1967 published his first book, *The Chinese Looking Glass,* which made the best seller list and became a selection of The Book-of-the-Month Club. In his next book, *An Eye for the Dragon,* he focused on Southeast Asia. He lived and worked out of Singapore.

Karel van Wolferen shook the world when he published *The Enigma of Japanese Power.*

Karel was destined to report on Asian affairs. He knew when he was in grammar school in Holland that he wanted to be a writer. "I remember, I was in the 5th grade," he said. "The teacher asked the entire class what each of us wanted to be when we grew up. I said a writer, and he said, 'Karel, let's be realistic. One just can't be a writer. You had better think about it.'"

Karel did think about it. That's all he thought about. And when he reached eighteen, he would make that wish come true. He set out from Holland to see the world and write about what he saw. Everything he owned was jammed into a rucksack, and this included what he thought were the essentials for a writer—an ink well, pen and paper. He even had a suit, so he could look presentable when the occasion arose for him to do so. Karel was prepared to tackle the world.

Karel was born in Rotterdam in 1941. His mother was one of the thirteen children of a dock worker; his father, who had been an active member of the Dutch resistance during the war, dedicated most of his postwar energies to keeping the memory of the resistance alive by helping publish a magazine for former activists.

At sixteen Karel began his travels. He hitchhiked to Paris and down through the Loire Valley to Barcelona. The next year he cycled across northern France.

Back home in Rotterdam, Karel spent more time in the Municipal Library than he did on his school studies and homework. "I was totally fascinated by the possibility that people in the world could still be living in the Stone Age," he said. "I read everything, even the great Chinese classics. I read *The Dream of the Red Chamber*, trying to sit in the lotus position, thinking that's how you read books like that."

Karel finished high school "without ever doing a stroke of homework" and after working in a bicycle factory and bookshop and delivering the newspaper whose Tokyo correspondent he would later become, he left Holland with plans to hitchhike to India. He had a hundred dollars in traveler's checks and eighty German marks. "I knew I could live on very little so I wasn't worried," he said. "In Europe I slept in orchards and hitchhiked everywhere I went. I was very romantic about my approach to the world."

When Karel let it be known to his family and friends that he was planning to hitchhike to India, no one took him seriously. "My father didn't believe I could make it," he said. "And my mother thought I'd be back after a week or two."

The morning of Karel's departure arrived. At 5 a.m. he woke his brother and two sisters to say goodbye. "I expected them to be all tears," he said. "Instead, they were angry that I woke them. But I thought I might not see them again."

He put on his rucksack and left the house. He chuckles when he tells the story. "My rucksack was so heavy it pulled me backwards and I could hardly walk," he said. "I had to get from Rotterdam to the German border via the autobahn, which meant walking several miles to the train station. I could only do twenty or thirty meters and I had to stop." Karel told me the story as we sat in the comfortable study of his home in Tokyo, more than thirty years later. "And every time I stopped, I would take off my rucksack, open it up and throw something away. I started off dreaming how the world was going to be mine, all mine. I was thrilled. I was going to become a great writer. The steps became shorter and the pack heavier, and I began to question what I was doing."

Karel took the train to where he could reach the autobahn. Victory was within sight. "I took a shortcut, across an open field, and half way there I found the field had just been newly plowed. I sank up to my knees in mud," he chuckled. "I stood on the autobahn and looked at myself, covered with mud, sweaty and grimy. I thought you're going to India like this, with a hundred dollars in your pocket. Suddenly my great thoughts vanished. Hadn't a truck stopped to pick me up I'd probably turned around and gone back home." He smiled. "Well, maybe."

It took two weeks for Karel to reach Istanbul. He had used up half his traveler's checks but found he could make a little extra money teaching English. He attempted to take passage aboard a pilgrim ship sailing to Bombay but couldn't pass for a Muslim. He did succeed in joining an American expedition traveling overland to Bombay. After driving across Iran, Afghanistan and Pakistan, he reached Bombay, his final destination. He was greatly disappointed.

In the early 1960s, a fair number of dissatisfied young Europeans and Americans were roaming around Asia looking for the "spiritual center" that they believed the West lacked. It didn't take Karel long to lose patience with the Europeans he met. He became an enthusiastic admirer of Arthur Koestler and his debunking of Indian mysticism. Karel soon lost his belief in the 'spirituality' of the East. "I discovered it wasn't as spiritual as we are taught to believe," he said.

Disillusioned, Karel left India and traveled to Burma and Thailand, two countries he loved, and down through Malaysia to Singapore. From Singapore he caught a ship to the Philippines.

"I was making a little money along the way," he said. "I could teach English almost anywhere, and I began writing for newspapers and selling some photographs in the Philippines. I did stills for a low-budget movie company in the Philippines."

Japan was the logical next stop for Karel. He heard the money was good there teaching English. It took him two years to get to Japan. "My English wasn't that great," he said, "but the best way to learn is to teach. I looked up a language school in the telephone book and went to see them. Ten minutes later I was standing in front of a classroom."

Like those of many Western travelers to the East, Karel's arrival in Japan was partly the outcome of an admittedly romantic fascination with the unusual and the exotic. However, when he arrived in Kobe, he was elated not so much by the exoticism of his new home as by the degree to which Japan in the early 1960s seemed bent on imbibing the best of Western culture.

"I went to a department store in Kobe," he says, "and the sound system was playing Bach's unaccompanied cello suites, so I thought well I'd come to the right country. In the early 1960s there were many classical music coffee shops. The Japanese were reading Tolstoy. You could have conversations with Japanese students on Russian literature. They watched serious movies. It was much better then than it is today."

Karel had begun contributing articles to newspapers in India and the Philippines, and now in Japan. He liked Japan from the very start. He admits, what attracted him most was the seriousness of the Japanese. "I left Japan a couple of times, always thinking I wasn't coming back, but I always did. With my teaching and writing I could do quite well in Japan. In those days I thought how nice it would be to go to the press club and have cheap meals, not thinking that one day I would be the president."

In 1968, Karel returned to Holland for a visit. It became a turning point in his life. A Dutch research institute commissioned him to do a study of student revolutionaries. He worked hard at the project, which required traveling to the United States. Subsequently his study was published in a Dutch magazine. This was his first large-scale serious piece of writing, and immediately it drew attention. It made Karel think of concentrating on serious writing.

The Herald Tribune praised that study as the best short introduction to its subject, and after contributing several more articles on Japan to the Dutch intellectual press, Karel was invited by *NRC Handelsblad*—which he loyally describes as one of the best newspapers in the world—to be its Tokyo correspondent.

Soon Karel had his own apartment in Tokyo and found himself covering all Southeast Asia.

"I covered Southeast Asia, including the Philippines. I

could choose any subject I wanted. The newspaper began paying my expenses. I was soon doing long stories as well, and I went as deeply as I wanted to in a subject." Karel covered Mrs. Gandhi and her career, and her death. He became a credited correspondent in Vietnam, and found himself more often than not in Cambodia, writing about the horrors of the Khmer Rouge. He was present in the Philippines for the People's Revolution. He interviewed President Fernando Marcos before he was forced from power, and Corazon Aquino when she gained power. He was aboard the last helicopter flight out of Saigon. "I had to leave my old Lettera typewriter behind during the evacuation," he lamented.

Karel got to know many foreign correspondents working in Asia, including a few women correspondents. The war in Vietnam was a tragedy for the men who fought it, but it brought triumph for women correspondents. For the first time in history, the U.S. Defense Department allowed women to cover combat on an equal footing with men, and they made the most of it. Two noted women reporters who were covering the war when Karel was there were Marguerite Higgins and Martha Gillhorn.

Higgins started her career covering the Korean war. She was there when a force of sixty thousand North Koreans attacked South Korea on June 25, 1950. And when trouble broke out in Vietnam, she was there to report it. On her tenth trip to Vietnam, she contracted a tropical disease. She was flown to Walter Reed Hospital in Washington for medical treatment where she died at the age of forty-five.

Reporter Martha Gellhorn, who married novelist Ernest Hemingway in 1941, left Hemingway in the bars in Hong Kong while she flew to China to cover the war there. In three days she covered fifteen hundred miles, to the terminus of the Burma Road and back. On her next trip she traveled to Shaokuan, China—her objective was to reach the Canton front—where the Chinese were fighting the Japanese. From Shaokuan, she traveled by truck, on horseback, by motorboat, and sampan. She later covered Indonesia's battle for independence against the Netherlands. In 1966 she went to Saigon to cover the war in Vietnam for *The Guardian* of England. She also wrote a series of five articles for her hometown newspaper, the *St. Louis Post-Dispatch.* They were so inflammatory that the *Post-Dispatch* printed only the two mildest, but she would have her say, and in her book *Travels with Myself and Another,* she struck out at American military leaders. She so angered the military she was denied a visa to return to Vietnam.

Wars and hostilities in Southeast Asia were Karel's concern, but what bothered him most was the West's misunderstanding of Japan. He was aware that the business of explaining Japan to the rest of the world has been an active and profitable one for more than a century. Many of the earliest foreign explicators earned their reputations by emphasizing Japan's quaintness. Often they sought not so much to explain as to revel in the supposedly inexplicable state of being.

The Second World War ended and Japan became the West's staunchest ally. They portrayed to the world that they were a bulwark of anti-communism in Asia and a beacon of democracy. They wanted to show they were a peace-loving, open-hearted, open-handed, rapidly internationalizing society that was hard-working, polite, inscrutable, cohesive, group-oriented, obedient, dependent, nature-loving, and that the Japanese were a sensitive people.

But Karel came to the conclusion that Japan is not a Western-style state at all. It does not belong to the club of nations operating a free market economy. Japan is not in the Western sense a free society in which its citizens are able to choose from among different courses and implement their choice through political or other action. He could readily see that a headlong and mutually destructive collision between Japan and its trading partners is clearly on the horizon.

Karel began to look for the roots of the problem. "America's belief that Japan, after centuries of feudalism followed by dictatorial misrule in the modern age, has become a democracy comparable to American democracy, is all wrong."

Karel was asked to partake in the recording of a discussion on Japanese politics on American public radio with American ex-ambassador to Japan, Edwin Reischauer. During the 45-minute program, Reischauer brought up the sensitive issue of the Recruit Scandal, the dissatisfaction among Japanese consumers, and other issues the press had been writing about, as evidence that Japanese society was indeed becoming more democratic. Reischauer then said that Americans had to be more patient because, eventually, all problems, including the conflict between the United States and Japan, would be solved by these changes.

Karel had respected Reischauer for some of the things that he had done, but on this occasion he was dismayed by his apparent ignorance of what was going on in Japan. Karel felt that most correspondents presented a picture of Japan that to a large extent was influenced by Japanese flattery. Journalists are blinded to the true state of affairs as officials pour them drinks at private dinners. Karel did not see Japan as Reischauer did. He stopped the recording as he did not want to be part of such a broadcast.

The only way that Karel could present a realistic picture of Japan was to put his thoughts down in a book. "I did not want to criticize," he said. "I wanted to analyze the Japanese system of government, and thus show how it functions, or how it doesn't function."

Karel found a publisher interested in his story, and he had enough money saved to hold him for a year. He rented a cabin in the mountains north of Tokyo and for the next eighteen months labored writing his book. "It was the greatest time in my life," he said. "I walked through the countryside with a small tape reorder in my hand, talking into it. I got used to the hermit life, and in doing so it changed my life."

Karel occasionally went back to Tokyo to do more research, and another time he took off for a few weeks to travel to Amsterdam to receive the Dutch Award for his coverage of the 1986 "People's Revolution in the Philippines," but the rest of the time he concentrated on *The Enigma of Japanese Power*. When finished, he sent the completed manuscript to Macmillan, his publisher in New York, and waited.

"I had no idea it would reach such a wide readership," Karel admitted. "At most we thought it might sell five thousand copies. Macmillan printed three thousand. It was soon in the hundreds of thousands. A book on the politics of economic power. No one expected the book to have such an effect in Washington."

The critics were quick to strike out at Karel. "The Japanese officials who are responsible for public relations with the United States have spent more to discredit me than on any other writer before," Karel explained. "I have been told if I had one percent of what they are spending I could retire for life on the Mediterranean or in a castle in Switzerland."

Nothing has riled him more than the attempts to suggest that his book is unscholarly. "There have been many voices trying to discredit me internationally," he believes, "but one Foreign Ministry official told me over lunch, out of the blue, 'Mr Wolferen, I hope you will continue writing in the way you are writing now.' Other highly-placed

Japanese have estimated in private correspondence that between seventy and eighty percent of the Japanese people agree with me."

In private life, Karel enjoys Japan as much as he ever did. He has a taste for good food and good music, and from time to time he has fallen in love with Japanese women, but he doesn't want to commit himself. He lives in a splendid house in Shitemathi, the oldest part of Tokyo. The four-story building has polished wooden floors throughout, heavy wooden doors and a music room that is equipped for sound. The room has a huge leather sofa and a black leather reclining chair. The closets are filled with old LP records. When he is in Tokyo, Karel spends much of his time here, listening to music. "Of course," he says, "Bach is the greatest composer ever."

Karel can recall the exact moment he became interested in fine music. "I was seven years old," he said. "I was in elementary school. Back then they had cars with billboards that drove through the streets advertising products or announcing coming events. We kids used to jump on and off the moving vehicles. I jumped on one and fell off. The next thing I remember was waking up in the hospital, and hearing Handel's "Messiah." It was the most beautiful thing I had ever heard. I have loved good music ever since."

Apart from his first love, music, Karel's hobby is large-format photography. He has a fully-equipped darkroom in his house and does all his own processing and enlarging. He works almost entirely in black and white. "It's much more beautiful," he claims, and then adds, "and much more difficult." His favorite camera is a Deardorf 8 x 10. I was with Karel once when he was in action. I stood in the middle of the road in the redwoods of northern California, flagging down traffic, while he set up his huge camera and tripod in an attempt to photograph the giant trees in the early morning. Even logging trucks thundering down the road couldn't disrupt him.

Karel speaks a half a dozen languages–Dutch, German, English, Turkish, Armenian, a bit of Thai, and, of course, Japanese. He's a voracious reader, in English. The study in his house is crammed with books. They fill the bookshelves and spill over his desk and on to the floor. They are stacked everywhere. Mostly they are books on political and economic thought: *The Market and the State, Political Thoughts and Polemics, In Defence of Politics, Conservative Capitalism, Essays on Politics and Literature, Consciousness Explained, The State in Capitalist Society.*

There are also books on music, such as *Experiencing Music.* On a corner of his desk are several disks: "Bach's Sonatas, and Partitas," performed by violinist Itzhak Perlman, and "Berlioz Requiem" with Luciano Pavarotti.

Karel continues to maintain his mountain retreat, a two-hour drive by car from Tokyo. "It's at the end of a deadend valley and is tucked away among Japanese cedar trees," Karel explained, without offering an invitation to visit him there. "A little bubbling brook runs through the property. The house is two stories, with endless bookcases and lots of sound equipment." No one knows exactly where the retreat is, nor does anyone know the telephone number. It was here, over a four-month period, that Karel wrote a book on the Japanese constitution, for the Japanese. Within two months it had sold over a hundred thousand copies.

Karel believes Japan does need a new constitution. "A new constitution would, of course, have to tackle Article Nine," he claims. Article Nine prohibits Japan to wage war. "It is perhaps the single biggest mistake of the American occupation," he said. "It demands something that is impossible for a country which is at the same time expected to participate as a full member of the international community, with responsibilities just like the other members. A nation that gives up the 'right' to wage war, gives up an essential element of its sovereignty."

Karel claims there is no evidence that General MacArthur gave much thought to the historical weight of what he was proposing when he helped draft the Japanese constitution. "We owe Article Nine to his desire to keep the Emperor in place," he says, "which he thought would make it easier for him to control Japan. He needed something in exchange, for calming down the fear in some Washington circles that Japan might become a threat again. The war-renouncing constitution was that special precondition ameliorating those fears. By adding Article Nine, General MacArthur also sealed the fate of the constitution as an unimpeachable document."

Comparing the Japan when he first arrived with the Japan he lives and works in today, Karel is not overly impressed by the progress of 'Japan's much touted internalization.' "The Japanese people as a whole were much nicer to foreigners back in the 1960s than they are today," he said. "There's more antagonism now than then. But maybe the major change is that, in the 60s, the Japanese had a great deal more hope. There was a feeling that things were going to work out in every way, that they were going to be different from what they had been. The youth were going to make changes. The Japanese were going to be politically more alert and significant. When I first arrived, there was still a sense that joining action groups or signing petitions could make a political difference. Today much of that feeling has disappeared."

Nor does Karel feel that foreign press coverage of Japan has much improved. "Foreign correspondents today speak better Japanese than they did then," he acknowledges, "but that doesn't mean they are better versed in their subject. On the whole, coverage of Japan is abominably bad. It's partly a problem of editors; editors are not ready to cope with the complexity nor do they want to understand Japan."

Karel admits he misses the tension of daily journalism, but success really hasn't changed him. He is on demand for lecture tours around the world, and he has more writing assignments, for books and magazines, than he can handle. "But I am going to continue to be a journalist," he said. "I will continue to work for my paper as a special correspondent. And I'm currently writing a book which will be an attempt at political philosophy, incorporating some of the ideas that have occurred to me in Asia into the theoretical discussion that has been going on for centuries. Maybe I can contribute."

Nor has Karel changed his views about Asia. "Today I still have very similar feelings about Asia to those I had when I first arrived," he explained. "Asia is the largest repository of humanity on Earth, with a great variety of cultures and experience. In Europe and the United States the economic process is completely divorced from the struggle for survival. In Asia it is not. That makes the difference."

The readiness with which the United States has extended economic favours to Japan, to the detriment of its own industries, continues to baffle Karel. "Never before had victors in a war between major countries been so eager to help in the economic rebuilding of the defeated as the United States was for Japan. I cannot think of any other instance in history in which one country has had it so easy in its strategic and diplomatic, and even economic, dealings with the world, simply by relying on the power, the goodwill, and the self-appointed task to maintain world order, of another country, while at the same time retaining its own political identity."

"Because of this extraordinary relationship," he said, "Japan was never forced to solve any internal political problems for the purpose of coping with a demanding external world."

"I admire Japanese politeness," Karel said when I asked what he liked about Japan after a quarter of a century of living there. "For all the Western contempt for form without content, form is important. Etiquette, the graceful way of doing things, the attempt not to cause the other person embarrassment—these are all important. But one must learn, as I have, to understand the Japanese one has to continue to peel away the onion skins. And I'm afraid that, when I've finished peeling, there'll be nothing left."

In the meantime, Karel van Wolferen continues to live happily in his adopted home and to explain to the world what Japan is all about—as he did to me on the road from Bangkok to the Burmese border those many years ago.

Singapore as it was yesterday.

Singapore as it is today. (Photo by Robert Stedman)

Street Scene. Bangkok (Siam).

See the old Siving

Bangkok, yesterday

Bangkok, today

Chapter 14

LIVING IN ASIA
The Realities

It's an intriguing idea, living abroad, especially in an exotic place where it's warm year round, where palm trees perpetually nip at the blue of the sky, and where living is easy, prices are right and servants are at hand to serve our every whim. We can easily find such a place in tropical Southeast Asia. But can we live there?

The people I have written about in *At Home in Asia* have found their niche in this foreign land; they have made a place, if not a home, for themselves in beautiful Southeast Asia. Some live in fine houses where tiny bells tinkle in the breeze, or other dwell high on mountainsides with views that are overpowering. Others live aboard their boats, and change scenery with the changing tides. They have all made a dream reality.

But the picture is not complete. What about those who have tried and didn't make it? Their numbers far exceed those who have succeeded. Remember Bill Heinecke, Bangkok's shining entrepreneur who loves to race cars and dive among great white sharks. He says for everyone who does connect in Thailand there are fifteen to twenty others who fail, especially in recent years. Higher costs, government regulations, greater competition from locals and big internationals are making the small foreign entrepreneur a rare species, as they already are in most corners of the developing world.

To survive as they did, the people I wrote about have come to accept Asia as it is. Survival in Asia for the foreigner, as they learned, means accepting things as they are. When we begin questioning the Asian way of life, we

315

lose the battle. We must not try to change things. When we go to a festival such as Thaipusam in Malaysia, where Hindu devotees perform self-mortification rituals, we learn to accept what our eyes are telling us even though it is seemingly impossible. Southeast Asia continues to be a land of mystery which an outsider may never fully understand.

The foreigner, the Western especially, must also accept that he or she can never fully integrate into the Asian scene. Make a mistake, even a grave one, and the Asian will say, "Oh, never mind. He is a foreigner." The Asian will forgive you, but only if you are a foreigner. Make no mistake about that. Perhaps you learn to speak an Asian language fluently, let's say it's Mandarin Chinese, and you talk to someone on the phone who also speaks Mandarin. You have never met him, and you get along splendidly. But when they meet you in person they are disappointed—"Oh, I thought you were Chinese." You feel slighted.

Southeast Asia is changing. The half dozen countries that make up ASEAN can hardly be called Third World "developing" countries anymore. They are prosperous and their people are well fed and well clothed, and they have money to spend. They wear designer clothes from New York and Paris and dine in gourmet restaurants and drive automobiles that cost as much as a house back home. The foreigner can no longer come and "live off the land" as he once did. He must toil, and struggle and be content that the land is not his. Foreigners—Americans and Europeans—underestimate the Asians. I remember living in Singapore in the mid 1960s when England pulled out. Brits who had to give up their private clubs and gracious government homes all muttered the same tune—"Wait till we leave, then see what happens to this place." As a port, Singapore then numbered twelfth in the world in the volume of shipping and trade. Today she is second, and a very close contender for first place. Singaporeans did it on their own. We can say the same about Malaysia and Indonesia. They have done remarkably well.

Still, and we must agree, Southeast Asia might be changing but it continues to offer a challenge for the foreigner. And for those who have taken up the challenge and become expatriates, it's a great place to live.